DATE DUE

GAYLORD			PRINTED IN U.S.A.

Traumatic Verses

Studies in German Literature, Linguistics, and Culture

Traumatic Verses

On Poetry in German from the Concentration Camps, 1933–1945

Andrés Nader

CAMDEN HOUSE
Rochester, New York

First published 2007
by Camden House

Camden House is an imprint of Boydell & Brewer Inc.
668 Mt. Hope Avenue, Rochester, NY 14620, USA
www.camden-house.com
and of Boydell & Brewer Limited
PO Box 9, Woodbridge, Suffolk IP12 3DF, UK
www.boydellandbrewer.com

ISBN-13: 978–1–57113–375–5
ISBN-10: 1–57113–375–5

Library of Congress Cataloging-in-Publication Data

Nader, Andrés José, 1968–.
  Traumatic verses: on poetry in German from the concentration camps,
1933–1945 / Andrés Nader
    p. cm. — (Studies in German literature, linguistics, and culture)
Includes bibliographical references and index.
ISBN-13: 978–1–57113–375–5 (hardcover : alk. paper)
ISBN-10: 1–57113–375–5 (hardcover : alk. paper)
  1. Concentration camp inmates' writings—History and criticism.
2. German poetry—20th century—History and criticism. 3. Holocaust,
Jewish (1939–1945) in literature. 4. World War, 1939–1945—
Literature and the war.   I. Title. II. Series.

PT509.C66N34 2007
831'.912080358—dc22

                                                    2007018166

A catalogue record for this title is available from the British Library.

This publication is printed on acid-free paper.
Printed in the United States of America.

To the memory of
Martita Elena Bestani (Martita),
tucumana desaparecida

Contents

Acknowledgments   ix

Introduction   1

1: Literary Activities in the Camps   33

2: Identity under Threat   71

3: "Everyday Life" in the Concentrationary Universe   94

4: Communicating Torture   127

5: Contemporaneous Poetry in the Third Reich   152

Conclusion   181

Appendix of Complete Poems   185

Notes   229

Works Cited   239

Index   255

Acknowledgments

THIS WORK HAS BEEN long in the making, and I have already expressed the gratitude I owe to many people for help with the earlier stage of this project — my doctoral dissertation at Cornell University. Here I want to mention again only the principal mentors of the crucial initial development of this book: David Bathrick, Sander Gilman, Biddy Martin, Dominick LaCapra, and Jonathan Monroe. I am also especially grateful to Michael Moll for kindly sharing so much of his research with me. More recently Eleanor Kaufman, Thomas A. Pepper, Kimberley Healey, Susan Gustafson, Gudrun Brug, Christian Gundermann, Stefanie Oswalt, and Reinhild Steingröver have provided generous help and critical feedback, for which I am very thankful. My family, especially Agnès Benoit-Nader, bore with me while this project seemed never to draw to a close. At Camden House, Jim Walker, Editorial Director, Katie Hurley, Editorial Assistant, and Jane Best, Production Editor, were a stupendously efficient and communicative team who made the final stages of this project a pleasure. I also want to thank Sue Innes, whose copy-editing was insightful well beyond what I had expected.

For their help I also thank the staff at the Interlibrary Loan Department at Rush Rhees Library, University of Rochester, and the archival staffs at the Dachau Concentration Camp Memorial Site, at the Memorial and Museum Auschwitz-Birkenau, and at the German Literature Archive at Marbach.

Sections of this book were published in an earlier version under the title: "The Shock of Arrival: Poetry from the Nazi Camps at the End of the Century" in a special issue of *Poetics Today* entitled *Aftershock: Poetry and Cultural Politics since 1989* and edited by Jonathan Culler (Vol. 21, no. 1, Spring 2000), copyright by the Porter Institute for Poetics and Semiotics and used here with permission from the publisher, Duke University Press.

The poems "Der Kamin" and "Auschwitz" by Ruth Klüger are reprinted with permission of the author. The English translation of "Der Kamin" is reprinted with permission of Sander Gilman. The poem "Theresienstädter Kinderreim" by Ilse Weber is reprinted with permission of Hanus Weber; its translation into English with permission of David Keir Wright. The poem "Die Häftlingsnummer" by Hasso Grabner (© Aufbau-Verlag Berlin 1959) is reprinted here with permission of Aufbau-Verlag. The poems "Unterwegs;" "Fünfundzwanzig," and "Friedhof Obodowka" by Alfred Kittner are reprinted with permission of Rimbaud Verlag. The poems "Der Häftling" and "Wenn sich müd die Glieder senken" by Fritz Löhner-Beda are reprinted with permission of Seemann Henschel Verlag.

A. N.
May 2007

Introduction

For example, what did poetry and music mean in the Warsaw ghetto?
In Auschwitz, how could one think?
  Up to what point can one remain human? Starting from what mo-
ment does one absolutely lose poetry? (literary genre?) Why poems in
these times of repression? Songs, when women are silenced? . . .
                    — Hélène Cixous, "Poetry is/and (the) Political"[1]

Reading Poems in German
from the Concentration Camps

THE GOAL OF THIS BOOK IS TO think about a selection of poems. These are disparate poems, but they are marked in two particular ways. The individuals who wrote these poems did so while they were imprisoned in concentration camps set up by the National Socialists, and they wrote in German, the language of their tormentors. These two historical factors alone do not determine the poems, but they condition our reading as they call attention with particular force to the creative act and to the aesthetic dimension in a context of extreme abuse and dehumanization. With the exception of Michael Moll (1988), critics have neglected these works by and large, preferring instead to engage philosophically and at great length with what, following Theodor Adorno, has come to be known as the question of the feasibility of "poetry after Auschwitz."[2] Such theoretical concern is not insignificant to the subject at hand, but the purpose of this book is to make space for the poems themselves, to linger with that we might call poetry *in* the camps.

Traumatic Verses closely examines a representative range of poems written in German in a variety of camp settings. Hasso Grabner, Fritz Löhner-Beda, and Karl Schnog composed poems in Buchenwald; Ruth Klüger in Christianstadt, a satellite camp of Gross-Rosen; and Edgar Kupfer-Koberwitz in Dachau. Georg von Boris wrote in Flössenburg; Ilse Weber in Theresienstadt; and Alfred Kittner in a variety of smaller camps in Transnistria. Their poems constitute a neglected but important intervention in the literature and culture of the period. This book presents a selection of poems by both Jewish and non-Jewish authors: more poems are available in print; most of the extant material has been published, as detailed in the final section of this introduction. The archival records at the sites of various former concentration camps, such as Auschwitz, Dachau, and Sachsenhausen, contain the same or slightly variant versions of the published material. The selection presented here is intended to give a sense of both the range and the commonalities in the corpus as a whole and to stimulate the examination of further poems.

Any analysis of these poems must take their history into account, and, beyond the "scene of writing," this includes the history of how the work of each of these poets was saved from destruction. An analysis needs to engage the discussions about representation and the Holocaust, and to think about the relationship between trauma and language. To some extent this book does all that, but the poems remain its focus. This book asks: Why did some inmates engage in aesthetic practices? Why did they work at the most stylized of literary forms, of forms of communication? — Despite the prevailing conditions, or because of them, or for some other reasons? What kinds of poetry did inmates compose? Why poetry? What did they write about in what we call "unimaginable conditions"? How did they write? Why would human beings deprived of their agency resort to creative expression, to language games — as we might call them — that adhere to established rules of versification? What do their verses tell us about poetry and language in extremity? What can they tell us about our relation to language and about the ways in which identity is bound up with aesthetic notions? More specifically: What is the significance of cultural production from the camps in the language of those who created the camps? What is the relationship between the language of the perpetrators and the language of the inmates whose works are treated here?

Conditions varied widely from one concentration camp to another, within a camp at different periods in its history, and they differed as well for individuals according to the category or categories that the Nazis assigned to inmates. Though these differences are significant enough that they raise the question of the very notion of a corpus of "poetry from the camps" since "the camps" refers to such a disparate set of conditions, an analysis of these poems shows that a number of rhetorical and narrative strategies, including traditional versification and often a marked rhythmic regularity, ironic distance, and an avoidance of emotional expression, were used by most individuals composing poems in the different camps, and that these individuals shared a resilient belief in the staying power of poetry. These common characteristics extend beyond the subset of camp poetry analyzed here, poetry in German. However, the literary traditions and cultural contexts of camp writers in languages such as Yiddish, Polish, or French warrant, and have received, separate treatment.[3] Any poems from the camps available to us now counter the Nazis' intentions to eradicate the traces of their victims. Additionally, poems in German, particularly those composed by Jews, directly defied National Socialist ideology that linked culture and language to race and claimed that Jews were incapable of understanding or composing poetry.

Austrian-Jewish author and camp-survivor Jean Améry has conveyed the particularity of the situation of speaking, writing, and even thinking in German in the camps. On the one hand, knowledge of German ensured that inmates could understand the rules and orders in the concentration camps and — with luck — might more easily avoid the ire of camp guards. At the same time, being culturally and linguistically "bound" to German meant that German-speaking inmates could not as easily take imaginative flight into another, less hostile, culture or create a private, intellectual realm of their own. Améry writes that "A special set of problems in connection with the social function or non function of the intellect arose for the Jewish intellectual of *German educational and cultural background*. No matter to what he turned, it did not belong to him, but to the enemy." He continues:

> A comrade who had once been asked about his profession had foolishly told the truth that he was a Germanist, and that had provoked a murderous outburst of rage from an SS man. In those same days, across the ocean in the USA, Thomas Mann, I believe, said: "Wherever I am is German culture." The German-Jewish Auschwitz prisoner could not have made such a bold assertion, even if by chance he had been a Thomas Mann. He could not claim German culture as his possession, because his claim found no sort of social justification. Among the émigrés a tiny minority was able to constitute itself as German culture, even if there was not exactly a Thomas Mann among them. In Auschwitz, however, the isolated individual had to relinquish all of German culture, including Dürer and Reger, Gryphius and Trakl, to even the lowest SS man. (8)

As Améry's anecdote and commentary suggest, German-Jewish inmates were forced to relinquish the canon of German high culture, whatever the cultural achievements of the specific inmate or the cultural interests of the SS guards.

Ruth Klüger is like Améry an Austrian-Jewish author and camp survivor, though her writings, more recent, are less well known than his. With the advantage of much hindsight and in English Klüger claims that "German, strange as this statement may sound, is a Jewish language" (2001, 205). As if she intended to undo the humiliation she endured in the concentration camps and to nullify the Nazi expulsion of Jews from German-speaking culture and territory, Klüger supports her "strange" statement by admonishing her readers: "Consider that until the Holocaust, most of the world's prominent Jews spoke it: Kafka, Freud, Einstein, Marx, Heine, Theodor Herzl (!), and Hannah Arendt, to name the first that come to mind" (2001, 205). However, in the camps, and before she had learned English and become a professor of German in the United States, Klüger felt bound to German as "the language of the perpetrators" in a manner akin to Améry's and perceived this as demeaning:

> I hated Theresienstadt: it was a mudhole, a cesspool, a sty where you
> couldn't stretch without touching someone. . . . Makes you feel like the
> scum of the earth. Which is exactly what we were. To belong to a pow-
> erless people who are either arrogant or self-critical to the point of self-
> hatred. To know no language other than what those who thought us
> subhuman spoke. To have no opportunity to learn another language,
> to learn anything. (2001, 87)

There is a tension here between her subsequent assertion that German "is a
Jewish language" and the earlier experience of the concentration camps as a
site in which the German-speaking Jewish inmate, treated as subhuman by
the Nazis, has recourse neither to a language, nor, consequently, to a cultural tradition other than the ones claimed violently by the Nazis as exclusively their own.

That any "claim" on the part of inmates, not just those about culture or
a specific language, "found no sort of social justification" in the camps is an
understatement, particularly with respect to Jewish inmates. Different memoirs and studies have shown that the Nazis actively sought to destroy even
the claim the inmates might make as to their own humanity or their individuality. In this context Hannah Arendt has identified three stages in the
incremental attack on the inmates' personhood: (1) killing "the juridical person" by "putting certain categories of persons outside the law" and "placing
the concentration camp outside the normal penal system," (2) murdering
"the moral person" by "making death itself anonymous" and by rendering
"decisions of conscience [for the inmates] absolutely questionable and
equivocal," that is, by forcing an "alternative" "no longer between good and
evil but between murder and murder," and (3) destroying "the individual,
his unique identity" mostly by manipulating "the human body — with its
infinite possibilities of suffering — in such a way as to make it destroy the
human person" (1958, 437–59[4]). While the Nazi attack on the inmates' individuality was massive, the cultural output from a variety of camps is testimony to the fact that the the Nazis did not succeed in completely silencing
their victims. Arendt writes of "individuality" as that part of the human person that is "hardest to destroy" (1958, 453). Occasionally, inmates in the
camps — Jewish and non-Jewish, men and women, in a variety of languages
— expressed themselves in a manner that exceeded the absolute contingencies of the moment: they composed poems. Some of those individuals survived, many did not. Their poems are examples of the ways in which inmates
tried to resist the attacks on their cultural identity and on their individuality.
While both the significance of the attack on the inmates' personhood, as well
as, ultimately, the murderous efficiency of the Nazi system itself must be
kept in mind, the poems discussed here both implicitly and sometimes explicitly resist the exclusion from culture, from the aesthetic realm, and from
the human community that the Nazis imposed upon these inmate-writers.

The poems engage questions of morality, agency, and voice, and can be read as rare occasions for self-reflection on the part of some inmates.

Thus, in the context of the concentration camps, to write a poem in German is automatically and a fortiori to claim some kind of mastery over the language, some level of control and creative agency in this medium, despite all obstacles and in defiance of the Nazis' intent. Moreover, the contested status of the creative uses of (the German) language, and of poetry in particular, was not confined to the camps. The issue of literary expression in German affected most clearly German and Austrian Jews and other German speakers whom the Nazis excluded from qualifying as Aryan. For an example from Nazi Berlin, we may turn to the German-Jewish poet Gertrud Kolmar. In a letter dated 23 July 1941, at which time her situation was rapidly becoming more precarious, Kolmar wrote: "Ich bin eine Dichterin, ja, das weiß ich; aber eine Schriftstellerin möchte ich niemals sein" (I am a poet, yes, that I know, but I would never want to be a writer; Kolmar 1970, 106). On its own, this claim represents the author's artistic self-understanding as one in which the creative act is seen as something spontaneous and quasi-sacred, concerned with the "essential" and "eternal," and, most significantly, encumbered neither by technical concerns over the mechanics of composition nor by interest in the public's response. This is characteristic of a German tradition that valued "the poet" over "the writer" (Jäger, 50). The former was aligned with "culture" and notions of "truth," "genius," and "transcendence," while the latter was connected to "civilization" and its implications of "artifice," "fashion," and "entertainment." As Gudrun Jäger has argued, for a German Jew the conception of the poet's role as one removed from politics and from the public has a particular dimension in the Third Reich. Nazi literary critics qualified Jewish authors as "mere writers." In the Nazi conception, the "essence of poetry" "touches the deeper layers of soul of the Germans and contributes to forming them." Furthermore, the Nazis understood poetry and "depth of soul" as "completely alien to the Jews" (Jäger, 52). Jäger interprets Kolmar's formulation as a "defense against ethnic discrimination, against her exclusion and the humiliation of her person." Thus Kolmar's claim to being "a poet" can be read as

> a desperate and deeply wounded call to belong in German culture and for a return to the conditions in which an assimilated Jew who had grown up in a German national milieu was not yet prevented from counting herself as part of the intellectual-cultural elite of the country. (Jäger, 52)

Nazi ideology claimed that Jews could not be bearers of German culture and that Jewish culture was intrinsically inimical and alien to the German nation. By composing poems in German, and poems that sometimes incorporate the most classical stylistic aspects of the lyric tradition, Jewish inmates implicitly and secretly insisted on a cultural role for themselves in German; they imaginatively returned, to follow Jäger's model, to a time when German poetry was part of their culture as readers, writers, or both. But Nazi policy and practice sought to enforce a severing of Jews from German culture with murderous thoroughness. In an incisive history of German literature, Heinz Schlaffer comments on the consequence of this severing for German literature in the following terms:

> If one understands "German" to mean not an ethnic species but rather a cultural character, then the emancipated [German-speaking] Jews should count as the more serious Germans. With their expulsion and destruction German literature consequently lost its status and its character. (140)

Schlaffer writes of the "downfall" of modern German literature in the second half of the twentieth century as, in part, a consequence of the Third Reich.

During the Third Reich the problem of language was also confronted by writers — Jewish or not — who had fled or been forced into exile (Schlösser 1962, 40–48). Indeed, speaking to the Alliance of German Authors in New York in 1939, Ernst Bloch claimed that the German language was under threat. In an essay tellingly entitled "Zerstörte Sprache — Zerstörte Kultur" (Ravaged Language — Ravaged Culture; Bloch 1970), he warns that the German language

> is in danger of suffocating in Germany, of freezing abroad. Its extraordinary descent in Germany is obvious. The German language now belongs to the devil. The devil is the father of the lie, in whose service the language now acts. The slime and bombast, the fog and howling, the stupidity and elephantiasis of superlatives serve the demagogy. The chloroform masks that unfortunately are missing in the concentration camps are used by Goebbels for the so-called mass of supporters outside [the camps]: the language becomes a narcotic, words lose their meaning, war is called peace, a pogrom an act of self-defense, the murderer Führer [leader]. (292)[5]

Bloch's rhetoric reflects the urgency with which the exiled author regarded the problem of the abuse of the German language by the Nazis. As Helen Kelly-Holmes writes: "The entire Nazi project took place through the language, the German language was used and manipulated to persuade people of the necessity of this project, the language of the Nazi project filtered through to almost every level of spoken and written culture" (47).

If during the Third Reich opponents of the regime saw in the Nazi dictatorship's ideology and propaganda a threat to or a perversion of German language and culture, the full insidiousness of the Nazis' use of language was revealed only later on, when it became public knowledge, for example, that "special treatment" meant gassing, and "final solution" mechanized mass murder. The Nazis abused the language, and after the war an agreement developed that ordinary language was inadequate to convey the full horror of the concentration-camp universe and of the type of murder carried out by the Nazis. More specifically, the German language was deemed to have forfeited some of its humanity in the process: "Use a language to conceive, organize, and justify Belsen; use it to make out specifications for gas ovens; use it to dehumanize man during twelve years of calculated bestiality. Something will happen to it" (Steiner, 101). In 1959 George Steiner wrote that the German language was "not innocent of the horrors of Nazism" and went on to claim that the language now is "dead" (Steiner, 99, 96). Citing Karl Kraus, Alvin Rosenfeld contended that in their brutality the Nazis "closed the space that formerly mediated between violent words and violent deeds" and consequently "effectively invalidated language and made it forfeit its usefulness as the primary means of social and cultural discourse" (Rosenfeld, 135). And in 2003 Susan Gubar argued that "literary responses to the Holocaust might seem particularly preposterous after the contamination of German signaled the failure of language, indeed the spoiling of the very concept of language" (4).

The effects of the Third Reich and the Holocaust on the German language were perhaps expressed with most haunting eloquence and sophistication by the poet Paul Celan, who had been uprooted by the Holocaust and whose parents had been killed in the camps. In 1958, in a speech he gave as he received the literary prize of the city of Bremen, Celan went from speaking of the loss of homeland to speaking about "our language," a formulation John Felstiner has characterized as a "finely tuned sarcasm as uttered by a Jew in postwar Germany" (Felstiner, 113), though German did remain the language of most of Celan's literary work. In his Bremen speech, Celan claims that the language "went through" the Nazi period and was changed by it:

> Erreichbar, nah und unverloren blieb inmitten der Verluste dies eine: die Sprache.
> Sie, die Sprache, blieb unverloren, ja, trotz allem. Aber sie mußte nun hindurchgehen durch ihre eigenen Antwortlosigkeiten, hindurchgehen durch furchtbares Verstummen, hindurchgehen durch die tausend Finsternisse todbringender Rede. Sie ging hindurch und gab keine Worte her für das, was geschah; aber sie ging durch dieses Geschehen. Ging hindurch und durfte wieder zutage treten, "angereichert" von all dem. (Celan, 3:185–86)

> [Reachable, near and not lost, there remained amid the losses this one thing: language.
> It, the language, remained, not lost, yes in spite of everything. But it had to pass through its own answerlessness, pass through frightful

muting, pass through the thousand darknesses of deathbringing speech. It passed through and it gave back no words for that which happened: yet it passed through this happening. Passed through and could come to light again, "enriched" by all this. (Celan here as translated in Felstiner, 114–15)]

As Felstiner points out, this speech is extraordinarily rich in allusions, but it does make clear that the German language had "gone through" "that which happened," that the language, and poetry, could not ignore the murderous history of the Third Reich: what is rendered here as "enriched" is "ange-reichert" in German, meaning "enriched" but containing the word Reich, a dark richness indeed.[6] Celan's perspective in his Bremen speech is one of hindsight. But the problem of the German language was felt earlier on, as is made clear by Bloch's claim, Kolmar's statement, and even by the final lines of the following poem composed by Celan in 1944, after the Nazis had killed his mother. Under the title "Nähe der Gräber" (Nearness of Graves) Celan writes in perfect metric regularity: "Und duldest du, Mutter, wie einst ach daheim / den leisen, den deutschen, den schmerzlichen Reim?" (And can you bear, Mother, as once on a time / the gentle, the German, the pain-laden rhyme? Celan, 3:20, here in Felstiner's translation, 24).

As they rhyme "daheim" (at home) with "Reim" (rhyme) the final lines from "Nähe der Gräber" articulate, in the context of brutal displacement and violence, a now damaged link between a sense of home and the "German rhyme." The poems analyzed in this book seek to create in and through German rhymes a sense of home, something the inmates were violently denied.[7] The poems seem to function for the most part as unselfconscious vehicles for self-assertion in a German-speaking cultural realm. Poems written in the camps are unlike "poetry after Auschwitz" in that they were not written with hindsight; they generally lack a sense of the temporal break marked by Auschwitz.[8] They are at times desperate literary interventions in German, and since they constitute an alternate use of German during this time or perhaps the use of literary German in an alternate context, they may alter our understanding of the literary history of the period. German was the language of the perpetrators, but, as the poems from the concentration camps remind us, it was as much the language of many of the victims of the Nazis. The experiences of violent persecution, displacement, and internment, as traumatic experiences, affected the inmate-writers' relation to language and narrative. It is now up to us to "discern the ways [in which the Holocaust] can be recognized and felt in the present," as Gubar argues (7), to engage in the present, for example, with these texts and to listen both for the ways in which the poems bear traces of the traumatic experiences their authors faced then and for the ways in which they speak to us now.

Imaginative Acts: A Methodology

Poetry therapy came into fashion in the United States in the nineteen sixties, but it never achieved the widespread popularity its proponents had hoped it would. The use of poetry for psychotherapeutic purposes usually involves one of two techniques: the therapist might quote a poem to provoke in the patient a particular affective response, to help the patient come to terms with an emotion, or to "teach" the patient how to cope with a given situation — a patient with an inability to make decisions might be presented with Robert Frost's "The Road Not Taken." This could help the patient to "learn how to make decisions" and, particularly, to "reconcile herself to the loss involved in every choice" (Jones, 12).[9] The other option in poetry therapy is to encourage the patient to write poetry, again, in order to help the patient to come to terms with difficult psychological situations.

Poetry therapy claims to have found a very practical purpose for poems: poems then become objects of use. In situations of extremity poetry may come to play an unexpected and psychologically helpful role. Verses then take on the role of "emergency poetry."[10] This phrase brings together the incongruous, disparate notions of desperate urgency and dire need on the one hand and, on the other, notions of the leisure of artistic craft and aesthetic ideals, of individual creative expression, intellectual contemplation, and the significance of subtle differences — these last-mentioned notions, which circle around the realm of the aesthetic, are precisely the kinds of things that are left out of the realm of use according to an ideology of classical utility. The dialectically related poles of need and desire are inseparable in the material studied in this book, for in these works the concrete brutality of the Nazi concentration camps, with their extreme violence, is inextricable from the purportedly less tangible and more fragile materiality of words strung together into poems by inmates in those camps, in other words, by people who were denied any measure of power over their own destinies.

Joost A. Meerloo was a professor of psychiatry who survived Nazi persecution as a member of the Dutch underground resistance.[11] In his contribution to an anthology, *Poetry Therapy*, Meerloo begins an essay entitled "The Universal Language of Rhythm" with the following personal anecdote:

> During the Second World War, I had a personal encounter with the healing powers of a kind of poetry therapy. It was during one of the most trying times in my life. I remember how three prisoners lay crowded across the one dirty cot in the cell, on a thin layer of straw where fleas and bed-bugs held their nightly feasts. We were from different lands and understood only a few words of each other's tongues. To make matters more uncomfortable, we had no idea whether the morning would bring death or liberation.

The humid summer night was devoid of sleep. After a while, one of us made a feeble attempt to hum, and then began to intone some lyrics in his own language. Gradually, we took over in turn each other's chanting of intimate thoughts in measured cadences. That was how we managed to soothe ourselves with a kind of verbal hypnosis, which took the place of sleep. We were lucky to have discovered something ecstatic in our playful rhythmization of words.

No great poetry was spoken that night, or on many another similar occasion. But it was my repeated experience in those stressful years that people in extreme anxiety, frozen by the enemy into complete passivity while awaiting their fate, would suddenly find a rhythmic voice inside themselves — a voice that spoke for their essential "me." It is a pity that more of this war poetry by non-poets has not been gathered. Almost written in blood, these verses were smuggled out of prison or concentration camp, while the authors waited for an echo in their silent isolation. With the liberation, the emergency poets stopped writing their verses. But they had found the secret of communion through rhythm and poetry, a form of communication usually used by more creative talents. (52)

Here Meerloo equates poetry to "verbal hypnosis." Because of its rhythm, poetry assumes a reassuring, soothing function in a situation of high stress and uncertainty. It is a rhythm the prisoners find "inside themselves." Though clearly those rhythms have been learned, Meerloo conveys the impression of spontaneity that arises in the face of uncertainty: an activity the inmates engage in of their own accord, one that perhaps serves no utilitarian purpose but creates communication, a transcendence beyond the level of the individual into a communion, even despite language barriers.

One could interpret Meerloo's idea of an "essential 'me'" that finds expression in poetry as a Romantic idealization of the lyric genre as a *cri de cœur*, of lyric poetry as the most direct route to the inner self — Meerloo refers to "intimate thoughts in measured cadences." This idealization may itself be operative in the poems from the camps, though few of them present themselves as intimate expression. Often they operate at a level of generality or within a structure that creates a distance between the speaker and the feelings or actions described. The "I," as we shall see, tends to be rather elusive in this particular set of poems from the late nineteen thirties and early nineteen forties.[12]

Meerloo's idea of an "essential 'me,'" of a "rhythmic voice inside," particularly in conjunction with his concept of a poetic "verbal hypnosis," can be read in terms of an imaginary — that is to say, transferential — connection.[13] In "emergency poetry" in general and in poetry from the concentration camps in particular, this is a connection to a "self" that is outside or beyond the terrible circumstances of the camps. A poem's persona or speaker maintains a link to another time frame, imagines communication with the past or the future and thus renders temporary the adverse circumstances of the present moment. Meerloo writes of "communion" and "communication." Those notions, even if phantasmatic when considered from a psychological perspective, seem crucial in poems from the camps.

One could say that Meerloo fantasizes that poetry implies a voice, rhythm, play, an author, and a community, an audience. Those powerful fantasies seem to be necessary components of the writings in the camps. "In those stressful years," "people in extreme anxiety, frozen by the enemy into complete passivity" managed to find some consolation in poems and songs they recited or composed. Meerloo claims that such activity gave at least temporary succor to their harrowed souls. We can speculate that, if nothing else, such "playful rhythmization of words" opened up a space for personal expression to individuals who were being deprived of even the most basic physical comfort and personal autonomy. In their transcendence beyond the self, the poems were likely "therapeutic," or in Meerloo's words, "ecstatic" and "soothing" in the midst of horror. The rhythm, we might argue as well, constituted a link to a familiar, even if unconscious, pleasure.

Thus, to make explicit what has also emerged from the foregoing, the form of the poem, seen from a point of view informed by psychoanalytic considerations, seems to provide a structure for bringing traumatic experience to articulation. Possibly it allows the author to create in or through the poem a "resonating other," in the terminology of psychoanalysts Dori Laub and Nanette Auerhahn (1989), an interlocutor who plays an essential role in the mechanisms that safeguard psychic identity and health. The stories the poems tell may be "necessary fictions" that create meaning, allow for distance (for the perspective necessary for reflection), or, at times, provide consoling closure or a limited sense of mastery. This book examines particular, individual attempts to "make narrative sense" — in Pascale Bos's phrase (38) — of a chaotic and brutally violent environment, an environment designed to deprive its inhabitants of a sense of voice, community, and connection, and, ultimately, to kill them. Beyond the narrative as well, the poems create a structure through the repetition of sound and rhythm, possibly providing a sense of mastery and of a familiar order and regularity in traumatic surroundings.

Most writings on trauma focus on its aftereffects — the psychological sequelae of traumatization — as the by-now popular and official acronym PTSD (for post-traumatic stress disorder) corroborates.[14] From a technical point of view, the concept of trauma has come to form part of a major psychological, psychiatric, or psychoanalytic nosology. By definition, in other words, the term is applied retroactively when certain clinical symptoms are detected. Usually such a diagnosis posits an event in the past that is regarded as an "influx of excitations that is excessive by the standards of the subject's tolerance and capacity to master such excitations and work them out psychically" (Laplanche and Pontalis, 465.) In its essence, then, trauma pertains to experience that cannot be psychically assimilated into consciousness and thus haunts the traumatized person. The notion of the "traumatic event" itself is further complicated by the fact that traumatization "cannot be defined by the event itself — which may or may not be catastrophic, and may not traumatize everyone equally — nor can it be defined in terms of a personal *distortion* of the event, achieving its haunting power as a result of distorting personal significances attached to it" (Caruth 1995, 4). At the same time, the Holocaust has been understood to have traumatic repercussions not only for those directly persecuted but also for others, including more generally for Western civilization. As Dominick LaCapra argues:

> The traumatic event has its greatest and most clearly unjustifiable effect on the victim, but in different ways it also affects everyone who comes in contact with it: perpetrator, collaborator, bystander, resister, those born later. Especially for victims, trauma brings about a lapse or rupture in memory that breaks continuity with the past, thereby placing identity in question to the point of shattering it. But it may raise problems of identity for others insofar as it unsettles narcissistic investments and desired self-images, including — especially with respect to the Shoah — the image of Western civilization as the bastion of elevated values if not the high point in the evolution of humanity. (1998, 8–9)

Some consideration of phenomena resulting from trauma is relevant to the reading of poems written in the camps, as these poems themselves to some degree are a response — as cultural interventions in language — to a radical threat to identity and existence, just as writings on trauma alert us to the indirect ways in which a psychically unassimilated or dissociated experience makes itself known. Traumatic effects can also become evident in the ethical demands placed on contemporary readers by these very poems, readers who risk getting caught between "insensitivity — a distanced objectification of the text that ignores its affective realities — and sentimentality — an uncritical empathic identification with its affect that ignores its historical relevance" (Kahane, 182–83). In this context the notion of "empathic unsettlement" offers perhaps a possibility for overcoming the impulse between sentimentality in the form of vicarious identification on the one hand and insensitivity on the other. LaCapra argues that empathy does and should play a role in processes of understanding, including historical understanding, and warns against attempts to do away with empathy altogether. Empathy is difficult to control, LaCapra admits, but

> empathy is bound up with a transferential relation to the past, and it is arguably an affective aspect of understanding which both limits objecti-

fication and exposes the self to involvement or implication in the past, its actors, and victims . . . desirable empathy involves not full identification but what might be termed empathic unsettlement in the face of traumatic limit events, their perpetrators, and their victims. (2001, 102)[15]

Gubar elaborates on the concept of "empathic unsettlement," making an important distinction between sympathy, "which supposes affinity among people," and empathy, "with its recognition of disparity" (243). Gubar sees "empathic identification" as "responsively interactive forms of subjectivity" that are "not aggressively coercive, not passively submissive," an affective "reciprocity" that is in stark contrast to the "act of Nazi annihilation" (243–44).[16]

Although the notion of trauma refers primarily to questions of memory and history, to a split or dissociation of the psyche and to a belated response to the traumatic event, the writings on trauma by Nanette Auerhahn, Dori Laub, and Daniel Podell provide a framework for an analysis of the different ways in which individuals who were victims of the Nazis expressed their psychic reactions to persecution and internment in their poetry. The work of these psychoanalysts is based on oral testimonies and clinical case studies, and it offers applied readings of individual responses to the experience of persecution during the Holocaust. Both the work with oral testimonies and psychoanalytic work with survivors involve an active mode of listening that would let the victims speak, would give them back in the present a voice that the Nazis denied them in the past, while simultaneously acknowledging the processes of interpretation and the importance of relevant historical knowledge. Here the model for literary criticism is a dialogic one: dialogic both in the Bakhtinian sense of a criticism that understands itself as historically bound and creative[17] and in the psychoanalytic sense of an awareness of the transferential relation to the object of study, what we can also call the critic's countertransference or subjective reaction to the material. LaCapra describes transference as "one's implication in the other or the object of study with the tendency to repeat in one's own discourse or practice tendencies active in, or projected into, the other or object" (2004, 74). An awareness of such transferential process implies critical self-reflection and possibly a self-critical hesitancy.[18] Gubar warns us: "Since not-writing about the Shoah would constitute a Nazi victory, one way to evade indulging in self-serving forms of recollection involves taking seriously the idea that our stake in the fates of the murdered must be considered along with the stake they have in us" (7).[19]

Whereas, ideally, possibly all literary interpretation would be dialogic, the work of the aforementioned psychoanalysts makes possible the search for the individually diverse and varied responses to traumatic experiences in a manner that takes into consideration both the fragmentation and desolation entailed by the trauma as well as the powerful need to reconstitute continuity and identity in the victims of trauma and also, differently, in ourselves, the critics. These psychoanalysts' attention to language and the imagination (for example, in the form of creative activity) as partially constitutive or restorative of identity can serve as a starting point for a literary analysis of poetry that arose in the chaos and brutality of the concentration camps. As a work of literary analysis this book does not present an attempt to diagnose the psychic structures of inmate-writers. Rather, psychological notions such as "self" and "identity" are used here to think about works created by such individuals while their most basic assumptions about the world and about their own place in that world were under extreme attack. As Caroline Garland reminds us, in the context of an individual's response to trauma it is also crucial to take into account the individual's embeddedness in his or her own culture (23).[20] James Young also emphasizes the role of an individual's worldview or culture in any response to the experience of Nazi persecution: "But each victim "saw" — that is, understood *and* witnessed — his predicament differently, depending on his own historical past, religious paradigms, and ideological explanations" (26).

In an essay entitled "Art and Trauma" Laub and Podell posit an "art of trauma" that, through its "indirect and dialogic nature," can "come close to representing the emptiness at the core of trauma while still offering the survivor the possibility of repossession and restoration" (993). They use the metaphor of an "empty circle" to figure the "core of trauma" as the "abandonment of listening and communication that characterizes trauma." Their focus is on the art of survivors and of those born later. With respect to those subjects, they propose that "when a person is subjected to a trauma, the only way he can maintain a connection between self and internal other is by exercising an inner capability to shape and order the coercive 'facts' that confront him. Art aids survival (as well as recovery) by widening one's vision and offering alternative perspectives and ways of seeing things" (998). The authors go on to describe imaginative acts that transform a world that threatens to become "devoid of meaning." These imaginative acts, which may be described as the inner creation of meaning and of perspective in the face of traumatic fragmentation, can "deepen the experience" and "invest it with significance, albeit a dreadful one." One of their most telling examples comes from the oral (videographic) testimony of Helen K.: "She tells of how her thirteen-year-old brother died in her arms by asphyxiating in an overcrowded transport wagon. At the moment in which she witnessed both visually and physically the death of a family member, she vowed: 'I'm going to live.' She testifies: 'I said to myself, "I want to live one day after Hitler, one day after the end of the war"'" (999).

Laub and Podell point to the importance of Helen K.'s assertion, to her determination to survive, to outlive Hitler. Of course, actual survival depended on a multiplicity of factors, including chance, and most of the time none of those factors could be influenced by the inmates. Obviously it would be wrongheaded to shift responsibility for the deaths from the perpetrators to the victims. Laub and Podell point to the psychological significance of Helen K.'s determination when they argue that "when confronted with death, with a situation that tears apart all previous meaning and trust," Helen K. created in herself the belief that she was "going to live." Through that imaginative act she gave "form and meaning to the arbitrary brutality that surrounded her":

> This is not a superficial attribution of meaning. It does not look for "reasons" for this arbitrary and unjust occurrence. Nor does it succumb to the utter void and loss of meaning that was to be the moral of the trauma. Rather, in her expression of the belief that she will, in fact, survive to outlive Hitler himself, she becomes important, significant, and, as such, accurately comprehends and unyieldingly defies the psychology Hitler sought to impose on the Jews, i.e. that each is merely a number and deserves his fate. Through that imaginative act that created a framework for the knowing and comprehension of the deadly, arbitrary circumstances that confronted her, she realised her intimate, undeniable and inextricable connection to life. This ability to transcend the immediate physical reality through a kind of poetic defiance *may* be what enabled the girl to survive through the camps in the face of physical deterioration. (999)

It is my contention in this book that the poems written in the concentration camps can be understood as another form of that "kind of poetic defiance" — not precisely because of their lyricism, nor necessarily because they might have played a role in the writer's survival, a claim of which one must be wary. Rather, they can be read in this manner because, in ways that are similar to Helen K.'s resolution, the act of composing a poem in the camps — like other artistic or creative endeavors exercised there, at times at the risk of one's life — involves "the inner capability to shape and order the coercive" circumstances of life there (Laub and Podell, 998) and to imbue those circumstances with significance. It is worth noticing in this context that the language Laub and Podell use in order to analyze the psychological process they call "poetic defiance" is related to literary criticism. Their notions of a "meaning" and a "moral" to be derived from the Nazi treatment of Jews evokes the idea of the interpretation of texts and most prominently fables that contain a morally edifying lesson. In Laub and Podell's reading, the moral the Nazis seek to impart is an immoral one. Thus an idea of competing narratives intrinsically connected to ethics is implicit in their theory of the creative responses to trauma. Poems written in the camps constitute narratives contrary to the actions and expectations of the Nazis.

Composing a poem constitutes a gesture that contradicts the humiliation, silencing, and dehumanization imposed by the perpetrators and thereby "widens one's vision." These poems take a position against the brutality of the conditions imposed by the Nazis, even if it is in a manner that is difficult to characterize because it is not always as explicit as in the case of Helen K. Additionally, much unlike the case of testimonies of survivors, the poetic defiance of poems from the camps is not a priori connected to survival. In terms of the individual writers the poems may help anchor a sense of identity. They may help reassert an author's sense of emotional and spiritual autonomy and capacity for individual expression by serving as a mental bridge to life before imprisonment, to the world outside the camps, or to worlds beyond the material constraints of life in the camps. The poems are thus private acts in an environment that sought to annihilate the personal sphere, to make people uniform, and to destroy their individual personality by denying them the most basic rights and freedoms. Not surprisingly, Aat Breur, a Dutch resistance fighter and former inmate of Ravensbrück, writes of the sixteen-century German protest song "Die Gedanken sind frei" (Thoughts Are Free), a song extolling freedom of thought despite external coercion, as one of the most popular songs among inmates in the camps (Breur, 150). Poems written in the camps can be understood as expressions of private creativity and freedom, just as they may seem bound to particular aesthetic ideologies — even if at the level of ideology critique they may seem particularly "unfree" in the conventionality of their form. By their very existence the poems testify to their authors' at times tenuous but enduring trust in the word, or, more often, to an attempted restoration of such trust. This trust in language would seem to imply the possibility of communication with the present and the future. In this book I propose to read poems from the concentration camps as "imaginative acts" and as self-representations by people who were being denied personal, political, civil, legal, and historical representation.

The project of examining poems written in the camps requires us to understand poetry as a literary genre with a number of different and overlapping functions and within a variety of interrelated cultural registers. For the authors on a personal level, again, the poems might have functioned as attempts to establish communication with an "other," possibly a particular individual or a group outside the camps, or with one's own past or imagined future. The poems then might be understood as an attempt to be in touch with one's own capacity for expression and as a means to reflect on overwhelming suffering, to create a witness to it, or to attempt an imaginary escape from dire circumstances, be it through rhythmic self-hypnosis, as is suggested in Meerloo's anecdote, or in the form of narratives of wish-fulfillment. Thus the poems implicitly create a cultural role for the inmates.

From a historical perspective poems from the camps can serve as yet another kind of psychological and sociological documentation of people's experiences and their attempts to somehow cope with such experience. Lawrence Langer, Geoffrey Hartman, and Dori Laub, among others, have argued forcefully and convincingly that oral testimonies by Holocaust survivors, when given adequate attention, will yield at least another and possibly a crucial dimension of the truth of the Holocaust. The same can be said of these poems. Poetry written in the camps entails a historical dimension and constitutes a significant archival trace of the individual voices of the victims. With respect to writing the history of Germany during the Third Reich, Saul Friedländer argues:

> The reintroduction of individual memory into the overall representation of the epoch also implies the use of direct or indirect expressions of contemporary individual experience. Working through *means confronting the individual voice* in a field dominated by political decisions and administrative decrees which neutralize the concreteness of despair and death. The *Alltagsgeschichte* of German society has its necessary shadow: the *Alltagsgeschichte* of its victims. (1994, 262)

The point here is not that texts that speak to us "from the events" are, as "direct expressions," more genuine or authentic than texts produced later. Taterka has shown the limitations and dangers of "authenticity" as a criterion for this province of literary criticism: not only does the vastness of the events preclude an absolute knowledge of what did and did not take place in the camps; more importantly, the fact that the experience of the camps was "as if from another world" renders our commonsense judgments highly problematic.[21] And at any rate: we depend on those representations whose authenticity we would judge in order to attain any knowledge of the camps (Taterka, 147–61). As fragmentary evidence of "contemporary individual experience," the poems from the camps bring out individual voices in the context of an insidious and systematic attack on the individual. Thus they may produce a change in our conceptual topology of the camps as the sites not only of mass murder and unimaginable (because extreme and for non-survivors abstract) suffering but also of concrete and possibly creative individual responses to humiliations and torments. In this context it should not be forgotten that the perpetrators produced the vast majority of documents about the ghettos, concentration camps, and extermination camps. Marianne Hirsch has written of the problematic role played by the perspective of the perpetrators in our iconography of the Holocaust (2000). Not only did the perpetrators produce the bulk of the original documentation of the events in the camps, but they also planned the destruction of memory, the distortion of the historical record. In Heinrich Himmler's secret, now oft-quoted speech to the SS of 4 October 1943, the "annihilation of the Jewish people" would be an "unwritten and never-to-be written page of glory" (cited in Davidowicz, 133). Writings, compositions, and paintings by inmates, along with testimonies and creative expressions from survivors, offer us a fundamental change of perspective, giving us a sense of the victims' own responses. Following Saul Friedländer, Gubar has demonstrated the importance of what she calls "minute incidents" that "express the excess" and in their seeming triviality and quirkiness "put the lie to the deceptive sense that the totality of the Holocaust has been or could be captured" (165). These poems report on "minute incidents" and, more importantly, constitute in themselves such "minute incidents" that have not found their way into "Holocaust museums and memorials" (171).

Poems from the camps are also a sociological indication of the endurance of learned forms of expression, and of the fact that our most basic needs are not only physical. Furthermore these poems may provoke us to rethink poetry as a human activity and lead us to consider seriously Adrienne Rich's provocative notion that poetry is not "more, or less, necessary than food, shelter, health, education, decent working conditions. It is as necessary" (xiv). Or as Primo Levi put it: "I had neither lied nor exaggerated. I would really have given bread and soup [in Auschwitz], that is, blood, to save from nothingness those memories" of a few lines of Dante's *Inferno* (1989, 139). According to Corinne Granof and David Mickenberg, surviving visual artists "claimed that art became a necessity for them during their imprisonment." Granof and Mickenberg go on to point out that the fact that prisoners engaged in creative activities in the camps "suggests that producing art represents a basic human drive and fulfills some ineffable need." They also point out, however, that art "is not always an endeavor apart from other motives, or an absolute, direct expression of a creative urge" (xv).

In terms of literary history these poems constitute a specific literary genre that emerged under repression in Nazi Germany: "modern concentration-camp poetry" or in German what Karl Schnog (1945, 14) calls "*moderne Lagerlyrik,*" a corpus of texts that has been ignored by the literary establishment. To posit a loose "genre" *a posteriori* for these admittedly diverse texts — texts that were never in a position to influence one another, texts whose authors at the time of writing were cut off from any literary environment that might have inspired self-conscious considerations of genre — is to enable a comparison of texts that allows us now to think of the phenomenon of literary production in the camps. These "historically specific" texts evince a number of commonalities, most tellingly for considerations of genre perhaps, the "communicational dynamic," which typically includes a sense of the dismal situation in the camps and of a distinct but not separate universe outside the camps.[22]

The readings presented here demonstrate that the examination of the literary production of the period should not limit itself, as it has done most often, to texts published either in exile or under the aegis of the National Socialist regime. When literary history restricts itself in this way, it becomes blind to less visible but nonetheless culturally significant uses of poetry. This "genre" of poetry, then, also reminds us that modern poetry, including poetry written in response to the Shoah, is more varied and diverse than we tend to imagine, and that, as Cary Nelson has argued, "traditional forms continued to do vital cultural work throughout the [modern] period" (23).

This poetry might be particularly relevant in contemporary society's attempts to work through that traumatic past, as one of the few available forms of self-expression and self-representation of the victims.[23] As such, these communications are personal and might allow readers to develop an intimate relation to the poems. In her concern with keeping the memory of the Holocaust alive as we get further and further from the events, Gubar cites Jorie Williams to point out that "poetry attaches itself to consciousness in a way no other language experience does" (255). Contemporary individual as well as collective relations to this kind of poetry would ideally aid in the complex and permanent process of working through the past. This would extend the concept of "poetry therapy" beyond the private and clinical realms, though "healing" still must not be understood simplistically as "putting the past behind."

Attention to the historical context of these poems as well as to the critics' relation to them seems crucial in the attempt to engage with the poems dialogically. Given the conditions under which they were composed, these poems powerfully appeal to the reader to empathize. Only a dialogic reading will be able to show both their situatedness and their representational limits without fetishizing their special status (treating the poems as sacred objects) or dismissing them as narratives that in their inevitable ideological embeddedness and narrative closure disguise the trauma we expect them to communicate. In an essay entitled "Yiddish Writing in the Nazi Ghettos and the Art of the Incommensurable," David Roskies points out that we stand "at a double remove" from the destruction of European Jews since we are "separated, as vicarious sufferers always are, from the actual victims and perpetrators, and further inhabiting a cultural landscape that bears no resemblance whatsoever to that which came before" (1986, 29). As a result, he argues, two tendencies arise in the critical relation to "literature of the Holocaust":

> To view as Scripture every scrap of paper rescued from the Holocaust (to the extent that these have been published, properly edited and adequately translated), or to seek the one response radical enough to render the apocalypse. Both the liturgical and the apocalyptic readings presuppose an event so qualitatively different from any other that it defies all modes of historical and critical analysis. The pious reading of the literature of the Holocaust (as distinct from the literature *on* the Holo-

caust) assumes that aesthetic standards cannot be brought to bear on texts written under such terrible conditions; so all works are treated as equally naive, primitive, and holy. The apocalyptic reading looks for premonitions, unintended ironies, and expressions of rage, based on a similar assumption, that the victims would not have known what we know. Neither approach attempts to contextualize. Both take a corpus of diaries, chronicles, poems, songs, stories and plays written under specific historical conditions by a distinct ethnic and religious group and lift that corpus out of time and place in order to cast light on the post-Holocaust predicament. Even basic chronology is cast aside as postwar recollections are confused with war-time accounts, as memoirs are mixed with diaries, as revised versions are taken to be originals, as death becomes the story of survival. (1986, 29)

Roskies thus identifies a liturgical or pious reading that would disable analytic considerations in the face of texts from the ghettos and camps — and would constitute a fetishistic treatment of the texts — and an apocalyptic reading that would seek a "radical response." An apocalyptic reading as a consequence would tend to dismiss texts it considers conventional as deluded, shortsighted, naïve. A dialogic engagement with the text would avoid the pitfalls of a fetishistic treatment that, in its unquestioning awe, makes impossible any critical perspective. At the same time, the dialogic approach practiced in this book treats the texts as literature worthy of consideration as such. Taterka points out that literary scholars too often write about the concentration camps as if they themselves knew better than the inmates or survivors what went on there, or how best to represent the experience of the camps (171). This at times takes the form of demands for radical representation, for deference to theories of unrepresentability. Following Taterka's admonition, the readings of the poems here will be just that: engagements with the texts, their language and their history, rather than a presumptuous critique of their content. The fetishistic reading is one-dimensional in that it disables the critic; the apocalyptic reading is one-directional in that it undermines the authority of the texts. A dialogic reading proposes to make space for both the literariness of these texts and the critical powers of scholarship.

The following section, the final part of this introduction, offers a genealogy of this literary critical endeavor by way of a history of the reception of poetry from the concentration camps. The next chapter moves from more general discussions of the role of culture in the camps to a consideration of the earliest example in the history of publication of poems from the camps. The story of Ruth Klüger's poems spans half a century and begins with their composition in Gross-Rosen. As Klüger writes in her memoir, there she was responding to impressions from her time at Auschwitz. The story continues with the publication of her poems from 1945 on. Klüger's case is one of the few instances of this poetry for which we have authorial commentary. As we have seen in the case of her relation to the German language, Klüger's memoir includes and considers both temporalities at issue in discussions of cultural production in the camps: a perspective from the camps as well as a post-Holocaust perspective. In addition, Klüger participates as a scholar in the debates about aesthetic creation in the context of the Holocaust. Thus her texts provide the strongest example in German of more general issues that arise in the discussion of poetry from the camps, issues such as an individual's motivations and explanations for their own creative endeavors in the camps, the cultural background of inmates who wrote poems there, and their rhetorical strategies. Significantly, Klüger's writings also illustrate the contested and problematic public uses of cultural products from the camps and the critical quandaries posed by an aesthetic approach to atrocity. Both in terms of the issues raised and in terms of the inclusion of biographical, historical, and critical information, the treatment of Klüger's writings in the first chapter exemplifies the interpretive mode applied in the subsequent chapters.

Chapter 2 examines poems by Hasso Grabner, Fritz Löhner-Beda, and Edgar Kupfer-Koberwitz that focus on situations common to most inmates in concentration camps, though not in extermination camps: being assigned a number, being away from home, having to wear a uniform. In all these poems the narrative involves a transformation that endows the experience with significance and suggests a sense of defiant hope. By contrast, the next chapter analyzes poems that confront more arduous situations and display a lack of such hope. The analysis moves from a poem by Kupfer-Koberwitz focused on the monotony of life in the camps to a series of hunger poems, and then on to a short but almost unbearable poem by Georg von Boris that describes an extreme reaction to hunger. That chapter also examines depictions of the inmates' relations to corpses as these are represented in a nursery rhyme by Ilse Weber and a love poem by Alfred Kittner.

Under the heading "Communicating Torture," chapter 4 discusses a variety of strategies used by authors to represent psychological and, more often, physical abuse. Some of these poems speak for others who were abused, while some of them defy the speaker's torturers and promise revenge. The fifth and final chapter then extends the scope of this study to discuss as well contemporaneous poetry published in the Third Reich. This comparison is intended to be both provocative and critically incisive since the distance separating "everyday life" in the Third Reich from "everyday life" in the camps is, on the one hand, enormous. At the same time these two universes were contiguous and mutually implicated. Such comparison is necessary if we are to consider the period and its legacy as a whole, even if the question of the critic's moral judgment looms large in such exercise. German Jews living under the Nazis temporarily occupied an intermediate zone, so to speak, between German society and the concentration camps, thus this chapter also includes a discussion of German-Jewish cultural activity in the Third Reich.

Finally, the conclusion revisits the question of posthumous or belated aesthetic judgment in the context of post-Holocaust poetry. This is another important axis of comparison. Whether with or without hope, poems from the camps evince in terms of both style and narrative a search for unity, for containment, and for some form of resolution. Such restorative impulse, which seems to predominate in poetry written in the camps, is replaced in post-Holocaust poetry by the need to render the unthinkable loss, to represent in poetry the shattering and its shadows.

The 1990s Anthologize the Camps: A History

In 1969 Meerloo lamented the loss of "war poetry by non-poets." But since then more of it has been gathered and examined, though concentration-camp poetry as a phenomenon in its own right failed to draw sustained attention until the 1990s. The history of the publication and reception of poetry from the Nazi concentration camps has reflected growing interest in the cultural activities of inmates in those camps. This growth took place amid shifting perceptions accompanying new developments in Holocaust studies as well as the turns of the Cold War. Through this process a disparate set of poems coalesced into a "genre" for the publishing industry; even so, publication and scholarship in this area have remained precarious and scattered. A brief historical account (here limited to the Western European languages) is therefore necessary and will serve as an annotated bibliographic guide to the field.

The year 1989 marked a major turning point in the history of Germany and of the competing sides in the Cold War. In some ways 1989 signaled the end of a century dominated by two world wars and the subsequent division of the world along irreconcilable ideologies maintained by the threat of nuclear war. The political changes that took place in 1989 brought an end to the partition of Germany that had been imposed after 1945 and consequently created the sense that some of Germany's historical debt had been settled. The apparent acceptance of a unified Germany as another "normal" European neighbor produced in that country louder calls to put the past behind once and for all. 1989 seemed to bring to a close a post-Holocaust period of penance. The new Germany's relationship to the past remains complex and highly conflicted, however, as demonstrated by recurring debates about the proper place and appropriate forms for remembering and memorializing the history of the Third Reich, including its history of persecution and war, in contemporary German society and in Germany's new and former capital Berlin.

In a manner reminiscent of Meerloo's concern about the loss of poetry written under persecution, the scholar of German letters Wolfgang Emmerich pointed in 1976 to the lack of attention granted to poems from the concentration camps. As he put it in the opening lines of a section on literature from the camps in an essay entitled "The Literature of the Anti-Fascist Resistance in Germany":

> In what follows I will report on a thoroughly literary phenomenon of the period 1933–1945 that — as far as I can see — has not been noted in any literary history: that is, the use of literature as a means of resistance in the fascist concentration camps and other prisons and detention centers. (1976, 441)

In keeping with the prevailing proclivities of the politicized, left-leaning West-German intelligentsia of the nineteen seventies, Emmerich emphasized the role of "literature as a *medium for resistance*" in the concentration camps. His essay explores a variety of forms of resistance to National Socialism in and through literature. In its section on literature in the camps, Emmerich seeks to broaden the scope of the term *resistance* to include what he implies are some of its less obvious (because less clearly political) manifestations, such as "the self-understanding and strengthening of identity of the individual resistance fighter, the encouragement of his fellow inmates, the sensory experience of solidarity" (442). Although Emmerich concentrated on political prisoners — that is, on those who by definition were resistance fighters — he points in the essay to a larger set of texts that constitute what he rightly called a literary phenomenon, one that had received scant attention then and has fared only slightly better since: the writings, and more specifically the poems, composed by inmates in the National Socialist ghettos, prisons, and concentration camps.

A related cultural phenomenon that similarly has failed to attract critical attention is the publication in Germany during the 1990s and beyond of several anthologies of such poetry, as well as several books by individual authors. Before then, only one large-scale study, Michael Moll's pioneering doctoral dissertation, *Lyrik in einer entmenschlichten Welt: Interpretationsversuche zu deutschsprachigen Gedichten aus nationalsozialistischen Gefängnissen, Ghettos und KZ's* (Lyric in a Dehumanized World: Attempts at Interpretation of German-Language Poems from National Socialist Prisons, Ghettos, and Concentration Camps), had appeared (1988).[24] It is therefore all the more significant that since the last decade of the twentieth century this poetry has reached a wider audience and that, although still largely ignored by critics, historians of literature, and Holocaust studies scholars, it has attained a limited popularity with the general public in Germany through readings, local newspapers, and its publication by some, albeit mostly smaller, publishing houses. To explain the current and unprecedented interest in poetry from the camps one must consider a number of interrelated yet distinct developments within academic disciplines, in mainstream culture, and in international relations:

Since 1945 there have been several waves of interest in the Holocaust and, since the 1970s and 1980s, a renewed international concern with its history and legacy. Alternatively, one can also speak of various attempts to counter tendencies to deny or forget the Holocaust. Gubar writes of how in the sixties "the conspiracy in the forties and fifties to nullify the Holocaust was brought to public attention and defeated by the first generation of Holocaust studies advocates" (3). Examples of interest in the history of the Holocaust range from studies of psychotherapeutic work with children and grandchildren of survivors to Steven Spielberg's popular film *Schindler's List* (1993) and the building of the U.S. Holocaust Memorial Museum in Washington, DC, or, in Berlin, the building of the Jewish Museum[25] and later the Memorial to the Murdered Jews of Europe. Such international interest was spurred further by the fiftieth anniversary commemorations of the liberation of the concentration camps in the mid-nineties (Kahane, 161).

Moreover, at the end of a massively violent century, the term trauma became common currency. Theories of trauma and the workings of memory were put to new clinical, academic, legal, and political use as different groups — from survivors of sexual abuse to veterans of the Vietnam War — sought recognition for, and healing from, the suffering they had endured. Post Traumatic Stress Disorder, or PTSD, gained official recognition in 1980.[26]

In addition, during the 1980s the new status of individual experience as a legitimate field of scientific and scholarly inquiry was manifested, for example, in the rise to prominence of oral history. Projects to record the experiences of survivors of the Holocaust have gained new urgency as these individuals near the end of their lives. Survivors themselves seem keener than they were before to tell their stories, and younger people, particularly those of the third generation, seem more willing to listen to survivors speak of their experiences. The "need to forget and move on" that survivors felt intensely after the war — and which at times was imposed on them — has given way to the need to bear witness, to know, and to remember (see also Gubar, 2). The Fortunoff Video Archive of Holocaust Testimonies at Yale University, started in 1979 and greatly expanded in the following decades, attests to this change. Folklorist Christoph Daxelmüller dates to the end of the 1980s the "discovery of the [concentration-camp] inmate as a cultural being," noting that although some publications containing cultural productions from the camps date from the 1940s, these were not taken into account in scholarly studies of the camps nor were cultural activities regarded as "strategies of identification and survival" (Daxelmüller, 256).

The following note in the preface to French author Jean Cayrol's poems from the concentration camp Mauthausen, however, reveals a persistent and widely shared belief that the writings from the concentration camps do not constitute literature properly speaking. At the same time, the publication of Cayrol's poems signals a change from the notion, held in the 1940s and 1950s, that such work should not be published to satisfaction with their "rediscovery" in the 1990s. In an anecdote that exemplifies more generally the variegated paths of the actual, material pages of poetry composed in the camps, and of its reception later on, Cayrol explains:

> Ces textes, que l'auteur se refuse à considérer comme de poèmes, ont été écrits dans un atelier d'une petite usine du camp Guzen-Mauthausen. Les détenus y vérifiaient des pièces entassées sur de grandes tables. En se cachant sous ces abris relatifs, l'auteur écrivait dans la pénombre, sans se relire, pendant que le travail se poursuivait au-dessus de lui.
>
> Perdus à la Libération, ses carnets lui furent restitués dix ans plus tard par un Allemand anonyme. Mais, en 1955, il était conseillé aux survivants d'oublier, de se taire . . .
>
> Oublié, donc, puis retrouvé par hasard cinquante ans plus tard, ce recueil est ici présenté sans corrections ni ajouts. (Cayrol, 5)

> [These texts, which their author refuses to consider poems, were written in the workshop of a small factory of the camp Guzen-Mauthausen. The inmates were carrying out quality control checks on machinery pieces piled on large tables. Hiding under such contingent cover, the author wrote in dimness, without rereading, while work continued above him. . . .
>
> Lost at the Liberation, the notebooks were returned to him ten years later by an anonymous German. But, in 1955, survivors were advised to forget, to keep silent. . . .
>
> Forgotten, then found again by chance fifty years later, this collection is presented here without corrections or additions.]

In Germany, the fall of the Berlin Wall invigorated scholarly inquiry into the period that had brought about that country's division. At the same time, new opportunities for research became available in Eastern Europe. In fact, in a prefatory note, editors Ellinor Lau and Susanne Pampuch attribute the inspiration for their anthology of poems and songs from the concentration camps to a meeting in Krakow with Aleksander Kulisiewicz, a survivor of Sachsenhausen who had dedicated his life to collecting artwork and poetry from the camps (Lau and Pampuch, 2).

From the point of view of literary history, numerous challenges to the canon have undone a dogmatically codified aesthetic order and encouraged archeological research aimed at recovering previously discarded authors. A critical sensibility less bound to modernist aesthetics and New-Critical formalism allows us to take seriously poetry that would otherwise appear "too contingent," too enmeshed in its historical context. Cary Nelson argues that "of all literary genres, poetry has the strongest tradition of being idealized as ahistorical, transcendent, self-referential and self-contained" (128). He proposes that we look beyond the canon for other uses of poetry. Nelson's arguments apply here as well. Like the works by "lost [American] poets" such as William Vaughn Moody and H. H. Lewis, which Nelson himself examines, the poems from the camps do not "generally display the surface indecision and ambivalence that many critics since the 1950s have deemed a transcendent, unquestionable, literary value" (Nelson, 44). Therefore, until recently, they have been ignored.

Meerloo writes that "no great poetry" was composed in the camps; Cayrol "refuses" to consider his writings poems. Jäger shows how in West Germany an initial interest in the German-Jewish poet Gertrud Kolmar, who had been deported by the Nazis and who perished most probably in Auschwitz, was quickly replaced by an indifference to her poetry while Gottfried Benn's aestheticist, radically anti-historical late poetry, on the other hand, was celebrated as the work of *the* modern German lyric poet. Poetry was to be regarded as "autonomous" and not primarily related to "ethics" (Jäger, 133–34). As these examples suggest, critics, authors, and, in some cases, the public have tended to react defensively to these poems. For instance, in the 1962 preface to *An den Wind geschrieben: Lyrik der Freiheit, 1933–1945* (Written to the Wind: Poetry of Freedom, 1933–1945), an anthology of exile and oppositional poetry that contains a number of poems from the camps, editor and compiler Manfred Schlösser concedes that "not every poem may appeal to our understanding of art" (9). He suggests that one might notice "at times, an embarrassing holding on to old forms and formulas"; but our attention is justified, he contends, because of the human significance of the poetry. I argue that such generalized discomfort with "old forms" stems from an unreflected and partial notion of aesthetic quality, one overly indebted to the aesthetics of avant-garde European modernism — and its erection into a form of critical defense — with its emphases on formal experimentation and on challenging narrative closure.

Individual memory itself, as well as the workings of mourning and melancholia, has recently become a topic of intense scholarly inquiry. To quote Friedländer again, what is necessary for the responsible writing of history is "the use of direct or indirect expressions of contemporary experience. *Working through means confronting the individual voice* in a field dominated by political decisions and administrative decrees which neutralize the concreteness of despair and death" (1994, 262). Rather than recollections of the past, as in the case of testimonies from survivors, poems written in the camps are direct expressions of individual attempts to come to terms with incomprehensible, traumatic events. As manifestations of individual voices and of the individuality of those voices, these poems convey a personal dimension of the horrors of the concentration camps. It is in this vein that they have been anthologized in the 1990s in Germany and elsewhere.

One could argue that this trend in the publishing industry is particularly noteworthy in Germany, the land of the perpetrators. But interest in these poems has international dimensions too. In the United States, for example, Frieda Aaron published what the book cover calls a "pioneering study of Yiddish and Polish-Jewish concentration camp and ghetto poetry": *Bearing the Unbearable: Yiddish and Polish Poetry from the Concentration Camps* (1990). Previously David Roskies had written about Yiddish texts from the ghettos and camps (1984; 1986). Four anthologies published in the U.S., though not dedicated exclusively to poetry by prisoners of the Nazis, all contain poems written in the Nazi camps: Carolyn Forché's voluminous collection, *Against Forgetting: Twentieth Century Poetry of Witness* (1993); Hilda Schiff's *Holocaust Poetry* (1995); *Beyond Lament: Poets from the World Bearing Witness to the Holocaust,* edited by Marguerite Striar (1998); and Aaron Kramer's *The Last Lullaby: Poetry from the Holocaust* (1998). Of these Kramer's anthology has the highest proportion of poems written (mostly in Yiddish) in ghettos and camps, as well as a complete translation of *Der Kaiser von Atlantis* (The Emperor of Atlantis), a German-language opera written and composed entirely in Theresienstadt by librettist Peter Kien and composer Viktor Ullmann.

In France 1995 witnessed the fiftieth anniversary republication of poems from Buchenwald, Verdet's *Anthologie des poèmes de Buchenwald* (Anthology of Poems from Buchenwald), as well as a major new compilation by Henri Pouzol under the title *Ces voix toujours présentes: Anthologie de la poésie européenne concentrationnaire* (These Ever-Present voices: Anthology of European Concentration-Camp Poetry). Here Pouzol, who had already edited an anthology of concentration-camp poetry in 1975, grants these poems the status of a European literary genre through the use of the definite article in French (*la*) and of "concentration-camp" as an adjective to modify "poetry." In 1993, Rachel Ertel published in Paris a study of poetry in Yiddish under the title *Dans la langue de personne: Poésie yiddish de l'anéantissement* (In No One's Language: Yiddish Poetry of the Extermination). Also in France, as cited earlier, poet and former concentration-camp inmate Jean Cayrol, *par hasard,* found again the poems he had written over fifty years earlier at Mauthausen and published them in 1997 as *Alerte aux ombres: 1944–1945* (Alarm in the Shadows: 1944–1945). And in 2001, Yves Ménager edited another anthology of concentration-camp poetry under the title *Paroles de Déportés* (Words of the Deported).

Interest in the cultural life of inmates of the camps extends beyond poetry. Artistic and personal expressions from ghettos and camps in a variety of media, from diaries (Reiter 2000, Laqueur 1992), painting (Mickenberg, Granof, and Haynes 2003), religion (Rahe 1999), music (Fackler 2000), and recipes (Silva 1996, Goldenberg 2003) to cabaret (Kühn 1989) and theater (Rovit and Goldfarb 1999) have also been researched. The music world in particular has experienced since the 1990s an international surge of interest in songs and poems from the ghettos and concentration camps, as exemplified in the Decca label's series "Entartete Musik: Music Suppressed by the Third Reich," which in 1994 brought out Ullmann's opera and other songs composed in Theresienstadt (Ullmann), or Arabesque Recording's own "Music from Terezín" series, which released an English-language recording of Ullmann's concentration-camp opera in 1996 (Ullmann). In addition, under the title *Composers of the Holocaust: Ghetto Songs from Warsaw, Vilna, and Terezín,* Mimi Stern-Wolfe released a CD of original compositions from the ghettos as well as some poems from those ghettos set to music later (Stern-Wolfe 2000). Similarly, Bente Kahan set to music poems written by Ilse Weber in Theresienstadt, and released recordings of them in Norwegian (Kahan 1996), German (Kahan 1997), and English (Kahan 2000). In 1997, Russian-Israeli composer Zlata Razdolina set to music Yitzhak Katzenelson's Yiddish epic written in Nazi internment, "The Song of the Murdered Jewish People" (Razdolina 1998). On the occasion of a review of a staging of Ullmann and Kien's opera in New York City, the *New York Times* carried an article entitled "Hearing Music Silenced by the Nazis" on 26 March 2003. In it, Allan Kozinn reported that the works of composers imprisoned and murdered by the Nazis had been simply "forgotten" until "the 1980s and 90s, when researchers who had heard about the composers came looking for their work." As Cayrol's words cited above illustrate, beginning in the 1980s the time for "forgetting" seems to be over; this was even more true in the following decade.

It would be misleading, however, to create the impression that none of this poetry was published before 1989. Certainly some of it was, but very often such publication occurred rather inconspicuously in volumes containing mostly poems written by authors who had been in exile or had been part of the *Inner Emigration* — the term Germans invented to refer to individuals who secretly opposed the regime but remained in Germany during the Third Reich, and who wrote texts that were either not published then or were somehow coded or ambiguous enough to fool the Nazi censors (see Schnell). *De Profundis: Deutsche Lyrik in dieser Zeit* (De Profundis: German Poetry in These Times), a collection by Gunter Groll published in Munich in 1946, is the earliest anthology dedicated to inner emigration that also contains a few poems written by inmates in the camps. Other anthologies of exile and inner-emigration poetry that include a few poems from the camps are Felmayer's *Dein Herz ist deine Heimat* (Your Heart is Your Homeland), published in 1955; the already mentioned anthology edited by Schlösser (1960, 1961, 1962); and Seydel's 1968 anthology, *Welch Wort in die Kälte gerufen: Die Judenverfolgung des Dritten Reiches im deutschen Gedicht*

(Words Shouted into the Cold: the Third Reich's Persecution of the Jews in German Verse). A collection that reproduces artworks as well as some poems produced by inmates of Buchenwald was published in Leipzig as *Kunst hinter Stacheldraht: Ein Beitrag zur Geschichte des antifaschistischen Widerstandkampfes* (Art behind Barbed Wire: A Contribution to the History of the Battle of the Antifascist Resistance; Schneider 1973, 1976). It was only after 1989, however, that this set of diverse and scattered texts coalesced into a "genre" deemed worthy of its own anthologies. For the most part, the poems had been available in print, but the cultural climate had relegated them to a gray zone as documents of dubious value, as contingent or old-fashioned poetry, or as artifacts of terrible memories or bad conscience best kept at a distance.

At the risk of sounding naïvely innocent about the ideological force of post-Cold War rhetoric, I suggest that the final decade of the twentieth century brought about a loosening of East-West ideological tension. In 1962 such tension, as well as the internal debates about the political and moral merits of exile, had led Manfred Schlösser, editor of the West German anthology *An den Wind geschrieben,* to assert that "in the selection we wisely refrained from any partisanship!" but then to emphasize that "the contributions of authors who, according to our information, fought or suffered for a different kind of totalitarian regime — and not fundamentally against the degradation of the human personality — those authors have no place here" (1962, 9). In other words, at the height of the Cold War, the work of such left-wing opponents of the Nazi regime as Communist inmates was not acceptable in this West German publication. Characteristically, the focus is on the "degradation of the human personality" (1962, 9) and on the "battle against barbarity" (1962, 10), and a more specific political engagement is seen as suspect. Schlösser writes of the "martyrs' legacy to our nation" (1960, 17) and of "martyrs in the camps and ghettos" (1962, 7). Post–Cold War interest similarly revolves around the personal and private aspects of the experience of the camps, with an emphasis on the suffering and on the persecution of Jews. Thus the perspective in West Germany has become the dominant perspective after unification, though in a different tone. Significantly, the remarks about "a different kind of totalitarian regime" appear in much milder form in the original, 1960 edition of the anthology, suggesting that the 1961 erection of the Berlin Wall may have affected the editor's attitudes.

East of the Iron Curtain, Wolfgang Schneider, the author and editor of the aforementioned anthology of concentration-camp artwork and poetry from Buchenwald (tellingly entitled *Art Behind Barbed Wire: A Contribution to the History of the Battle of Antifascist Resistance*), highlights the heroic resistance of the "righteous" — in other words, the Communist inmates in the camps. Schneider minimizes the extent of the senseless suffering by emphasizing the resolve of artists with revolutionary consciousness. As Schneider's subtitle suggests, the anthology presents the works of art not in terms of the torment individuals endured in Buchenwald but rather in terms of their fight against a political enemy — a battle, one might add, retroactively linked ideologically to the Soviet Union's eventual position in the war against Hitler's Germany. Schneider manages to obliterate any reference to Nazi racial policy by pairing Christians with Communists, rather than with Jews, in the supposedly all-inclusive list that answers a question couched in definitely humanist and positive tones ("the new day in the development of humanity"):

> Who were the righteous ones, who in the fascist night lit the light of true humanity and carried it over into the morning of the new day in the development of humanity? They were Communists and Christians, proletarian revolutionaries and bourgeois democrats; representatives from many nations with differing worldviews and divergent conceptions of art, but united in their repudiation of the fascist dictatorship and in their resolve to fight against it. (1973, 15–16; 1976, 15–16)

The implied message in Schneider's introduction is that the Jews suffered passively under the persecution of the Third Reich, but Schneider intends, at least explicitly, only to tell a story of antifascist resistance — by 1973, a story clearly couched in a Cold-War East German rhetoric that understood the West German government as the heir to and continuation of the Nazi regime and saw the German Democratic Republic as the peaceful alternative (see Herf, especially 162–200). Certainly, the only collection of poems specifically on the topic of the persecution of the Jews in the Third Reich was published in East Berlin, but the introduction, again, puts this persecution in the acceptable context in official East German history: the persecution of Jews is only a section (*ein Ausschnitt*) of the "hell of the Third Reich," and anti-Semitism is to be understood in terms of a class antagonism to which East Germany understood itself to be the solution (Seydel, 9). In agreement with Soviet foreign policy and a year after the Six-Day War in the Middle East, Seydel's introduction to *Words Shouted into the Cold: the Third Reich's Persecution of Jews in German Verse* manages as well to include a strongly worded critique of Israel, elegantly accomplished through the citation of critical verses written in Jerusalem in the early 1940s by a German-speaking Jewish-Czech exile, Louis Fürnberg: "The young generation dreams of bombs, / the swastika turns into a star of Zion" (Seydel, 21).

Cold War editors on both sides of the divide underscored the ideological value and purity of the contributions they gathered in their respective publications. In 1990 there was a faint remnant of that type of international politics in the first anthology dedicated exclusively to poems from the camps, but political ideology is no longer a criterion for inclusion or exclusion in Hanna Elling's 1990 anthology *Mitten in tiefer Nacht: Gedichte aus Konzen-*

trationslagern und Zuchthäusern des deutschen Faschismus, 1933–1945 (In the Middle of Deep Night: Poems from Concentration Camps and Prisons of German Fascism, 1933–1945). Elling was a political opponent of the Nazi regime who was interned at a small camp near Moringen; the collection seems inspired by her scholarly work on the history of women under National Socialism, particularly women of the resistance (Elling 1978). The book has a documentary flair that comes through in its academic organization and the considerable historical background provided at the beginning of each section. In her introduction Elling explains that the texts come from men, women, and children and represent "different political convictions and a variety of worldviews. These were people from all levels of society, among them workers, intellectuals, artists as well as people filled with a deep religiosity; numerous among them were convinced antifascists" (1990, 11). The rhetorical terms and the perspective have changed: no longer, as for Schneider in East Germany in the 1970s, "united in their resolve to fight against fascist dictatorship," the authors now *may* have been political opponents of the regime. The point here is not to validate supporters of the regime, which none of the anthologies do, but to show how the focus of interest shifted from the nobility and heroism of political opposition to personal trauma.

The anthologies of the 1990s are interested in inmates of the concentration camps as victims, as people who suffered, who endured traumatic conditions. To bear witness to the suffering and to memorialize the humanity of the victims are the stated purposes of such publications. To help him obtain publication of a selection from the extensive compilation he had gathered for his master's thesis in the early 1980s (Moll 1983), Moll joined forces with Social-Democratic Bundestag representative Barbara Weiler. Together, they convinced Schüren Presseverlag, a small, progressive publishing house with ties to her party, to bring out *Lyrik gegen das Vergessen: Gedichte aus Konzentrationslagern* (Poetry against Forgetting: Poems from the Concentration Camps) in 1991 (Moll and Weiler, 7). In the preface Weiler writes about those who suffered through the inhumanity of the Nazis rather than about those who struggled against fascism. She emphasizes that the reason for publishing the poems, despite the extensive literature already available on the Holocaust, is precisely that "they are not about the victims but rather by the victims." She is interested in the feelings of inmates and in the shocking force of their individual stories: "The feelings of those who suffered, which are not included in factual historical accounts, the personal destinies that spring out of the namelessness shock us all the more deeply" (7).

Fischer is among the most important publishing houses in Germany, particularly for modern German literature.[27] Thus, when it brought out a collection of poetry from the camps in 1994, its imprimatur made it clear that what we might call the "genre" of concentration-camp poetry had become established. *Draußen steht eine bange Nacht: Gedichte und Lieder aus*

Konzentrationslagern (Outside a Frightful Night Awaits: Poems and Songs from the Concentration Camps; Lau and Pampuch 1994) is divided into sections by language (German, French, Polish, Yiddish, and Czech) and prints the original side by side with the German translation. Like Weiler and Moll, its editors want to bring the reader closer to the victims, their humiliation, and their suffering, as well as to the creative forces they found in themselves for consolation. The collection makes no allusion to the political or ideological leanings of the concentration-camp writers. Lau and Pampuch write: "As we were working on this project, again and again we were surprised that in this world of hunger, sadism, humiliation, torture and mass murder, the creative broke through like a light" (2). The focus on the heroics of resistance of the 1960s and 70s gave way in the 1990s to an interest in the creative forces in the catastrophe. Thus a tendency to stress a positive aspect, against which Langer warns repeatedly (1991, 1–2; 1998, 1–22), finds expression in very different cultural and ideological contexts.

Beyond the aforementioned anthologies that gathered poems from a variety of camps, numerous collections of poems from a single camp[28] also appeared in the 1990s, as did books of poetry by a single author.[29] Nevertheless, despite their repeated publication, on the whole these texts have been accorded secondary status: by literary critics, as aesthetically second-rate and historically contingent, and by historians, as of questionable documentary value. *Traumatic Verses* seeks to rectify the situation. As was already intimated above, the question of aesthetic value is itself historically and very contingently determined. This book is about the multiple ways in which these poems speak to us now. The historical import of these poems has less to do with their direct relation to any particular event and rather with how they function as archival traces of the perspective of the victims, with how they enable us to engage now with individual reactions then.

1: Literary Activities in the Camps

DISCUSSIONS ABOUT THE ROLE PLAYED by the literary and the aesthetic in the concentration camps have tended to revolve around the dichotomy between transcendence and immanence. This focus has had at least two distinct though not unrelated registers, one centered around the experience of inmates and the other, more general, centered around questions of historical rendition. At one level discussions about literature in the camps make claims about the function of the aesthetic in the psychic life of inmates and more generally about the relevance of the aesthetic realm for people in extreme conditions. Given the abject material constraints and the inhospitable conditions in the camps, the question goes, was it possible for inmates to transcend their physical surroundings through creative endeavors, via the imagination or through culture? In this context faith too counts as a significant example of culture, whether faith is conceived as religious, political, or metaphysical. Were cultural artifacts of use in the inhuman and dehumanizing situations in which inmates found themselves? On this question the memoirs of survivors such as Primo Levi and Jean Améry have given us a range of conflicting answers. Rather than adjudicate the question it seems more productive to hold together the contradictory claims about the value or irrelevance of culture and of the intellect in the camps in order to arrive at a complex conception of the experience of the camps, one that accommodates both a sense of the futility of the intellect in the isolation and brutality that inmates faced and a sense of the vital importance the intellect or imagination took on for inmates as a way for keeping or recreating a connection to the world outside the camps. Such multifaceted representation of the Nazi camps provides a framework for a discussion of Ruth Klüger's claim that composing and reciting poetry constituted for her a mode of keeping her sanity in the camps.

Assertions about the ability of inmates to transcend the horrible conditions of the camps through the imagination are implicated as well in the more general level at which the question of transcendence relates to the representation of the Holocaust: The events of the Holocaust have been conceptualized as constituting a reality that transcends our cognitive, cultural, and even linguistic capacities for representation — capacities inextricable from considerations of aesthetic practice and narrative emplotment. Such extremity is thought to preclude or annul cultural connections for those who experience it. A break is posited that puts the events of the Holocaust outside the ordinary course of history. There is then a tendency at times to make of the Holocaust a negative transcendental. Ruth Klüger resists that tendency, one that she understands as a (negative) theological (and masculinist) impulse to create a quasi-sacral conception of the Holocaust. As Claudia Liebrand writes:

> For Klüger what happened at Auschwitz is not unspeakable, like the name of the Jewish God, and she accepts neither the injunction against representation . . . nor the injunction against comparisons: "without comparisons we can't get by" she states plainly (110). Klüger's distance to the quasi-sacredness that she sees attributed to Auschwitz by Adorno, for example, or by Lanzmann, goes together with a fundamental rejection of transcendence, a rejection that connects a critique of religion with a critique of patriarchy. (204)

Klüger thereby opens the way for an approach to the intellect or culture in Auschwitz focused on the pragmatic rather than the metaphysical and offers a depiction of the Holocaust that avoids sentimentality by holding together the everyday and the extreme without seeking redemptive resolution or heroic meaning.

Disagreements about the ability of inmates to transcend psychically the horrible conditions of the camps and about the proper historical place of the Holocaust are reflections of the deadlock described by Michael Rothberg between realist and antirealist modes of representing the events of the Holocaust, modes that founder on the difficulty "of thinking through the relationship between the everyday and the extreme" (108). In *Traumatic Realism* Rothberg describes the impasse in the following terms:

> On the one hand, a demand that representation of the genocide be realistic registers the desire for an undistorted documentation of history and the fear that flights of the imagination or of philosophical speculation will trivialize the events, mock the "literalness" of the victims' suffering, and lend ammunition to Holocaust negationists. An antirealist tendency within Holocaust studies, on the other hand, argues that the reluctance to attempt epistemologically challenging analyses of the Nazi genocide has blocked from view the very aspects of the Holocaust that constitute its specificity. Indeed, just as frequent as the calls for realism and "the facts" are assertions of the Holocaust's uniqueness and exteriority to understanding and normalizing writing practices. Here, instead of calls for realism, are found attacks on realism and calls for silence. (108)

Ironically for my argument, the "realist mode" here, which keeps the events of the Holocaust grounded in their historical and sociopolitical context, would allow for a cultural or imaginative flight of the imagination for the inmates, while the "antirealist mode," aligned to the "negative transcendental" critiqued by Klüger, would preclude any continuity for the inmates between the camps and the world outside and would disregard, as a consequence, a sense of cultural or intellectual connection on the part of the inmates.

In his reading of Ruth Klüger's memoir Rothberg proposes to overcome the deadlock through a "new understanding of the concentrationary universe of the Nazi camps as a borderland of extreme and everyday elements," an understanding Rothberg terms "traumatic realism" (109). My argument in this section parallels Rothberg's powerful analysis of the ways in which critics Lawrence Langer and Tzvetan Todorov delimit and thereby limit an understanding of the Holocaust. Rothberg's analysis of Langer and Todorov focuses on how the two critics include or exclude considerations of morality and ethics in their writings about inmates of the camps, whereas my focus here is on the aesthetic. Nevertheless, questions of both ethics and aesthetics reflect directly the more general question of the continuity or discontinuity between the concentrationary universe and so-called "normal life." I follow Rothberg's lead in reading Klüger's text as a particularly apt instance of a representation of the Holocaust in which "extremity and everydayness coexist and abut each other, but without resolving into a new unity" (Rothberg, 129).[1] This perspective facilitates an understanding of poems from the camps as negotiations of the complex borders and crisscrossing lines in the concentrationary universe between the extreme and the everyday, rather than as renderings of extremity that are banal because of their narrative closure and their aesthetically conventional poetic exertions. Significantly, here the everyday includes what goes ordinarily under the name of culture, that is, not only conscious traditions and values but also unspoken assumptions about society and one's role in it.

In 2001 Ruth Klüger published *Still Alive: A Holocaust Girlhood Remembered*.[2] In 1992 Klüger had published *weiter leben: eine Jugend* (Going On Living: A Youth; 1994), a memoir that made its author famous and was translated into several languages. Klüger calls her US publication "neither a translation nor a new book: it's another version, a parallel book, if you will" (2001, 210).[3] Her account spans her childhood in Vienna, her time at Theresienstadt, Auschwitz-Birkenau, and Christianstadt (a satellite camp of Gross-Rosen), the immediate postwar period in Bavaria under US occupation, and her eventual emigration to the United States. In the following pages quotations in English are taken from the English version. For sections of the German book that do not appear in the English edition, citations are provided in German followed by my translations into English.

In *weiter leben* Ruth Klüger posits a direct relationship between sanity or reason (*der Verstand*) and poetic form (*die gebundene Sprache*). In a passage in which she reflects on her experiences as a twelve-year-old in one of the freight cars bound for Auschwitz, she writes:

Wer nur erlebt, reim- und gedankenlos, ist in Gefahr, den Verstand zu
verlieren, wie die alte Frau auf dem Schoß meiner Mutter. Ich hab den
Verstand nicht verloren, ich hab Reime gemacht. (1994, 128)

[Those who experience, without rhyme or reason, are in danger of losing their sanity, like the old woman on my mother's lap. I did not lose
my sanity, I made rhymes.]

Furthermore, she explicitly takes issue with philosophical deliberations about
the role and feasibility of poetry "after Auschwitz" by stressing her own very
practical use of the lyric mode *in* Auschwitz as a way of saving herself, her
sanity, "um sich seelisch über Wasser zu halten" (to keep oneself psychologically afloat; 1994, 127).

Klüger joins in a tradition in West German letters sparked by the 1951
publication of Theodor W. Adorno's essay "Cultural Criticism and Society,"
in which he wrote: "to write poetry after Auschwitz is barbaric" (Adorno
1995, 34). Like others, she refuses to accept this as a moral injunction, as a
prohibition:

So gut reden hab ich wie die anderen, Adorno vorweg, ich meine die
Experten in Sachen Ethik, Literatur und Wirklichkeit, die fordern, man
möge über, von, und nach Auschwitz keine Gedichte schreiben. . . .
Und was ist das überhaupt für ein Dürfen und Sollen? Ein moralisches,
ein religiöses? (Klüger 1994, 127)

[I can speak as well as the others, especially Adorno, I mean the experts
on ethics, literature, and reality who proclaim that one may not write
poetry about, from, and after Auschwitz. . . . What is all this should and
must? Is it moral, religious?]

Authors from Hans Magnus Enzensberger, Alfred Andersch, Paul Celan,
and Hilde Domin to Marie Luise Kaschnitz, Wolfdietrich Schnurre, Stefan
Heym, and Günter Grass all agree in their disagreement with Adorno. Literary historian Petra Kiedaisch sums up these authors' reactions in her introduction to the 1995 collection of essays entitled *Lyrik nach Auschwitz?
Adorno und die Dichter* (Poetry after Auschwitz? Adorno and the Poets) in
the following manner:

They [the above mentioned authors] explain, in more or less defensive
manner and mostly without paying attention to Adorno's dialectic intention, that literature must continue to exist. The basic conception of
all contributions [to the debate] is most clearly represented in the final
sentence in Günter Grass's lecture on poetics: ". . . one cannot speak of
the end of literature after Auschwitz, unless, that is, the human race
were to give itself up." (20)

Yet Adorno's provocative sentence has helped establish the wisdom in literary circles that literature and art must now demonstrate an awareness of the Holocaust, that "the autonomous art-object put forth by modernist theory has a limit imposed by historical trauma, that even fifty years after the event, the sheer fact of the Holocaust impinges on any aesthetic object that claims to represent it" (Kahane, 161). Nevertheless, quite how aesthetic representations can and do show awareness of the enormity of the Holocaust is highly contested. Indeed, it has been argued that Adorno recognized that art and poetry were necessary to give expression to the suffering that must not be forgotten: "The abundance of real suffering permits no forgetting" (Adorno 1992, 88). Furthermore Adorno proposed that the breakdown of civilization represented by Auschwitz made art and poetry necessary after the Holocaust as viable reminders of its horrors: "But because the world has outlived its own downfall, it nevertheless needs art to write its unconscious history. The authentic artists of the present are those in whose works the uttermost horror still quivers" (Adorno 1998, 48).

On the other hand, poetry *in* and *from* the Holocaust, rather than *after* the Holocaust, represents a challenge to the cultural critical apparatus of a different order. The connection to the "uttermost horror," even if complex and not always explicit in the text, is more direct than Adorno's belated "quivering" (*nachzittern*). For contemporary readers poems written in the concentration camps may remain an echo from a terrible past. However there are important differences between poetry written *in* and poetry written *about* or *after* the Holocaust: each "set of works" now evokes the past in different ways. The texts written by inmates, many of whom did not survive, change our temporal perspective in thinking about these traumatic events. It does not seem productive to think of these texts as post-traumatic reactions. In this respect these poems differ as well from Holocaust testimonies and the literature of survivors. Qua texts these poems are "belated" by definition — they are always composed *after* the fact — but their relation to hindsight does not easily fit into a dichotomy of past danger and present safety, death and survival. There is at least an attitudinal difference between poems written during persecution and those written later, in particular with respect to the question of the representation of one's own history and one's own position, and to the depiction of the perpetrators. Not surprisingly the "scene of writing" is a crucial aspect of the corpus.

Klüger's own practical use of poetry in the concentration camps takes on two distinct forms: she recites previously memorized poems mostly to herself and occasionally to others, and, as we shall see, she composes poems. The recitation of poetry has practically become a topos in the canon of survivor literature. Its earliest, paradigmatic example is Primo Levi's poetry lesson at Auschwitz-Monowitz, in which he teaches another inmate, his French camp-friend Pikolo, some lines of canto 26 from Dante's *Inferno:*

As if I also was hearing it for the first time: like the blast of a trumpet, like the voice of God. For a moment I forget who I am and where I am.
    . . .
    perhaps, despite the wan translation and the pedestrian, rushed commentary, he has received the message, he has felt that it has to do with him, that it has to do with all men who toil, and with us in particular; and that it has to do with us two, who dare to reason of these things with the poles for the soup on our shoulders. (1961, 103–4)

Levi recounts that he later discovered that his interlocutor at the time was not interested in Dante's poetry but in Levi's own "naive and presumptuous effort to transmit Dante to him" (1989, 139). Nevertheless, in the literature about survivors' writing this scene has become an exemplary moment of transcendence, one in which the dehumanizing conditions of the camps are momentarily overcome through the idiosyncratic use of language, through the act of sharing the memory of a great poem. The civility, loftiness, and intellectuality implied by a conversation about poetry offer a stark contrast to the location at which the dialogue takes place. The scene then represents a temporary imaginative escape from the camp. In *Facing the Extreme,* his 1991 study on moral life in the concentration camps, Tzvetan Todorov sees in this scene a "moment of spiritual transcendence" without which "the world would have lost one more fragment of beauty" (1996, 93). According to Todorov the connection to literary tradition helps Levi to reach imaginatively beyond the confines of the camp's limiting reality and thus leads him to attain a moment of intellectual or spiritual inspiration in a dreadful environment. Taterka's book-length study about references to Dante in the literature of survivors (1999) suggests that the inspiration described by Levi has to do with a connection to literary tradition, as Todorov would have it, but significantly as well with the specific content of that connection, Dante's *Inferno.* Dante's work may have allowed Levi to find a context through which to give his experiences of Auschwitz some narrative meaning since Dante's *Inferno* describes a hell that, unlike the Nazi concentration camps, makes sense, one in which the punishments meted out are thought to correspond to and be in proportion with the sins committed.

Lawrence Langer, possibly a more guarded critic, finds irony where Todorov sees the confirmation of his thesis about the heightened visibility of moral life in the concentration camps. In Langer's view Levi's narrative enacts as a warning the danger to which Todorov falls prey: "And this is precisely the point: when literary form, allusion, and style intrude on the surviving victim's account, we risk forgetting where we are and imagine deceptive continuities" (1991, 45).

Here Langer is intent on maintaining an absolute distinction between "everyday" existence and life in the camps. However, while it is crucial to keep in mind that the extreme experiences of the camps cannot be assimilated into the range of "normal" life events, it is also necessary to realize that when talking about inmates from the camps we are dealing with individuals with a history, people who may have experienced continuities, deceptive or not, as well as traumatic disruptions.[4] In other words, though the "scene of writing" is in some sense and in many cases unimaginable, the individuals who take refuge in writing or composing poems are not aliens, however much their experiences may have alienated them from the society they thought they inhabited. Such individuals may have drawn connections between the camps and the world outside, and some of these become evident in the poems. A poem relies on and constitutes such a connection.

Langer's notion of an "intrusion" of literary form is misleading, moreover, insofar as it can create the impression that there *were* non-literary written versions of life in the camps, or that oral testimonies are not rhetorically inflected. Langer's approach to videotaped Holocaust testimonies, however, hinges on the less mediated, though, as Langer admits, never completely unmediated language of oral testimonies. According to Langer, written testimonies always present a "reassuring" "*appearance* of form" in which the "literary *transforms* the real in a way that obscures even as it seeks to enlighten" (1991, 17–19). Langer claims that oral testimonies unsettle our traditional notions of narrative and require us to "accept the complex immediacy of a voice reaching us simultaneously from the secure present and the devastating past" (21).[5] Camp poems may provide a "reassuring appearance of form," but I argue that such form is another and possibly a necessary element in a complex reaction to trauma. Such "reassuring appearance" need not relieve readers from the task of reading carefully these texts, and it is plausible to interpret the "reassuring appearance of form" as an attempt to establish a sense of security in the midst of devastation, an attempt that takes place as a confrontation with such overwhelming devastation rather than as a ploy to disguise or repress it.

The literary analyses presented in this book consider poetry the most palpable of literary transformations. Arguments have been made that these poems may "take the sting out of suffering" in their pursuit of aesthetic achievement.[6] There has been concern as well that poetic renditions may render "normal" what must be beyond imagination. Such critiques become relative when we consider that inmates indeed rightfully may have sought consolation in their circumstances but that it is not for solace that readers now turn to these poems. As was suggested in the introduction, to read these poems now requires us to be vigilant of our own tendencies either to look for redeeming meaning in them or to seek evidence of the "ultimate" horror. Also, it is important to emphasize that mediation is necessary and inevitable in this context, both in the poems and in the analyses. There can be no direct access to the "reality" of the camps, not only inasmuch as that reality belongs to the past, to history, but more significantly because we are dealing with a situation of extremity, with a limit case. As Dominick LaCapra argues, the Shoah was

> a reality that went beyond the powers of both imagination and concep-
> tualization, and victims themselves could at times not believe what they
> went through or beheld. It posed problems of "representation" at the
> time of its occurrence, and continues to pose problems today. It is in
> this sense a paradigmatically traumatic series of events related in a com-
> plex fashion to the question of silence that is not mere mutism but in-
> trinsically related to the problem of representation. (1994, 220)

Nevertheless, there is a danger in an exclusive or excessive focus on what we speculate would be the "beyond" of a "reality" that "went beyond the pow-ers of both imagination and conceptualization." Such focus risks denying deserved attention to individual experience and to individuals' attempts to resist the fragmentation and mutism generated by the experiences of the concentration camps.

The question as to the possibility of transcending the physical reality of the camps through a flight of the imagination gets contradictory answers from different survivors. Some survivors contradicts themselves on this ques-tion. Thus for instance, as Langer points out, Charlotte Delbo "speaks of the value of literature in sustaining her during her ordeal" (cited in Langer 1991, 4), while insisting, later on, that "au camp, on ne pouvait jamais faire semblant, jamais se réfugier dans l'imaginaire" (in the camp one could never pretend, never escape into the imagination; Delbo, 12).

Jean Améry, who had also been imprisoned at Auschwitz-Monowitz, re-fers to Levi in *At the Mind's Limits* as "my barracks mate Primo Levi from Turin" (3). In that book Améry writes about the inability or impossibility of "transcending," of hearing "the voice of God." The emotional rapture he had known in connection with poetry, in his reading of the final lines of Hölderlin's poem *Hälfte des Lebens* (Half of Life) is missing in the camp. There he feels nothing: "But nothing happened. The poem no longer tran-scended reality" (7).[7] For him, this reduction of the individual to his or her bodily self, his hungry stomach — often, as in torture, a body in intense physi-cal pain — leads to a profound transformation in the person's intellectual at-titude: the spiritual dimension or mental faculty becomes unreal and there is a loss of the very capacity to transcend the materiality of the moment:

> So it was that in Auschwitz everything intellectual gradually took on a
> doubly new form: on the one hand, psychologically, it became some-
> thing completely unreal, and on the other hand, to the extent that one
> defines it in social terms, a kind of forbidden luxury. Sometimes one
> experienced these new facts at deeper levels than those one can reach
> during a bunk-bed conversation; then the intellect very abruptly lost its
> basic quality: its transcendence. (7)

Unlike Levi, Améry fails to find another person with whom to share his inspiration, his ideas. Améry suggests that this is no minor difference: "Perhaps the Hölderlin feeling, encased in psychic humus, would have surfaced if a comrade had been present whose mood would have been somewhat similar and to whom I could have recited the stanza. The worst was that one did not have this comrade . . ." (7).

Todorov uses this lack of a comrade in order to explain the difference between Levi's attitude and Améry's experience. He attributes Améry's inability to find "the good comrade" to a certain "intellectual" arrogance, to elitism: he calls Améry a "professional intellectual." Levi, by contrast, appears to Todorov "down to earth" and humble, and thus, paradoxically, able to attain internal freedom, even if only for a moment, in that inhuman world:

> But perhaps Améry himself was in large part responsible for that impression. A professional intellectual, he kept trying to establish a high-minded relationship with a peer, someone with whom he could share his delight in the beauties of the mind. . . . Indeed, it is perhaps because Levi considered the life of the mind an ordinary virtue and not something reserved for an elite that he was able to keep faith in it and safeguard its power. (1996, 94)

Todorov fails to point out, however, that Levi's apparent ability to enjoy a "life of the mind," as Todorov calls it, can also be linked to the fact that Levi is able to resort to the masterpiece of Italian literature in spite of any Fascist attempts to claim such cultural heritage. As was already discussed in the introduction, Améry faces the meaninglessness and emptiness of culture as a result of the particular problem of intellect or *Geist* of the "Jewish intellectual of *German intellectual and cultural background*" precisely because all of his cultural resources "belong to the enemy" (8). In an essay on Améry, Levi comments on this linguistic difference:

> [Améry] suffered from [the mutilation] of the language *because* German was his language, because he was a philologist who loved his language, just as a sculptor would suffer at seeing one of his statues befouled or mutilated. Therefore the suffering of the [German] intellectual was different from that of the uncultivated foreigner: for the latter the fact that the German of the Lager was a language he did not understand endangered his life; for the former, it was a barbaric jargon that he did understand but that scorched his mouth when he tried to speak it. One was a deportee, the other a stranger in his own country. (1989, 135, translation corrected: see Levi 1986, 109)

Levi and to a lesser extent Améry are among the canonical writers of Holocaust survivor literature. The apparent difference in their attitudes has become a question that touches on core issues in the conceptual understanding of the Holocaust. As we have seen, there is the claim that a link to a broadly defined "culture," or more specifically, to literary tradition, offered meaning and a possibility of transcendence despite or in contrast to the surrounding horror. Thus Levi still writes affirmatively about the role of culture in *The Drowned and the Saved,* albeit in more somber tones than in his first book:

> Culture was useful to me. Not always, at times perhaps by subterranean and unforeseen paths, but it served me well and perhaps it saved me. . . .
>
> [The memories of poetry] made it possible for me to reestablish a link with the past, saving it from oblivion and reinforcing my identity. They convinced me that my mind, besieged by everyday necessity, had not ceased to function. They elevated me in my own eyes and those of my interlocutor. They granted me a respite, ephemeral but not hebetudinous, in fact liberating and differentiating: in short, a way to find myself. (1989, 139–40)

On the other hand, Améry maintains that there was no possibility of meaning, of transcendence, of a link to the world outside the camp, whether past, present, or future:

> Only rarely did thinking grant itself a respite. But it nullified itself when at almost every step it ran into its uncrossable borders. The axes of its traditional frames of reference were then shattered. Beauty: that was an illusion. Knowledge: that turned out to be a game with ideas. Death veiled itself in all its inscrutability. (19)

It is possible to impute intellectual arrogance to Améry, as Todorov does, or to critique survivor and author Viktor Frankl for blind affirmation or naiveté, as Langer does: "Frankl's strategy is to minimize the atrocities he himself survived, and to stress the connections between pre- and post-Auschwitz reality . . . He has managed to transform his ordeal in Auschwitz into a renewed encounter with the literary and philosophical giants who preceded its existence . . ." (1995, 90). As on other occasions Langer alerts us here to the dangers of too facile a production of connections between the camps and life outside the camps. The difference of opinion between Améry's stated conception of the role of the intellect in Auschwitz and Primo Levi's sheds light on different aspects of camp experience and on varied individual circumstances. One possibly obvious but crucial outcome of considering this tension is the necessity of paying close attention to the multiple differences between Améry's and Levi's writings, and to the different situations described. Langer claims that videotaped Holocaust testimonies "impose on us a role not only of passive listener but also of active *hearer*" (1991, 21). Poems written in the Nazi camps require *active readers.* We must refrain from final or sweeping generalizations about "life" in the camps. As already suggested this implies an awareness of the critic's "belated" position, of the dangers and temptations of the "redeeming" narrative (as Langer calls it), of the pitfalls of the search for a "radical" representation (as Roskies discusses), and of the risks of the compulsive, vicarious perpetuation of a "communal wound" that will not heal (as LaCapra warns). It implies careful scrutiny of these poems while relying on historical sources and survivor testimonies to create a context in which these poems may resonate more fully.[8]

"Central Europeans" in the Camps: Some Types

Even though in the camps Ruth Klüger found humiliating her dependence on the national idiom the Nazis considered their own, she claims to have been able to make use of and derive pleasure from the "life of the mind" in German, as it were, through her recitation of Schiller's poetry, for instance. She circumvents the discussion about transcendence by attributing to the recitation of poetry a very pragmatic function, that of helping time go by: "Ist die Zeit schlimm, dann kann man nichts Besseres mit ihr tun als sie zu vertreiben, und jedes Gedicht wird zum Zauberspruch" (When times are bad, then one can't do anything better than to make time pass, and every poem becomes a charm; 1994, 124).

Klüger demystifies her own relationship to language by comparing it to her mother's relationship to objects. She makes words into the equivalent of material possessions, "things" to which one may develop a neurotic attachment, but which are a long way from notions of abstraction, concepts such as "spirit," "intellect," "beauty," "transcendence," or Levi's "voice of God": "[my mother] always clung to things, as I cling to words" (2001, 94). Klüger calls her own childhood habit of reciting poems out loud "a bit of an addiction" and continues: "while walking the unsafe streets [of Nazi Vienna], I would mutter verses as if they were a magic spell. It was as much a neurotic symptom (I now say in retrospect) as an early sign of a literary turn of mind" (2001, 19).

With the iconoclastic humor typical of her writing, Klüger compares her habit of reciting poetry to herself during roll call at Auschwitz to her earlier habit of passing the time with Schiller's ballads, for example, while at the dentist. She speculates about the function of reciting poems in the camps, asking herself why inmates sought and found consolation in poetry (Klüger 1994, 123). After pointing out that most examples provided in discussions about the issue refer to the religious, emotional, or ideological content of the poem, she goes on to suggest that the form of the poem itself offered support. She concludes, as cited above, by stating that poems make the time pass by. She maintains that therefore verses without "deep meaning" are the most adequate in such circumstances: "In gewissen Lagen, wo es einfach darum geht, etwas durchzustehen, sind weniger tiefsinnige Verse vielleicht noch geeigneter als solche, die das Dach überm Haus sprengen" (In certain situations, when what counts is simply to withstand something, less profound verses are possibly more appropriate than those that blow your mind; 1994, 124).

Todorov conveys a similar notion about the relatively lesser importance of the "content" of literature while discussing the process of reading in the camps, though the similarity to Klüger is limited, since she does not idealize literature as "beauty." Todorov writes:

> Reading has a powerful effect, and it appears that, given writing of adequate quality, that effect is independent of the book's particular content. The important thing is not whatever messages the book may seek to convey but the beauty it incarnates and the freedom of mind and spirit the reader experiences in entering in communication with its creator, and through that person, with the world at large. (1996, 92)

Other critics claim just the opposite: that content was the crucial aspect of literary activities in the camps. In a book on the literary production at Sachsenhausen, Katja Klein writes that "much more often it is the case that form becomes subservient to the content, becomes secondary: 'Artistic value was less important than ideological and emotional content,' asserts Dunin-Wasowicz" (Klein, 124).

Although all three write about literature in the camps, the processes described by survivor Klüger and by critics Todorov and Klein differ greatly from one another: remembering poems as a way of passing time; reading for emotional or intellectual inspiration; composing poetry. In the first case, form, as in regular metric and rhyming patterns, seems best suited to fill an unforeseeable length of monotonous time. Poetry functions here as a good method to divide up time, because "Verse, indem sie die Zeit einteilen, im wörtlichen Sinne ein Zeitvertrieb sind" (verses, because they divide time up, are literally a device to pass time; Klüger 1994, 124). This requires a fixed, continuous, easily remembered flow of lines, rather than less memorable contemplative highs with their corresponding variations in form that might end in the shock of a return to the unbearable present.

Todorov more broadly understands form as the "literary" itself. Form functions as a marker of an intellectual dimension that is otherwise denied to the inmates. The literary stands in for "beauty and freedom of mind." In the material studied by Katja Klein, on the other hand, what matters is the message, the content, not because of the different nature of the process (composing poems), but because of another significant distinction that Klein does not elucidate: that is, the difference between explicitly political or religious texts, and texts that are most easily defined in the negative: not religious, not explicitly political. Klein analyses Communist poetry from the camps: in that poetry there is indeed a focus on the message. Such poetic work seeks to encourage comrades, to reassure both the speaker and the audience of the impending defeat of the Nazi enemy.

If what presents itself as non-political corresponds to the bourgeois, liberal, or humanist conception of itself as "non-ideological," what is significant here is that what this apparent "non-ideology" lacks is a grand scheme or theory to give narrative meaning to or somehow render understandable an inmate's experiences in the camps. There seem to be two options left for humanists in the camps: blindness, that is, outright denial of reality, or despair and sorrow. Klüger's warmly sardonic portrayal of a "humanist" in Auschwitz illustrates the first option:

> Central Europeans in Birkenau. There was a woman high school teacher who shortly after her arrival, in the face of smoking, flaming crematoria, lectured us with touching conviction on how the obvious wasn't possible, for this was the twentieth century and we were in Europe, that is, at the heart of the civilized world. And I recall how ridiculous she seemed to me. Not because she didn't believe in genocide — that refusal was comprehensible, for this business wasn't plausible (why kill all the Jews?), and every objection was welcome to my twelve-year-old love of life, or fear of death. But her reasons were ridiculous — the bit about culture and the heart of Europe. (2001, 100)

In most accounts, as soon as the usual coordinates of a broadly conceived bourgeois existence disappear, nothing takes their place to provide orientation in that new, inhuman universe. As Levi puts it: "[Culture] was definitely not useful in orienting oneself and understanding. . . . Reason, art, and poetry were no help in deciphering a place from which they were banned" (1989, 142). This lack of orientation is represented in Améry's figure of the "intellectual" who is not bound by an explicit political or religious "ideology" and is, in Améry's view, clearly at a disadvantage when compared to the "believer":

> Whoever is, in the broadest sense, a believing person, whether his belief be metaphysical or bound to concrete reality, transcends himself. He is not captive of his individuality; rather he is part of a spiritual community that is interrupted nowhere, not even in Auschwitz. (14)

Levi echoes the notion of the disadvantage of the unbelievers and goes on to explain how faith, whether religious or political, creates a sense of understanding, becomes a point of reference in the catastrophe, or rather, makes of the catastrophe a battle to be fought, a Calvary to be endured, a repetition of past pogroms, always with a view to the future:

> The believers lived better, both Améry and I observed this. It was completely unimportant what their religious or political faith may be. Catholic or Reformed priests, rabbis of the various orthodoxies, militant Zionists, naive or sophisticated Marxists, and Jehovah's Witnesses, all held in common the *saving force* of their faith. Their universe was

vaster than ours, more extended in space and time, above all more *comprehensible:* they had a key and a point of leverage, a millennial tomorrow so that there might be some sense to sacrificing themselves, a place in heaven or on earth where justice and compassion had won, or would win in a perhaps remote but certain future: Moscow, or the celestial or terrestrial Jerusalem. . . . Sorrow in or around them was decipherable and therefore did not overflow in despair. (1989, 146, my emphases)

The notions of a "continuum" beyond and through Auschwitz, of a "universe" "vaster than ours," are likely idealizations of the position of the "other." These notions also point to the particular situation of those who were persecuted because of Nazi racial categorizations regardless of political affiliations or activities. While some Communist inmates might on occasion have suffered similar, or even the same physical treatment as Jewish prisoners — and some inmates belonged to both categories — political prisoners were perhaps better prepared to face the atrocities than non-political ones, since from early on they had understood the Nazis as their enemy and they could often keep at least imaginary, if not also actual, connections to a circle of friends, family, nations, and a Soviet Army increasingly effective against the Wehrmacht. Non-political, non-religious Jews very often remained uncertain about the destiny of their families and friends, or knew that they had been murdered: they felt that they were suffering in a vacuum, feared that no one would ever know what was being done to them, and their connections to a fighting army were, at best, tenuous. As Rahe formulates it in his study of Jewish religiosity in the camps:

> In this respect the agnostic or atheist Jews were psychologically different from [Orthodox Jews]: their self-definition, their self-respect depended essentially on their position in the non-Jewish world before they were persecuted, on the social resonance that they found there — and from all that they were cut off in the camps, without finding a real replacement for it. Jews with a religious orientation were much less affected in terms of their identity by such external definitions, and persecution and suffering as part of the religious destiny of Jews was rooted in their collective memory. (112–13)

The inability to find a replacement for their social role before the persecution is particularly acute with non-political German and German-speaking Jews who, unlike French or Polish Jews, were furthermore deprived of the opportunity to construe for themselves an allegiance to a subjugated nation fighting to resist the Nazis. What matters in this case is not necessarily the "real" situation in a country, as in the level of anti-Semitism and of cooperation with the National Socialist occupiers in France or Poland, but rather the possibility of an "imaginary" connection. Annette Wieviorka discusses for instance the situation of French Jewish survivors who report on their ordeal indistinguishably from non-Jewish French survivors: "For even during this racial persecution, there persisted a model of civic emancipation that arose out of the French revolution and was transmitted by a Communism which, viewing Nazism as a modality of capitalism, did not admit the specificity of Nazi anti-Semitism. The Jewish testimonies are indistinguishable from the testimonies of French deportees on the whole" (20). By "imaginary" connection, then, I do not mean fanciful or belonging to the world of hallucinations; rather, I refer to a person's self-understanding, to a conception of one's place in the world, within "imagined communities" such as a nation, a culture, or a social group.[9]

Christian prisoners could understand their suffering through reference to the iconic sufferings of Christ or to divine providence. For instance, Hermann Lange, a Catholic clergyman in Lübeck condemned to death in 1943, writes in a poem included in a good-bye letter to his parents from his prison cell in Hamburg: "Ganz der Wille Gottes / Soll auch dann geschehen" (God's will alone / must also come to pass; cited in Moll and Weiler, 107). Believing Christians were thus able to give some narrative meaning to their experience: the experience was made to correspond to a will beyond that of the National Socialists. As Moll's analyses show, texts composed by Christian inmates in the camps exhibit a tendency to dismiss the reality of torture and dehumanization in order to subsume that reality under the greater reality of faith; the authors make their physical reality subordinate to the religious sphere (Moll 1988, 162–78). By contrast Moll finds a duality of vision in Jewish religious poetry written in the camps: "Jewish religiosity does not show itself through an inner self-forgetting, in an assimilation to faith or to God that ignores the self, but rather, on the contrary, in an obstinate holding on to God despite everything" (179). Jewish religious poetry then displays a dual perspective: the preservation of faith as well as despair at the incomprehensible horror, as in the following section of a poem attributed to an anonymous Jewish author in Buchenwald:

> Du bist mein Gott! Und darum muß ich rechten
> Und darum zweifeln, spotten, und dich kränken —
> Und darum an dich glauben und verstummen
> (cited in Moll 1988, 179)

> [You are my God! And because of that I must argue,
> Because of that I must doubt, mock, and offend you —
> And because of that I must believe in you and be silent.]

Even some non-religious Yiddish- and Polish-speaking Jews formulated narratives of the persecution and the genocide in terms of mythological history. Frieda Aaron argues that this stands in direct relation to a long-standing Jewish tradition of bearing witness to the violence suffered by Jewish communities:

Both in the concentration camps and the ghettos, most of the [Yiddish-language] poets created poetry less as a means of self-expression than as succor, a vehicle for mitigating daily disasters. This phenomenon reflects the tradition of Jewish literature that responded to over two millennia of Jewish suffering with poetry, threnodies, and liturgy of consolation. (3)

In other words Jewish inmates with ties to Jewish culture could find a resource in the forms, stories, and invocations available in the Jewish testimonial tradition, whether the emphasis was religious or secular. David Roskies points out:

That unbelieving Jews would transmit the traditional response to catastrophe — in however dialectical a way — is consistent with the collective ethos of East European Jewry. That the techniques of Jewish memory were still viable, even as the whole culture of East European Jewry was being destroyed, testifies to the power of that fusion of sacred and secular. The eyewitness chroniclers of modern Jewish catastrophe — Bialik, Ansky, Tcherikower, Ringelblum, Auerbach and others — found new and even subversive means to merge the events they witnessed into an ongoing saga. Despite their loss, or lack of faith in a God of History, they revived the archetypal reading of that history. (1994, 40)

Note that Roskies writes of the "ethos of East European Jewry." In general, recourse to a Jewish testimonial tradition or to an archetypal reading of history is not as readily available to assimilated German-speaking Jews. As the autobiographic account of assimilated, Austrian-Jewish Améry shows, he had practically no connection to Jewish culture. Reflecting on his childhood in his essay "On the Necessity and Impossibility of Being a Jew" Améry writes:

I know very little about Jewish culture. I see myself as a boy at Christmas, plodding through the snow-covered village to midnight mass; I don't see myself in a synagogue. I hear my mother appealing to Jesus, Mary, and Joseph when a minor misfortune occurred; I hear no adjuration of the Lord in Hebrew. The picture of my father — whom I hardly knew, since he remained where the Kaiser had sent him and his fatherland deemed him to be in the safest care — did not show a bearded Jewish sage, but rather a Tyrolean Imperial Rifleman in the uniform of the First World War. (83).

Other German-speaking Jews similarly lacked a connection to the testimonial tradition despite a possibly more intense relationship to Jewish culture and customs. Ruth Klüger describes her own family as "emancipated, but not assimilated" (2001, 43). She writes about celebrating the Jewish holidays at home ("Passover in Vienna and the ritual seder meals"; 44). In Vienna,

Klüger recounts, there was a sense that the impending catastrophe would not affect the locals: "My people knew about the pogroms of the past (they wouldn't have been Jews if they didn't), but these were dark, historical, preferably Polish and Russian matters — nothing to do with us" (21). She describes her background as "bourgeois," with all the deeply ingrained values of the bourgeoisie, down to the firm belief that "nobody would hurt an old woman. Or a child, like her [the old woman's] youngest granddaughter Susi" (42). Because of such belief at times it was felt that it was more urgent for men to emigrate. Given the difficult situation, sometimes women and children were left behind and were later deported to the camps. Historian Joan Ringelheim writes: "Even after 1941, it was common to believe that men were in danger, not women or children. . . . Believing this meant that all kinds of decisions were made which put women and children in even greater jeopardy than they already were" (392).

Instead of turning toward more traditional Jewish testimony or archetypes, German-speaking Jews with a bourgeois or a liberal intellectual biography turned toward the traditional canon of German poetry as a possible source of succor during their harrowing experience, or sought expression for their suffering by writing in poetic forms that were familiar to them and reached back to the Classicist and Romantic models of the eighteenth and nineteenth centuries. After all, even as a failed cultural resource Hölderlin's poetry remains Améry's frame of reference. Klüger refers to Schiller and Uhland.

Believers had a more readily available set of references through which to give narrative sense to their suffering. East European Jews had recourse to a Jewish testimonial tradition. Levi felt inspired by Dante. The point of these comparisons is not to rank victimizations nor to measure up behavior or weigh up cultural traditions. The objective rather is to delineate differences among inmates so as to begin to establish a tentative and incomplete sociocultural field to enable the analysis of the poems. The differences (for example, between "believers" and "non-believers") should not make us forget the context of our study, however. As Joan Ringelheim reminds us about comparing categories of victims as she reconsiders the study of women in the Holocaust:

> It is interesting to look at differences between women and men. It is even interesting to see, if we can, whether women maintained themselves either better than or — perhaps more accurately — differently from men. However, the discovery of difference is often pernicious because it helps us to forget the context of these supposed strengths — oppression — and to ignore the possibility that they may be only apparent. To suggest that among those Jews who lived through the Holocaust, women rather than men survived better is to move toward acceptance or valorization of oppression, even if one uses a cultural and

not a biological argument. Oppression does not make people better; oppression makes people oppressed. (387)

Whereas Améry presents himself as decidedly agnostic before, at, and after Auschwitz, some individuals evince a metaphysical belief that is, however, not central to their self-understanding, and they remain in the category of the non-believer. For example, Klüger reports about a "last bout of religiosity" on a night spent in mortal fear, in which she tells herself:

> Surely God had other plans for me; God would let me live, or he wouldn't have let me make poems. Perhaps I had composed poems mainly to ingratiate myself with God, so he would make an exception for me. (2001, 11)

In some sense, this is an attempt to establish a self-understanding that might assure her of her own survival, that is, a conception of the world beyond the concentration camps within which her life would have a different, and special, meaning — in contrast to the debasement of the individual and to the annihilation of meaning in the camps. The magic or ritualistic power of poetry, of writing, of the written word, of the willful, conscious, individual use of language, is an important factor for other inmates as well. As secular Yiddish poet and survivor of the Vilna ghetto Abraham Sutzkever put it during an interview for a German radio station in 1985:

> The point of creative activity in the ghetto is very complex. No one has got to the bottom of this; it was like a prayer with the firm conviction that one would be heard. I believed that I could not die while I was writing. I believed in that from the beginning to the end of my time in the ghetto. That was not only my case, it was like that for everyone who wrote in the ghetto. (cited in Moll 1988, 131)

Indeed, Roskies argues that as the final "liquidation" of the ghettos was taking place, writing took on a very special significance for individuals engaged in it. Roskies cites the cases of Chaim Kaplan, a "retired pedagogue," who kept a diary in Hebrew, and Emanuel Ringelblum, "a militant Socialist-Zionist historian," who wrote an account of *Polish-Jewish Relations during the Second World War* in Polish, and concludes that "both saw their writing as the most sacred of all tasks, the sign of their chosenness, the key to their personal and collective mission" (1986, 33).

A writer-inmate's own expressions of judgment about his or her motivations for writing and about the results of his or her efforts, as well as a literary analysis of the writings, may help us elucidate the complex relations between language, fantasy, identity, and trauma in that particular period. Klüger, as cited above, and Sutzkever make it clear that individuals who composed poetry in the ghettos and camps regarded their poetry as an essential activity.

A Case Study: The Publication of Klüger's Poems from the Camps

In prison he [a cousin] learned one of the camp songs, the so-called "Buchenwaldlied." The lyrics translate roughly, "Buchenwald, I can't forget you, because you are my destiny. Anyone who has entered here becomes conscious of the wonders of freedom." It is a famous song, but the lyrics are not very good. No great poetry was composed in the concentration camps. If it were not so, one might entertain the idea that the camps were good for something, that they were, for example, a kind of catharsis, producing fine art. In fact, they weren't good for anything. Of course, right away I memorized the words of the song. (Klüger 2001, 36)

Like other camp poets and critics Klüger maintains here that "no great poetry was composed in the concentration camps." In so doing she points to the danger of a retrospective valorization of the camps, as if the aesthetic endeavors that might arise from the camps could somehow justify the atrocities. Of course this would not be the case, even if "great poetry" had been produced there. At the same time she reveals an intense fascination with the song from the camp: "Of course, right away I memorized the words of the song." On the one hand the eagerness to learn the words simply could be part of a neurotic compulsion to memorize poetry and a childish fascination with knowledge (about the camps) that the adults were keeping from her. At the same time her confession of interest in the poem reveals that poetry of questionable literary quality might be of use, and raises the question as to the aesthetic judgments we might use to think about poetry. At any rate the poem — which apostrophizes the Buchenwald concentration camp — as well as the circumstances surrounding it were good enough to capture her attention and through her writing that of her readers.

In *weiter leben* we first encounter one of Ruth Klüger's own poems from the camps on the second page of the section entitled "Auschwitz-Birkenau" (Klüger 1994, 107). On the corresponding second page of the section entitled "Death Camp" in *Still Alive*, Klüger reports about writing the poem but does not offer a translation of it: "The *Muselmänner* were walking dead men who wouldn't live long, I was told. I composed poems about them and the camp in slick rhythms and rhymes which were inappropriate for the subject but good for memorizing — an important asset, since I couldn't write them down, lacking pencil and paper" (2001, 90). Although other poems, some of them youthful, appear in *Still Alive*, none of Klüger's camp poetry is reproduced in the English version.

As if to suggest a connection between the paradigmatic extermination camp and the lyric mode, poetry is a crucial issue in the Auschwitz-Birkenau section. Klüger explains that she composed (but did not yet write down) her two poems about Auschwitz while at the next location in her internment, Christianstadt, a satellite-camp of Gross-Rosen, where she had been taken as part of the slave-labor force. However, in the German version of the book, the poems themselves and the story of their creation, as well as Klüger's discussion about the meaning and use of poetry in the camps, appear in the Auschwitz section (1994, 106–39) and not in the next section entitled "Christianstadt (Groß-Rosen)" (140–70). Although the poems are set in Auschwitz-Birkenau, Klüger claims in retrospect that she could not have created them there. At Birkenau that would have meant a confrontation with reality bound to overburden the psyche:

> Da war die Sache noch zu hautnah, der Kamin löste panisches Entsetzen aus, und der Impuls zur dichterischen Bewältigung wäre dem stärkeren Bedürfnis nach Verdrängung erlegen. (1994, 126)

> [There [at Birkenau] the whole thing was too close to the bone, the chimney made me panic, and the impulse to work it through poetically would have given way to the need to repress.]

At the forced labor camp Christianstadt, while still at the mercy of the SS, though no longer within visual proximity of one of the National Socialist "extermination factories," she wished to give expression to her traumatic experience. Through a creative act with words, she attempted to make sense of what she has just experienced, to gain some emotional mastery over it:

> Im nächsten Lager war es umgekehrt, da wollte ich mein Erlebnis verarbeiten, auf die einzige Weise, die ich kannte, in ordentlichen, gegliederten Strophen. (1994, 126)

> [In the next camp it was the opposite; there I wanted to work through my experience, in the only manner that I knew, in orderly, well-structured stanzas.]

The deferral between the actual experience (of witnessing the chimneys of the crematoria, in this case) and the psychological process of coming to express the experience in verses has a material parallel: at Birkenau she could not have thought out the poems; at Christianstadt she composed the verses, but was not able to write them down:

> Zwei Gedichte über Auschwitz habe ich noch im Jahre 1944 verfaßt, aber erst im nächsten Lager, Christianstadt, ein Außenlager von Groß-Rosen. Eines habe ich dort aufgesagt für Häftlinge, die nicht unbedingt davon erbaut waren. Aufgeschrieben habe ich sie erst 1945, nach dem Krieg, als ich wieder Stift und Papier hatte. (1994, 124–25)

[I composed two poems about Auschwitz as early as 1944, but in the next camp, Christianstadt, a satellite camp of Gross-Rosen. I recited one of them there, for the inmates, who were not exactly enthusiastic about it. I only wrote them down in 1945, after the war, when I had pen and paper again.]

Only after the war did she write the poems down, in Straubing, near Munich, after the American forces had conquered Bavaria and she was no longer in danger, lived in a house, and had some measure of privacy.

The motivation behind the poetry is psychological: confronted with the abandonment of hope, of the survival instinct, of the desire to live represented in the phenomenon of the Muselmänner, she seeks to find expression for her feelings. "Muselmann," the singular of "Muselmänner," was one of the most commonly used terms in concentration-camp jargon to describe individuals who had become so weakened and emaciated that they had lost even the most basic survival instinct and the desire to live.[10] In her poems Klüger tries to counter the hopelessness symbolized by the Muselmänner. She calls this attempt to come to terms with the "Trauma der Auschwitzer Wochen" (trauma of the weeks at Auschwitz) a

> poetischer und therapeutischer Versuch, diesem sinnlosen und destrukt-
> iven Zirkus, in dem wir untergingen, ein sprachlich Ganzes, Gereimtes
> entgegenzusetzen; also eigentlich das älteste ästhetische Anliegen.
> (1994, 126–27)

> [poetic and therapeutic attempt to oppose to that senseless, destructive
> circus, in which we were being destroyed, a linguistic whole, a rhyme;
> in other words, in fact, the oldest aesthetic intent.]

In language more philosophical than psychological, though following a similar line of thought, literary scholar Michael Moll describes the desire somehow to respond to those events, to counteract the silencing, destructive effect of cumulative, traumatic experience, in the following manner:

> The assumption seems plausible that many people who had never writ-
> ten before wrote partly under mortal danger in the prisons, ghettos,
> concentration and extermination camps in order not to succumb com-
> pletely to the unspeakable events. (1988, 131–32)

But the story of the poems does not end with their composition. Klüger describes the results of her first attempt to publish the poems shortly after the end of the war. She writes up both poems and sends them to a newspaper, along with a letter "certifying" that they are authentic texts composed in the concentration camps. Her expectation is that she will be treated with the respect due to a poet: that she will be contacted by the editor, informed of the decision to publish, and that her poems will be published as literary pieces.

To her surprise and dismay, she writes, she eventually finds two stanzas of one of her poems in that newspaper, framed by a sentimental description and a portrait drawn not "of a young poet who had been in the camps" but rather its opposite "a former child prisoner who had written some heart-wrenching verses":

> Instead of a modest column I found half a page that dealt with me. In the middle was a photo of my cover letter, which had been carefully ripped, so that the jagged edges, together with the awkward hand-writing of a girl who hadn't spent much time in school, evoked the im-pression of an emergency SOS, a kind of message in a bottle. To make matters worse, they had added a drawing of a ragged, terrorized child, who accidentally happened to look a little like me. What I minded most was that they had eviscerated my poetic output without asking, omit-ting one poem altogether and printing only two stanzas of the other, and these were embedded in a maudlin, hand-wringing text, in effect asking the public for pity. (2001, 154)

Klüger's dissatisfaction with the newspaper publication stems from a num-ber of factors. She has not been perceived as a poet. The editors have trun-cated her poem. They have touched up visual evidence to create not only a sense of authenticity but also a confirmation of the innocence and "heart-wrenching" helplessness of the child-victim. Most important, they have sought to manipulate the public, to restrict the readers' reaction to the feel-ing of pity. The poetry is not allowed to "speak for itself." Vicarious pain — or sentimentality — becomes the escape route out of a more sustained con-frontation with complex issues. The visual cues of the child's unpracticed handwriting and the drawing of a frightened child in tattered clothes under-score the desire to evoke pity. Of course the "accidental" similarity between the illustration and the author suggests that to exclude pity altogether from the range of appropriate responses to such situations might be inadequate as well.

An examination of the newspaper article confirms Klüger's critique. On 23 June 1945, two papers, one in the city of Munich, one in the state of Hessen, both listing the publisher as "the 12th Division of the US Army for the German Civilian Population," (Die amerikanische 12. Heeresgruppe für die deutsche Zivilbevölkerung), published practically identical articles with the title "Ein Kind schrieb aus Auschwitz . . ." (A Child wrote from Au-schwitz . . .") The illustration shows a starved and terrified young girl, be-hind her we see what we assume must be a crematorium, flames shooting out the side, with smoke from the tall chimney descending in a black serpen-tine cloud to reach in front of the girl almost as if to strangle her. Clearly she cannot escape the smell of the burning bodies. The text reinforces the im-age: the "small young girl, not yet fourteen years old," had been at "possibly the worst of the concentration camps, the death camp Auschwitz," where "day and night the air was full of the smell of burning human flesh." The girl was born in Germany, the article claims, and her only fault (Schuld), like that of many other children, was to have been "born of Jewish parents." As one of the headlines announces and the article explains, one of the poems carries a dedication, "To my friend Hanna Ungar";[11] the article speculates: "probably one of the burnt children." The article's main focus is the fate of children: the reader is constantly reminded of the young age of the writer — who is referred to as "small young girl," "child," "Ruth," or "thirteen-year-old Ruth" — of her lack of guilt and that of her countless fellows (Kameraden und Kameradinnen) who did not survive. The paper reports that this "child" regained her freedom, and goes on to claim that that "freedom can not make good the crime committed against a child, not even against a child who escaped" (Die Freiheit kann nicht gut machen, was an einem Kind verbrochen wurde — an einem Kind das noch entkam). The article concludes with the statement that the newspaper editors consider the poems "shocking" documents that take their place among the other documents about "the darkest Middle Age, which for twelve years had spread itself over Germany and Europe."

The intent of the newspaper publication, with its appeal to the "child-loving" public, recalls an anecdote from Adorno's essay "What Does Coming to Terms with the Past Mean?" He quotes "a story of a woman who, after attending a performance of the dramatization of *The Diary of Anne Frank*, said in a shaken voice: 'Yes, but really, at least *that* girl ought to have been allowed to live'" (1986, 127). This type of reaction, in Adorno's story, as characterized by Klüger, and as evident in the newspapers' article, effects a pernicious displacement: by lamenting the destiny of the one child (that is, innocent) victim, the fate of the other victims is overlooked if not actually vindicated. Can the Nazi crimes committed against adults, whether or not they survived, be made good, one asks after reading the article on Klüger's poems, and were the Jewish parents not just as innocent as their children?

One could reasonably object that it was a naive mistake to expect more than "sentimentalities" from a newspaper. Nevertheless, Klüger's story brings to light an attitude that existed and exists beyond the arena of journalistic sensationalism, one that affects the overall reception of texts from the camps. In effect writing about the reception of Anne Frank, not coincidentally another young female writer victim of the Nazis, Catherine Bernard identifies a "new manifestation of morality" that evinces itself in the form of "identification with victimization" (Bernard, 217). Bernard cites Ian Buruma, who argues that a tendency "to identify with suffering itself, to, as it were, gain virtue from vicarious victimhood, is our modern form of sentimentalism" (cited in Bernard, 217). In some sense the pity evoked in the newspaper article foreshadows the more general identificatory relation to the "innocent child-victim" in the later reception of such texts.

Klüger calls the newspaper episode "an anecdote from the early stages of Germany's attempt to come to terms with the Nazi past," and her dissatisfaction with the public uses of her poems continues: "I am told that they exhibit my Auschwitz poems in [the museum at Auschwitz], against my express wishes" (2001, 155 and 111). Subsequent episodes in the publication history of these poems involve the inclusion of the two stanzas from "Der Kamin" — whose title Klüger translates as "The Chimney" (2001, 127) — as well as one stanza from the poem entitled "Auschwitz," that is, the same selection as in the newspaper, in a journal with very limited circulation published in 1956 (Euler) and in the two early anthologies of exile, oppositional, and camp poetry. In the journal *Ariel*, the poems appear under the title "Gedichte aus Auschwitz" (Poems from Auschwitz) and on the same page we are given the author's date of birth (30 October 1931) and 1944 as the date of composition (Euler, 12). There is no mention of the poeticizing "child," but the poems are accompanied by the only illustration in that edition of the journal — one dedicated to poetic writings from the camps: a sketch by Alexander Bogen dated 1943 that carries the description: "Drawing from the ghetto." The drawing shows a forlorn-looking girl with a "Jewish badge" holding a doll by the arm. The same selection from Klüger's poems appears in *An den Wind geschrieben* with the indication that the poems were written in 1944 in Auschwitz (Schlösser 1960, 121 and 123). The author's date of birth is provided in the biographical section at the back of the book (346). The paperback edition reprints them as "children's poems written in the concentration camp Auschwitz" (Schlösser 1962, 73–74). *Welch Wort in die Kälte gerufen* reprints the two same stanzas from "Der Kamin" as a poem "written in Auschwitz, 1944," making only indirect reference to the author's age by providing a year of birth in the biographical section (Seydel, 320 and 549). In the first anthology exclusively of poems from the concentration camps, *Lyrik gegen das Vergessen*, the same selection as in *An den Wind geschrieben* is presented as the poetry written in 1944 by a thirteen-year-old girl at Auschwitz; it is not included in the book's section of "Poems For and From Children" but rather under the heading "Deportation — Death — Destruction" (Moll and Weiler, 131–32). The 1994 anthology, *Draußen steht eine bange Nacht*, though published after the appearance in 1992 of Klüger's memoir, again includes only the two stanzas from "Der Kamin" as a poem written in 1944 at Auschwitz, and does not indicate the author's age except in the biographical information in the back of the book (Lau and Pampuch, 56 and 191–92).

The sections of "Der Kamin" that were published in the original newspaper articles, in the anthologies, and in Klüger's German-language biography (1994, 125–26) are the following two stanzas as printed in *weiter leben* and in Sander Gilman's translation, in which "Kamin" is not translated as chimney (Klüger's choice), but rather as "furnace" (Gilman 1991, 229–30):

Täglich hinter den Baracken
Seh ich Rauch und Feuer stehn.
Jude, beuge deinen Nacken,
Keiner hier kann *dem* entgehn.
Siehst du in dem Rauche nicht
Ein verzerrtes Angesicht?
Ruft es nicht voll Spott und Hohn:
Fünf Millionen berg' ich schon!
Auschwitz liegt in meiner Hand,
Alles, alles wird verbrannt.

Täglich hinterm Stacheldraht
Steigt die Sonne purpurn auf,
Doch ihr Licht wirkt öd und fad,
Bricht die andere Flamme auf.
Denn das warme Lebenslicht
Gilt in Auschwitz längst schon nicht.
Blick zur roten Flamme hin:
Einzig wahr ist der Kamin.
Auschwitz liegt in seiner Hand,
Alles, alles wird verbrannt.

[Daily behind the barracks
I see smoke and fire.
Jew, bend your back,
No one can escape *that*.
Do you not see in the smoke
A distorted face?
Does it not call out, full of mockery and sarcasm:
Five million I now contain!
Auschwitz lies in my hand,
Everything, everything will be consumed.

Daily behind the barbed wire
The sun rises purple,
But its light seems empty and hollow
When the other flame appears.
For the warm light of life
Has had no meaning in Auschwitz.
Look into the red flame:[12]
The only truth is the furnace.
Auschwitz lies in his hand,
Everything, everything will be consumed.]

In her memoir Klüger presents one further stanza. As indicated earlier, she explains that this is a psychological elaboration, in "sleek rhythms and rhymes which were inappropriate for the subject" (2001, 90) of her encounter with the phenomenon of the Muselmänner (1994, 107; translation Gilman 1991, 230):

> Mancher lebte einst voll Grauen
> Vor der drohenden Gefahr.
> Heut kann er gelassen schauen,
> Bietet ruhig sein Leben dar.
> Jeder ist zermürbt von Leiden,
> Keine Schönheit, keine Freuden.
> Leben, Sonne, sie sind hin.
> Und es lodert der Kamin.
> Auschwitz liegt in seiner Hand,
> Alles, alles wird verbrannt.

> [Some have lived full of horror
> Faced with threatening danger.
> Today he looks with equanimity,
> Offering up his life.
> Everyone is depressed by suffering,
> No beauty, no joy,
> Life, sun are gone,
> And the furnace glows.
> Everything, everything will be consumed.]

Additionally in *weiter leben* Klüger prints the ending section of a fourth and final stanza (1994, 164; translation Gilman 1991, 230, amended):

> Keiner ist mir noch entronnen,
> Keinen, keinen werd ich schonen.
> Und die mich gebaut als Grab
> Schling ich selbst zuletzt hinab.
> Auschwitz liegt in meiner Hand,
> Alles, alles wird verbrannt.

> [No one has yet outrun me,
> No one. No one will I spare.
> And those who built me as a grave
> I will consume at last.
> Auschwitz lies in my hand,
> Everything, everything will be consumed.]

In *Inscribing the Other* (1991), which predates Klüger's German memoir, Sander Gilman includes his translation into English of all four complete stanzas (229–32), although the only source he lists is Seydel 1968, which contains only the two first stanzas (Gilman 1991, 352 n. 19). The beginning of the fourth and final stanza — that is, the section that precedes the one cited immediately above and that Klüger omits from her memoir but that is included in a study manual on *weiter leben* — reads as follows (Heidelberger-Leonard, 38, translation Gilman 1991, 230):

> Hört ihr Ächzen nicht und Stöhnen,
> Wie von einem, der verschied?
> Und dazwischen bittres Höhnen,
> Des Kamines schaurig Lied:
>
> [Don't you hear the moans and the groaning
> As from someone who is dying?
> And between them bitter mockery,
> The furnace's horrid song:]

It is significant that the last two stanzas are excluded from the German-language anthologies of poems from the camps. Following the newspapers' initiative, the journal as well as all four anthologies would have us read only the first two stanzas of "Der Kamin" as if it were the complete poem. In so doing they exclude from Klüger's text a range of issues that may conflict with or at least complicate the image promoted by the newspapers of the innocent victim worthy of pity. Furthermore, one should point out that nothing in the text reveals that the author is a child. The first stanza shows a "chimney" in a metonymic relation to the perpetrators: it is full of the threatening scorn and derision commonly associated with the latter's attitude toward inmates. Irène Heidelberger-Leonard calls it "the Anti-God, the dictatorial death-machine [which] takes the word" (38). The chimney has power and stands in contrast to the subjugated Jew who should "bend" his back in recognition that there is no escape. Although the stanza begins with a first-person speaker who observes the events ("I see smoke and fire") and addresses a representative (male) victim ("Jew," "Do you not see"), it ends with the voice of the threatening chimney: "Auschwitz lies in my hand." The second stanza carries on the metonymy while it renders the metaphor abstract and absolute: "The only truth is the furnace." The violence perpetrated is caused by an infernal and anonymous machine: a "red flame" overpowers the natural light of the sun. The "red flame" threatens to destroy "everything, everything." This moves towards a desolate ending, but the full consequence of the powers of the "dictatorial death-machine" is only spelled out in the final two stanzas. The third stanza raises the specter of the figure of the "passive sheep" led to the slaughter: "he" who "offers up his life."

More problematic for the image of the innocent child-victim, the fourth stanza presents a fantasy of revenge. The "furnace" runs out of control and destroys literally everything, that is, specifically, also those who had created it. Here there is only a quick reference to the perpetrators: "those who built me." This makes the abstraction less all-encompassing: someone actually built the flaming entity that destroys everything from behind the barracks. In terms of the narrative voice this reference to "those who built me" raises more general questions about how victims portray perpetrators. References to the perpetrators are often elliptical in the poems written in the camps: in "Der Kamin," the perpetrators are referred to only once their own mortality is imagined, once they too can be seen as victims, or, to put it differently, once an end to their rule is in sight. Significantly as well, here the reference to the perpetrators is not in the speaker's own voice, but in that of the personified "chimney," whose voice grows from three lines in the first stanza to six lines in the final stanza as if it were overpowering or consuming the narrative voice of the poem as well. The revenge on the perpetrators is produced by an extension of the perpetrators' own actions. The truncation of the poems by the newspapers completely leaves out this crucial aspect of the poem. In fact Klüger calls "The Chimney" a "revenge poem" in her memoir:

> In this poem the personified death machine proclaims that when it has consumed all who have come its way, it will in the end consume those who built it. I recited these verses with much verve and the secret thought, "You'll get your comeuppance, you [SS] creep who hit me, just wait." That was a comfort of sorts, but of course it was nonsense, too, for one can be pretty sure that he didn't get his comeuppance. (2001, 127)

While the author understands the poem as an expression of "revenge," the truncation and emplotment of the poem in the newspapers and the anthologies focus on the destiny of a pitiful sufferer. Though an inmate's desire for revenge would not have come as news to German readers in the U.S. occupation zone in June of 1945, just over a month after the capitulation of Germany, its public declaration would most likely have met with hostile rejection and possibly expressions of anti-Semitism, such as the attitude that Klüger's narrator senses in the newspaper salesman who gives her the paper: "not so much giving me a present as removing some seemingly malodorous thing from his home" (2001, 154).

Of the other poem, entitled "Auschwitz," the single stanza that was published in the newspapers in 1945, and subsequently in some of the anthologies, does not appear in *weiter leben;* however, it appears in Euler 1956, 12, in Schlösser 1960, 123 and 1962, 74, and in Moll and Weiler, 131:

Fressen unsere Leichen Raben?
Müssen wir vernichtet sein?
— Sag, wo werd ich einst begraben —
Herr, ich will nur Freiheit haben,
Und der Heimat Sonnenschein.

[Will ravens devour our corpses?
Must we be destroyed?
— Say, where will I be buried —
Lord, all I want is to have freedom,
And the sunshine from home.]

Calling the "Auschwitz" poem no less "shocking" than "The Chimney," the newspaper editors claim that the other stanzas of this poem are not suitable for publication because "they reveal the whole, indescribable misery to which the soul of a child was condemned." It is not clear why the editors feel entitled to write of the smell of "burning human flesh" while leaving out the other stanzas of this particular poem. However, that this particular stanza was selected by the newspaper editors seeking to arouse pity for the "small girl" (das kleine Mädchen) is not surprising. Terms such as "Freiheit" and "Heimat" are generic enough to allow for easy identification. "Heimat" in particular would have resonated in ears trained by Nazi rhetoric. The traditional vocative "Herr" and the humble plea "ich will nur" create a victim-speaker with whom it is easy to identify, particularly in a largely Christian society. The despairing question "must we be destroyed?" is counterbalanced by the longing plea for a restoration of an original order: "der Heimat Sonnenschein" (the sunshine from home [or the homeland]). The last two lines seem to foreshadow a "Hoffnungssonne" (sun of hope) that, as Klüger explains, comes out at the end of her poem. The poem follows here a tradition of hopeful last lines as Klüger knew it from the camp song she had learned from her cousin, the "Buchenwaldlied" (Song of Buchenwald).[13] Klüger points out that another camp song, "Die Moorsoldaten" (Peat-Bog Soldiers, or Soldiers of the Marshes, a name that makes reference to the marshlands surrounding the Börgermoor concentration camp),[14] the quintessential camp song, ends in hope too, thus she claims that a happy end is part of the genre. Different concentration camps had their own songs written by inmates: sometimes on orders of the SS, as in the "Buchenwaldlied" (Heilig, 44–46) sometimes as well in defiance of the camp administration, as in the case of "Die Moorsoldaten." Practically all camp songs, some of which inmates were forced to sing while marching to and from work, end with an invocation of the freedom and home that will be regained.[15]

Bibliographic notes at the end of the second, revised edition of *An den Wind geschrieben* explain that the editors had learned that Klüger's stanza quoted above was only the fifth of six stanzas after their book had gone into print (Schlösser 1961a and 1961b, 346). Klüger actually reports that of her "two Auschwitz poems," one had eight stanzas and the other four (2001, 154). In fact the poem "Auschwitz" has eight stanzas, of which the one published in the newspapers is the seventh or penultimate one. In Klüger's *weiter leben* only the two beginning stanzas of "Auschwitz" are printed (1994, 125):

> Kalt und trüb ist noch der Morgen,
> Männer gehn zur Arbeit hin,
> Schwer von Leid, gedrückt von Sorgen,
> Fern der Zeit, da sie geborgen,
> Langsam wandern sie dahin.

> Aber jene Männer dort
> Bald nicht mehr die Sonne sehn.
> Freiheit nahm man ihnen fort.
> Welch ein grauenvoller Mord,
> Dem sie still entgegengehn.

> [Cold and gray is still the morning,
> Men go to work,
> Heavy with sorrow, depressed with worries,
> Far away is the time when they were safe,
> Slowly they walk away.

> But those men there
> Will soon no longer see the sun.
> Freedom was taken away from them.
> What a horrible murder
> Are they quietly approaching.]

The other six stanzas are printed in Heidelberger-Leonard's study (37):

> Gott, du allein darfst's doch nur geben,
> Das große, heilige Menschenleben,
> Du gibst das Dasein und Du gibst den Tod.
> Und du, du siehst dieses endlose Morden,
> Du siehst die blutigen, grausamen Horden,
> Und Menschen verachten dein höchstes Gebot!

> Wir haben die herrliche Heimat verlassen,
> Bleiben wir ewig in Elend und Not?
> Willst Du, daß alle Menschen uns hassen,
> Daß wir im Staube der schmutzigen Gassen
> Leiden den elendsten, niedrigsten Tod?

Hinter den Baracken brennt
Feuer, Feuer Tag und Nacht.
Jeder Jude es hier kennt,
Jeder weiß, für wen es brennt,
Und kein Aug, das uns bewacht?

Sag, wofür muß ich hier büßen?
Nenn mir eines Unrechts Spur.
Darf ich nicht das Leben grüßen?
Darf mich nicht der Morgen küssen
Und die Schönheit der Natur?

Fressen unsere Leichen Raben?
Müssen wir vernichtet sein?
Sag, wo werd ich einst begraben?
Herr, ich will nur Freiheit haben
und der Heimat Sonnenschein!

Fern im Osten liegt ein Dunst,
Und Natur zeigt ihre Kunst:
Sieh, die Sonne bricht hervor.
Zeigt mir diese Strahlensonne
eine neue Lebenswonne,
Zieht die Freiheit still empor?

[God, only you alone can give it,
The great, holy human life,
You give existence and You give death.
And you, you see this endless murder,
You see the bloody, brutal hordes,
And people despise your highest law!

We have left behind our lovely homeland,
Will we remain forever in misery and need?
Do You want all people to hate us,
Want us, in the dust of the dirty alleys,
To suffer the most miserable, despicable death?

Behind the barracks fire
Burns, fire day and night.
Every Jew here knows it,
Every one knows for whom it burns,
And no eye watches over us?

Say, what must I expiate here?
Tell me of one trace of wrongdoing.

May I not greet life?
May not the morning and the beauty
Of nature kiss me?

Will ravens devour our corpses?
Must we be destroyed?
— Say, where will I be buried —
Lord, all I want is to have freedom,
And the sunshine from home.

Far in the East there is a mist
And nature shows her art:
Look, the sun comes through.
Does the sparkling sun show me
A new joy of life,
Is freedom quietly rising?]

Both poems were written at about the same time (Heidelberger-Leonard, 38) and are thematically close to each other: note, for example, in the fifth stanza of "Auschwitz" the "fire" burning constantly "behind the barracks" like the "smoke and fire" of "The Chimney." Nevertheless the two poems evince significant differences. Heidelberger-Leonard finds in "Auschwitz," chronologically the earlier poem — Klüger calls it the "first" of two (1994, 124) — a "helpless revolt that turns into a hope that is just as clumsy." Heidelberger-Leonard points out that "The Chimney" is much less conciliatory because it is "godless" (37). There is a hope in "Auschwitz" that is absent in the other poem, even if in "Auschwitz" the hopeful end is posed as a question. The poem "Auschwitz" seeks to make sense of the murder and of the abuses through claims about injustice — it calls on a higher power to confirm the speaker's sense of justice.

The sun is a central symbol in both poems. Perceptions of the sun are a theme in numerous accounts by survivors. In the concentrationary universe, where existence usually was marked by the dreary monotony of exhausting physical labor, by a landscape devoid of the usual colors of nature, and by exposure to long, cold winters or scorching summer heat without anything near to adequate protection, the sun becomes a primordial sign of change, of the passage of time, and, eventually, of the arrival of another season. As spring approaches, Levi reports, attention focuses on the movement of the sun: "the rising sun is commented on every day." He continues:

It is a Polish sun, cold, white and distant, and only warms the skin, but when it dissolved the last mists a murmur ran through our colourless numbers, and when even I felt its lukewarmth through my clothes I understood how men can worship the sun. (1961, 64)

In an environment designed to deprive people of their individuality and of satisfaction of their most basic bodily needs, the sun becomes a tangible representation of something beyond the confines of the camps, a symbol of nature, of the "positive rhythms of existence" (Langer 1991, 105–6). In "Auschwitz" the sun is a conventionally positive symbol, on the side of freedom and, by implication, of life. In the second stanza, the men have been robbed of their freedom and will soon no longer see the sun — "freedom" and "sun" are almost causally linked. In the final two stanzas, the narrator's wish is to regain both freedom and the sunshine from home, and the sunrise is interpreted as a possible sign of the arrival of freedom. "Auschwitz" invokes God as a witness and as an external power, and God's inscrutability — rendered in the rhetorical questions such as "do you want all people to hate us . . . ?" — is given a positive if tentative interpretation in the final stanza.

In "The Chimney" the sun is a key image but a further negative development has taken place. Along with "God," "freedom" has completely fallen out of the picture and the symbolic proximity between "sun" and "life" has become a negative one — in other words, the relation between the two terms is the result exclusively of the negation of both: "Life, sun are gone"; the rhyme to "warme Sonnenlicht" (warm sunlight) is "nicht" (not). Next to, or more precisely behind, the chimney the sun pales and loses its vitality: sunlight has become empty and hollow. The life force of the sun is attenuated by the light of the flame, the smoke, and also by the barbed wire behind which the sun rises. The image of the sun behind barbed wire in a sense excludes the sun from participation in the life of the inmates. The "chimney" takes the place of the sun and comes first. The chimney instead of the celestial body marks the passage of time: "Daily behind the barracks / I see smoke and fire." That in the second stanza the sun also rises "Daily behind the barbed wire" produces a shift, whereby the sun is placed at a further remove from the speaker and becomes derivative. The configuration that gives priority to the "chimney" over the "sun" is reinforced by the rhyming structure later in the poem. In the second stanza, lines seven and eight read "Blick zur roten Flamme hin: / Einzig wahr ist der Kamin." In the next stanza, lines seven and eight repeat the rhyme, but now instead of being called upon to look at the "red flame" in the seventh line, we find out that "life, sun are gone." Sun and life have become secondary, almost imitative of the "chimney." This desolate, barren, lackluster sun calls to mind the oral testimony of another survivor of Auschwitz, Edith P., only in her testimony the sun finally loses all connection to the life-giving forces and turns into its opposite, a symbol of destruction: "I swear to you, the sun was not bright. The sun was red, it was black to me . . . The sun was never life to me. It was destruction. It was never beautiful. We almost forgot what life was all about" (cited in Langer 1991, 105).

In Edith P.'s testimony no connecting transition seems necessary between the negative sun and forgetting "what life was all about." This negative link is also present in Klüger's poem: in the Muselmänner stanza, having lost their fear, the men's "Gelassenheit" (equanimity) indicates as well the abandonment, not only of hope, but also of a more basic investment in life: joy, beauty, life itself along with the sun have lost their validity or meaning. The sun's life force succumbs to the more powerful destructiveness of the furnace or chimney, that is, the crematoria, which become the "only truth" and the center in the universe enclosed by barbed wire.

In the poem "Auschwitz" the third stanza begins with the word "God," introducing the concept of an entity beyond the camps and thus opening the dreary scene of the first two stanzas to a new dimension and, through the vocative, creating an audience. The perpetrators are referred to only in that stanza — as "bloody, brutal hordes" and as people who "despise [God's] highest law" — and in connection with God, as if by naming the murderers the poem might stir God into action. The reference to the perpetrators occurs in a context that creates some distance between them and the speaker. The perpetrators are named in conjunction with God as an external witness rather than in connection to the first-person plural or singular pronoun of the later strophes: this provides distance between the victims, which implicitly include the narrator, and the perpetrators. Moreover, the first two stanzas of "Auschwitz" speak of "men" and in the third-person plural when it depicts the victims who are "heavy with sorrow" and "walk toward their own murder." Partly this might follow from the nineteenth-century literary background that informs the poem. It also seems shaped by traditional perceptions of "men as strong, as protectors of women," perceptions then that make men more particularly and poignantly "pitiful" figures when perceived as victims (Bos, 38). Perhaps not without a trace of projective identification, the narrator in "Auschwitz" speaks of a time long since past in which the men were "geborgen," meaning safe or sheltered: the men might then have been able to shelter the poet herself. In this poem the depiction of men as the victims also functions as a protective mechanism that distances the victims of murder from the girl-witness. In the second stanza of "Auschwitz" the men are moving toward their own murder. Grammatically speaking they are represented as agents with respect to the murder. The fourth stanza opens with the declaration that "*we* have left behind our homeland," again attributing agency, and thereby responsibility, to the victims. In the sixth stanza, the second line — "Must we be destroyed?" — is a passive sentence: again it refers to the perpetrators only through the grammatical elision of the agents of destruction.

Writing about Sutzkever's ghetto poetry, Ruth R. Wisse claims that "in their reluctance to name the enemy, [Sutzkever's] poems are also special acts of aggression, annihilating the foe by denying him existence" (14). While we might plausibly understand the vengeful ending of "The Chimney" as an "act of aggression," the treatment of the perpetrators in "Auschwitz," with the one brief mention in the stanza that is preoccupied with God, seems rather to function as self-protection on the part of the narrator from too stark a confrontation with the reality of the perpetrators, with their arbitrary power. At the same time, the "personified death-machine" in "The Chimney" might be a more dignified enemy and somewhat more abstract than a banal and brutal SS man.

Whereas the emplotment of these poems in the original newspapers' article and in the successive anthologies follows a sentimental or martyrological strain, Klüger's own emplotment is defensive, as if to prevent serious literary scrutiny, or at least, as Eva Lezzi points out, to gain a level of control over the texts and their reception (234). In an echo of the attitude Klüger critiques in the newspapers, she herself calls the poems "Kindergedichte" (children's poetry) and "aalglatte Kinderverse" (eel-smooth children's verses) marked by "Unbeholfenheit" (helplessness) (1994, 107 and 126). She blames her literary influences up to that point for the structure and language of her poems:

> Ich war leider belesen, hatte den Kopf voll von sechs Jahren Klassik, Romantik, Goldschnittlyrik. Und nun dieser Stoff. Meinem späteren Geschmack wären Fragmentarisches und Unregelmäßigkeiten lieber, als Ausdruck sporadischer Verzweiflung zum Beispiel. Aber der spätere Geschmack hat es leicht. Jetzt hab ich gut reden. (1994, 127)

> [I was unfortunately well-read; my head was full of Classical, Romantic, and gilt-edged anthologies. And so this stuff. My taste later would have preferred fragmentary and irregular poetry, as an expression of sporadic despair, for example. But taste with hindsight has it easy. It's easy to say that now.]

In her characteristic two-pronged attack Klüger manages to distance herself from her poems and to preempt later critics who might know better now that their aesthetic judgment has the advantage of "hindsight." Here she makes it clear that she "knows" that a different, more fragmentary, experimental, more abstract style might be considered more appropriate in the context of what has come to be understood as an "unrepresentable" historical event. In so doing she disarms the simplistic literary critic who might approach these poems with the aesthetic standards of the present. In addition to creating authorial discomfort, these poems, whose afterlife leads Klüger to compare them to "verstoßene, doch hartnäckige Kinder auf der Suche nach ihrer Mutter" (abandoned but stubborn children in search of their mother; 1994, 201; see also 2001, 155), create a problem for critics as well, as I discussed in the introduction. Scholars feel compelled to defend these kinds of poems as documents even if they find their literary value questionable.

Adorno's sentence labeling the act of writing poetry after Auschwitz "barbaric" can be understood within a philosophical tradition that finds the pursuit of aesthetic goals in the face of the grossest abrogation of ethical values problematic. Adorno worries about the consumption of artistic products: how such consumability and its implied enjoyment are an affront to the respect for and memory of the victims:

> The victims are turned into works of art, tossed out to be gobbled up by the world that did them in. The so-called artistic rendering of the naked physical pain of those that were beaten down with rifle butts contains, however distantly, the possibility that pleasure can be squeezed from it. (Adorno 1992, 88)

The problem of enjoyment and consumption is pertinent as well in the case of the works that the victims themselves produced, though in this case we cannot easily make the claim that the "victims are turned into works of art" in a gratuitous or disrespectful manner. Instead the poems reveal a sense of agency, however limited, on the part of the inmates akin to the agency that Bos, by acknowledging "the constructed nature of testimony," attributes to survivors in their recollections. As Bos writes: "These constructions suggest that survivors are able to renegotiate the past and produce meaning as subjects" (31). Nevertheless, enjoyment and consumption are part of the contemporary public's relation to those artistic products, for example, as they have been commercialized since the 1990s. In "Anne Frank: The Cultivation of the Inspirational Victim," Bernard shows the kinds of moral, historical, and commercial manipulations to which the purged versions of Anne Frank's diaries were subjected. Similarly Klüger's poems, especially in their purged versions, can be read for easy consumption, but they also bring us to a number of central issues in the representation of the Holocaust: questions about the appropriate level of abstractness and generality, the problems of narrative voice and aesthetic choices, the problem of agency in the representation of the inmates of concentration camps. To ignore those works or to give them a fetishistic treatment can hardly count as respectful of the victims. As discussed earlier, Roskies argues about the need to "contextualize" our analyses of writings from the ghettos and concentration camps and identifies two tendencies in the scholarship on writings by victims of the Nazis, a liturgical and an apocalyptic one. Clearly neither tendency does justice to the writings in question. Within Adorno's rather apocalyptic critique of ideology, the search for sense or meaning contradicts or obfuscates the extent of the horrors perpetrated in the concentration and death camps. This notion leads him to the conclusion that "The only legitimately meaningful artworks today are those opposing the concept of meaning with the utmost recalcitrance" (1998, 45). Adorno's essay "Those Twenties" was originally published in 1962 (Adorno 1998). In the decades since, scholars of the Holocaust have focused on the "unfathomable" aspects of the Holocaust to such an extent that Kathrin Bower could rightfully argue in 2000:

> In the contemporary effusion of words about rupture and the fracture of language there is an observable fetishization of the signifier over the signified, a fascination with tropability in an ethereal realm of aesthetic abstraction, that threatens to obscure the real victims' legacy through a new game of smoke and mirrors. By codifying the conviction that, as Nelly Sachs once wrote, "Silence is the dwelling place of the victims," Holocaust literary scholarship has proclaimed speech an impossibility (thereby denying the victims a conventional voice) while simultaneously privileging a certain kind of language, a poetics of horror, fragmentation, and silence for which Paul Celan has been celebrated ever since Adorno's proclamation in his *Aesthetic Theory:* "Celan's poetry seeks to express the most extreme horror through silence." This concentration on silence and its representations point to the increasingly self-referential nature of Holocaust literary studies. (137)

The stories told in Klüger's poems are rendered in conventional lyric form. The language is old-fashioned and the structure is conventional: iambic tetrameter and intricate and exact rhyming patterns (for example, in "The Chimney," *ababccdd* with a refrain, *ee* and a repetition of words and rhymes from the first to the second stanza [*nicht*], and the second to the third stanza [*hin / Kamin*]). The poems also imagine an end to the suffering: optimistically the return to the freedom and sunshine of home in "Auschwitz," more darkly in "The Chimney," a fantasy of revenge in an image of complete destruction. As Klüger's poems and memoir show, the search for meaning played a vital role for many of the victims of the National Socialists. Often this search is reflected in the form of the poems as well. Gilman argues that

> In the camps the need for sanity, for a sense of stability, often drove young writers to search for the most stable, conservative forms to express the horrors they were living. The use of strict meter, of classical poetic form, of traditional images, was a means of grasping the sanity of the schoolroom that had existed before the corruption of literature and art by the Nazis. (1991, 229)

Adorno's dictum against "meaning" speaks of "artworks today," that is, works of art created after the Shoah, and his theories might prove somewhat inflexible in their understanding of aesthetic theory and in their indebtedness to the aesthetics of avant-garde European modernism. What comes through in poems from the camps are the self-representations, perceptions, perspectives, and psychic processes of some inmates in the camps.

The experience of those who wrote cannot be taken to represent the experience of all victims of the Holocaust — indeed, as Primo Levi insists: "the history of the Lagers has been written almost exclusively by those who, like myself, never fathomed them to the bottom" (1989, 17). Poems from the camps sometimes reveal attitudes to the experiences in the camps that are more widely spread among inmates, as we encounter them in the memoirs or testimonies of survivors. Sometimes the poems reveal an author's complicity with aesthetic assumptions of systems such as the one that oppressed them. Even then the individual details of the poem work against a totalizing view that would reduce the "trauma" of inmates to a monolithically silencing, inexpressible event, and those details give concrete shape to the history of internment. Klüger's poems show, for example, complex negotiations between hope and despair, anger and fear and evince an indirect approach to referring to the perpetrators, though they do not shy away from calling murder murder. These poems also demonstrate an understanding of the chimney, or crematorium, as the center of the concentrationary universe, a universe that replaces our heliocentric galaxy. Such details in the articulations of experience on the part of inmates while in the Nazi camps reveal creative processes in the concentration camps that prefigure later memoirs and testimonies and give texture to the life of the mind in the camps.

With respect to the horrific events people endured during the Holocaust, Geoffrey Hartman writes:

> For us, who were not there, the classical axiom holds that "Nothing human is alien"; for them [the survivors], "Nothing human is entirely familiar." The sense of the human has always to be restored. (133)

In whatever limited manner this may be possible we need to hold on to both those axioms as we read poems from the concentration camps, in order to keep in mind the ways they speak to us of those experiences and what they cannot convey. This is not tantamount to advocating a moderate position between philosophic or aesthetic extremes. Rather, it seems crucial to remember that any overgeneralizing account of the Holocaust does a disservice to the memory of the victims and impairs our possibly already limited ability to confront the events with responsibility and sensitivity.

2: Identity under Threat

A MONG THE CUMULATIVELY traumatic experiences in the concentration camps the attack on individuality was one that victims felt immediately. Brought by force into the concentrationary system, prisoners were robbed not only of their freedom and their civil rights but also of almost all external attributes that indicate and in some sense can be said to constitute a person's individuality. Circumstances varied greatly by time, location, and the category to which the National Socialists assigned a particular inmate. However most inmates lost their residence, their professional and social status, all contact with family and friends, their possessions, their clothing, and even their head- and body-hair. They were assigned numbers to replace their names and were allowed no self-determination. Depending on the camp, such humiliating treatment might include perverse elements such as being forced to ask for permission — often denied — to relieve one's bowels.[1] Jean Samuel, a survivor from Auschwitz-Monowitz and Levi's companion "Pikolo" there, describes the beginning of life in the camp:[2]

> I would like to tell you about the first humiliations quickly. The loss of all our personal belongings, the undressing in a group, the boiling shower, shaving the body from head to toe with blunt blades that grazed the skin, tattooing our number on us, for me 176397, my new identity, oh, how difficult to accept, my name and surname had vanished, the grabbing of two clogs taken running which could take you to your death in a few weeks through infected wounds they had provoked. The first example of the importance of luck or no luck, nobody could hope to survive without a lot of luck. All this imposes a great deal of humility on those who came back.

This account is fairly typical of the first experiences of inmates selected to work in a concentration camp. Bos reminds us, however, that like everything else in the camps, individuals experienced such events differently, in part due to their social conditioning. For example, the shaving of the hair tended to be more traumatic for women than for men: Auscwitz survivor Judith Magyar-Isaacson "describes the shaving as a violation, and the effects are much more dramatic [than in Elie Wiesel's description], for she no longer recognizes the other female inmates as women, not even her own mother" (Bos, 48). Orthodox Jewish men, one might add, would also experience the loss of head and facial hair differently from non-religious men (Rahe, 43–45). Despite the differences in experience and perception the struggle to retain a sense of individual identity and dignity is a theme in a number of writings and poems from the concentration camps. The site of struggle varies greatly. The issues range from a concern with the loss of one's name and consequently one's individual identity and the loss of connection to the world outside the camps (as in the poems in this chapter) to existential questions about what it means to retain one's humanity, even if not usually in those terms (as in the poems in the next two chapters). Faced with extreme degradation, what are the limits of human dignity, of "properly human" experience? What is at the core of identity when all external attributes are stripped away?

The Power to Name and Unname

Identification numbers were sewn onto the inmates' uniform in the breast area on the left-hand side, below or next to colored signs (and letters for the nationality) that indicated the category or categories the SS had assigned to the prisoner. Inmates were forced to use that number any time they needed to report to the different administrative offices in the camps or to talk to a guard or supervisor as well as during the daily roll calls. Officially the number replaced the name, and at Auschwitz it was tattooed onto the left arm of inmates (Kogon, 50); "only non-Jewish German prisoners were exempt" from having the number tattooed onto their arm (Levi 1988, 118).[3] Primo Levi writes: "Nothing belongs to us anymore . . . They will even take away our name: and if we want to keep it, we will have to find in ourselves the strength to do so, to manage somehow so that behind the name something of us, of us as we were, still remains" (1961, 22). Note that Levi writes here of "us as we were." The identity to be salvaged is the pre-camp identity. All four poems analyzed in this chapter confront the task of finding the strength to retain or regain identity in a variety of ways. In terms of their rhetorical strategies, the poem by Hasso Grabner and the poem by Edgar Kupfer-Koberwitz strive for a reversal of signification. Both poems take an element from the camps designed to deny the inmates their individual identity and they imbue that element with a meaning that counters or reconfigures such denial. By contrast the other two poems, both by Fritz Löhner-Beda, enact connections to the outside world and through such external relations restitute a sense of individual identity and connectedness for the speaker.

Hasso Grabner's poem "Die Häftlingsnummer"[4] (The Prisoner's Number), written in September 1938 in Buchenwald, is one attempt to find "the strength" to resist the dehumanization implied by the imposition of the number. The poem carries out a transformation of its title character: the prisoner's number. The first of its four stanzas focuses on the imposition of the prisoner's number and reveals the perpetrators' intent — to "extinguish" (löschen) the person through the number and to render the individual name meaningless.

Sie möchten gern, daß sie den Menschen lösche
· und seinen Namen ins Vergessen trägt,
verlorner Ruf, der keinen Hall erregt,
ein grauer Strich auf einer grauen Fläche.

[They would like it to extinguish the person
and to carry his name into oblivion,
a lost call that evokes no response,
a gray line on a gray surface.]

"They *would* like [the prisoner's number] to extinguish the person": the SS-administration relies on a system — assigning numbers to prisoners — in order to break the prisoners' resistance and their identity. There is no direct portrayal of the physical violence perpetrated by the SS officers; indeed, the SS seems to lack the power or the will to annihilate the inmates more directly. With this poem the speaker claims to see through the administrative ploy of the SS and creates a sphere of resistance to it — this resistance becomes clearer as the stanzas progress. It is well known that the National Socialists kept fastidious records (in the camps as well as outside) and that administrative tasks and accuracy were given inordinate importance in the concentration-camp system.[5] Furthermore the SS counted prisoners in terms of pieces (*Stück*), as one might take inventory of objects in a depot or count cattle on a farm (for example, see Levi 1961, 12). This poem doubts not the immediate impact but the ultimate effectiveness of such linguistic and administrative procedures.

The threat is radical: to extinguish, annul, or erase the person, the human. The representation of such radical danger to the self seems to necessitate some form of mediation: the "players" are external. The speaker stands at a distance from "the prisoner" and dis-identifies with the "Mensch," who appears in the third-person singular — *his* name, not "mine," is threatened with oblivion. Grabner's only direct reference to the perpetrators is a vague *they*, the first word of the poem, while a less direct reference to the SS is rendered as "dark will" in the third stanza. In the poem's first sentence the predicative verb is in the subjunctive, *möchten gern,* and is thus inflected with doubt. This subjunctive expresses the speaker's skepticism about the feasibility of what the SS — referred to as "they" — intends.

The second stanza continues to depict what the SS would like to achieve by imposing the number on the prisoner. Again the text concentrates on the administrative actions designed to replace the vital person (heart) with a lifeless record, a number or cipher, a "gray line," an index card.

Ein windverwehtes Nichts in seiner Schwäche,
vom Leben als Karteiblatt abgelegt,
ein Schatten, wo sich sonst ein Herz bewegt,
damit das Herz an dieser Zahl zerbreche.

[A wind-blown nothing in its weakness,
discarded from life like an index-card,
a shadow, where otherwise a heart would move,
so that the heart will break over that cipher.]

Grabner creates a sphere of life to which the heart and its movement belong and opposes that sphere to the bureaucratic imposition of the numbers and index cards ("So that the heart will break . . ."). In the first two stanzas, the name and the person are inseparable, almost indistinguishable. There is a slippage between "name" and *Mensch* (human being): by replacing the name, consigning it to oblivion, the number is supposed to "wipe out" the person. The name would become a "lost call," an appellation that no longer interpellates, that "evokes no response." *Verlorener Ruf* (lost call) evokes here a call that gets lost (goes missing) — a call the inmate cannot answer, an address that fails. Once the name had been eradicated, there should be, in the logic of the SS, no one there, no person, to answer to the call. *Ruf* also connotes reputation: the reputation that is lost with the loss of the name. The loss of reputation worried some inmates in the camps, at least initially.

Gray is the only color in the poem, and the imagery at the end of the first stanza is a trope for disintegration, for erasure: a gray mark on a gray surface. The prisoner's name becomes invisible. Along with his name the prisoner himself vanishes in the gray monotony of the camps, becomes lost in lists on which a person's only substance is as a number.

While the last two lines of the first stanza deal with the prisoner's name, in the next stanza and without explicit transition not the name but the person becomes a shadow, a feeble "nothing[ness]" (*Nichts*) blown about, scattered by the wind. The shadow, the gray line, the number, the index card are all elements of a system designed to replace the person, the heart. Vitality, albeit threatened, is aligned with the inmates in this poem, and the bureaucratic will of the concentrationary system seems to lack not just a heart but even muscle power. The third stanza is joined to the fourth by the rhyme scheme (abc cba) and by the sentence structure: the last sentence of the poem begins on the second line of the third stanza and constitutes the finale. It constructs the administrative failure of the SS and reaffirms the prisoners' identity and resistance. In the Nazi camps, this poem implies, to exist is to resist:

Nichts kann dem dunklen Wollen Sieg verleihn.
Es nimmt die Nummer jeden an die Hand,
als einer großen Kette dienend Glied,

als voller Ton in unserm hohen Lied,
das Millionen unzertrennbar band,
das Lied: Ich war, ich bin, ich werde sein.

[Nothing can give victory to that dark will.
The number takes each one by the hand,
as a link beholden to a great chain,

as full sound in our high song
that united millions inseparably,
the song: I was, I am, I will be.]

Here the narrator reverses the meaning, the function of the number: the number remains the character with the most agency in this poem, but it now becomes clear that the number is on the side of the inmates: "the number takes each one by the hand." It is as if the prisoner's number undergoes a transformation from a bureaucratic, humiliating, and oppressive instrument for record keeping into a positive, binding force that creates unity, makes of each prisoner another link serving a big chain, a chain of millions. In the end the narrator responds to the virulent attack on the individual *name* with a linguistic affirmation. All inmates are now united in a "high song" — "I was, I am, I will be!" — as if the commonality of the number had created a shared purpose. "Ich war, ich bin, ich werde sein!" is also the slogan with which Marxist revolutionary Rosa Luxemburg ended her last text, which she published on 14 January 1919, the day before her assassination in the midst of political turmoil after the end of the First World War. In Luxemburg's text it is the socialist "revolution" itself that reaffirms its existence through those words (Luxemburg, 209). Integrated into Grabner's poem these words acquire an almost magic connotation: Words are one of the individual poet's last refuges in the face of extreme degradation and mortal threat. This "song" is then an illocutionary declaration of selfhood, of identity in language. In this poem the first person pronoun is only introduced in a quotation in an affirmation of victory over the perpetrators' "dark will." The "I" as it were is thus variously protected: by the quotation marks, by its communal declaration, by its iteratively affirmed existence. The repetition of *ich* with the past, present, and future conjugations of *sein* establish a positive meaning or purpose in the poem and for the prisoner's existence. The poem posits an identity both prior and subsequent to the time defined by the number; it thus defies and counteracts the ways in which the imposition of the *Häftlingsnummer* would render people anonymous, less than human. Ironically it seems as if under threat the expression of enduring individual identity only emerges when the individual is a part of the larger unit. Is this an indication of the difficulties faced by the lone resister? Is this an indication of the author's political leanings? While the concentrationary universe was designed to make solidarity virtually impossible, this poem extracts one of the items intended to have an alienating, disaggregating effect and rhetorically turns that element into an occasion for unity, a solidarity predicated on existence in common, the shared existence of the inmates: "I was, I am, I will be."

The tenuousness of the poem's affirmation of identity in language is suggested as well in the repeated use of the word *Nichts* (nothing). In the second stanza, *Nichts* refers to the prisoner or, more accurately, to what the SS would like the prisoner to become. But *Nichts* is also the first word of the third stanza. There it declares the failure of the SS's dark designs. The first *Nichts* renders the second one equivocal, for the first sentence of the third stanza then turns around to mean that either the "inmate" or "nothing" "can give victory to that dark will." This simple deconstructive move shows the textual ambiguity in the poem's trajectory. It makes clear the element in language that is beyond intentional control and may serve as well to highlight the crass difference in power between a song and an administration conducted behind barbed wire and machine guns.

Born in 1911 in Leipzig, Hasso Grabner became an active member of the German Communist Party in 1930. He worked in the underground resistance from 1933 on and was imprisoned in 1936 in the Waldheim prison in Saxony at first. He was later transferred to the concentration camp Buchenwald, where he remained from September 1938 until June 1940. On arriving at Buchenwald he received the prisoner's number 5334; the dating of his poem indicates that he wrote it shortly after being assigned a number. He was released from Buchenwald to be ordered to *Strafdivision 999* (punishment division) — also known as *Strafbataillon 999* (punishment battalion), and officially as *Bewährungsbataillon 999* (probation battalion) — a unit of the Wehrmacht in which German men under 45 years old who were considered physically, but not morally and politically, fit to serve nonetheless were forced into military service.[6] After the war Grabner worked as a radio editor and economy functionary in the German Democratic Republic. From 1958 onward Grabner worked as a writer: he published a number of novels and two collections of poetry. He died in Potsdam in 1976 (Kirsten and Kirsten, 306).

Most of Grabner's camp poems are not explicit about his political leanings; nevertheless they do reveal some of the attitudes common among Communist prisoners: most prominently the idea of comradeship, as well as the idea of a struggle between the Nazis and the inmates (as in the opposition "dark will"/"great chain"), and the belief in a victory through unity and resistance (the "high song / that united millions inseparably.")

Indeed, this particular poem has been received as a poem of resistance. For example on 28 January 2000 the painter and Jewish survivor of Dachau and Auschwitz Max Mannheimer was welcomed to a meeting with students at a Bavarian high school (FOS u. BOS Ingolstadt) with a reading of Grabner's poem. Picking up on the defiant affect in "Die Häftlingsnummer" the speaker, teacher Birgitt Schärtel, went on to claim that although the number was indelibly imprinted onto Mannheimer's left arm, "they" did not manage to extinguish Mannheimer's humanity (Schärtel 2000).

Imagined Connection

Not surprisingly, the significance of the personal name and its loss is a theme in a number of poems from the camps. Fritz Löhner (born 1883 as Fritz Löwy), also known as Beda — his pseudonym — and as Dr. Fritz Löhner-Beda, was a well-known Jewish satirist, poet, songwriter, and librettist in Vienna until the National Socialists deported him days after they annexed Austria in 1938. He was most famous for a number of very popular songs in the 1920s and 1930s and for his work with Franz Léhar, who became Hitler's "favorite" and privileged composer. He is practically unknown now, mostly because in the process of the "aryanization" of music, National Socialist music historians and administrators ensured that his name and those of his coauthors, all Jewish, were deleted from their popular and profitable hits. A critic of Jewish assimilation, Löhner-Beda had been outspoken from early on about his contempt for the Nazis. He was arrested on 13 March 1938 and detained at first in Vienna, then deported to Dachau with the first deportation of prominent Austrians. In the autumn of 1938 he was taken from Dachau to Buchenwald. Deported to Auschwitz-Monowitz in October of 1942, he died there in December. A beating was most likely the immediate cause of death (for more extensive biographical information about Löhner-Beda, see Denscher and Peschina 2002; Schwarberg 2000). Karl Schnog was a fellow political and Jewish inmate and like Löhner a published satirist. In a recollection of Löhner's character and behavior at Buchenwald, Schnog writes of the kind of humor Löhner managed to muster despite the degradation of his camp existence (the cause of death mentioned by Schnog, who remained in Buchenwald until the liberation of that camp, does not jibe with accounts by witnesses from Auschwitz-Monowitz. For another account of Löhner-Beda's death, see also Hilberg, 3:930):

> Dry humor and spiritual superiority were demonstrated as well by Franz Léhar's librettist, the poet of "The Land of Smiles" [Land des Lächelns], "Friederike," "Giuditta," the author of "Gladly Have I Kissed the Ladies" [Gern hab ich die Frau'n geküsst] and "Yours is my Whole Heart" [Dein ist mein ganzes Herz]: Dr. Fritz Löhner-Beda. With this author from Vienna, amusing even in the greatest misery, I

shared a table in Buchenwald for one and a half years — until he was transported to Auschwitz and died there of starvation in December of 1942. One morning during roll call someone tried to point out to Beda the special beauty of the sunrise, to which he replied (after five years of internment): "My dear, I have had enough sunrises for the next ten years." If someone tried to tell him of even more horrible conditions for us in the future, Beda would say: "How can vinegar go more sour?"

But when on occasion after work the camp radio played one of his songs (these "non-Aryan" but successful texts were broadcast as — Léhar's works), then, in that barrack filled with inmates, the old man in his zebra suit would turn to the radio and declare festively: "The author would like to express his gratitude!" (Schnog 1945, 14–15)

Humor, like poetry, is an affect, an attitude, an activity that is experienced as personal, as free. In a different context, psychoanalyst Adam Phillips argues that the "joke is so important for Freud because it is the most ingeniously efficient way of rescuing our pleasure from the obstacles" (85). Wolfgang Sofsky writes of "eccentric positionality" — the "self-distance from which a person can observe himself or herself at a remove" — as necessary for humor and irony and a precondition for a sense of the passage of time, a positionality that gets lost with the deterioration of an inmate's psychic life (Sofsky, 201–2). That Löhner-Beda was practiced at confronting complex and difficult situations — though clearly less extreme than in the concentration camps — with a degree of irony and self-humor is evident from his satirical poetry, as can be seen in the titles of his two earliest collections: *Getaufte und Baldgetaufte* (The Baptized and the Soon-To-Be-Baptized; 1908) and *Israeliten und andere Antisemiten* (Israelites and Other Anti-Semites; 1909), which earned him a reputation as the "first Zionist satirist" (Otto Teller cited in Denscher and Peschina, 25).

At Buchenwald Löhner-Beda wrote a number of poems as well as the famous "Buchenwaldlied" whose happy ending Klüger emulated. Löhner-Beda's poems grapple with conditions in the camps: loneliness and separation from the family, tiredness, and hunger, as well as the imposition of the inmate's number. In the poem "Der Häftling"[7] (The Inmate) the speaker proceeds from having neither an identity nor a "belly" to finding a connection to the world outside the camps. This leads him, in turn, to hope about the future.

> Ich bin ein Häftling, sonst bin ich nix,
> hab' keinen Namen, die Nummer X.
> Gestreift ist mein Rock, die Hose auch,
> Ich schnüre den Riemen um gar keinen Bauch —
> und warte!

Ich schaffe am Tag an die vierzehn Stund',
ich kriech' in den Stall und bin müd' wie ein Hund.
Dann ess' ich die Handvoll verkrümeltes Brot
und fall' auf den Strohsack und schlafe wie tot —
und warte!

Das Weib und die Kinder, die sitzen zu Haus'.
Bald sind es fünf Jahre! Wie seh'n sie wohl aus?
Ich sehe die große verdunkelte Stadt,
da sind sie verkrochen und werden nicht satt —
und warten!

Doch mich schlägt kein Tiger, mich frißt kein Hai,
der Tod geht täglich an mir vorbei.
An mir beißt der Teufel die Zähne sich aus.
Ich fühl' es: Ich komm' aus der Hölle heraus!
Ich warte!

[I'm an inmate, nothing else,
I've got no name, the number X.
Striped is my jacket and so are my pants,
I tighten my belt around no belly at all —
and wait!

I labor for fourteen hours a day,
I crawl to the stable, tired like a dog.
Then I eat my handful of breadcrumbs
and fall onto the straw sack and sleep like I'm dead —
and wait!

The wife and the children are sitting at home.
Soon it will be five years. What do they look like?
I see the city, big and darkened,
there they crawl about, always hungry —
and they wait!

But no tiger will attack me, no shark'll devour me,
Death passes me by every day.
The devil himself will break his teeth on me.
I feel it: I will get out of hell!
I'm waiting!]

The central movement in this rhyming poem (aabb and one-line refrain) concerns the tension between the exhausting, deadly monotony of life in the camps and the increasing sense of resistance to it, of hope, on the part of the speaker. The poem begins with a first-person description of the circumstances: the uniform the speaker has to wear, the number in place of the proper name, the lack of nourishment. The speaker describes himself with a generic label ("inmate") and a number whose specific value is not important. The word inmate (Häftling) was used to refer specifically to those who were detained without having been convicted in a court of law, which was generally the case in the concentration camps (Kupfer-Koberwitz 1997, 470). Arendt points out the importance for totalitarian regimes of the legal limbo in which detainees were kept, and regards this as the "first step on the road to total domination." She also writes of the paradoxical plight of "innocent" inmates who are more (thoroughly) disenfranchised by being placed outside the penal system than individuals convicted of a crime (1958, 447; see also 1948, 752). The first stanza of Löhner-Beda's poem states that both his physical and his formal, nominal, legal existence are denied to the inmate-speaker. His whole identity seems determined here by his "legal" status outside the law and by his uniform: "I'm an inmate, nothing else." His "belly" has disappeared because he is treated as if he did not have a stomach, and his identity is threatened along with his name. The next stanza describes the brutalizing effect of conditions in the camps: working fourteen hours, being in a state comparable to animals: "I crawl to the stable, tired like a dog." The degradation progresses from non-human to non-living: "sleep like I'm dead." Despite the threat to human and individual identity, despite the perception that he is in a state comparable to dogs and to being dead, one thread of hope or defiance remains marked by the repetition, at the end of the first and the second stanzas of "and wait!" Even in sleep the speaker "waits." In the beginning the only option left open to the speaker is "to wait," a minimal connection to an unlikely future, to the future itself.

The speaker's death-like sleep is followed by the return of memory, and then by a flight of fantasy, or possibly a dream. Suddenly the speaker makes a leap to a place outside the confines of the Buchenwald concentration camp: "The wife and the children are sitting at home." After a moment's reflection on his own miserable condition the inmate-speaker now turns to his close relations outside the camp. It has been five years since he has seen them. He asks himself: "What do they look like [now]?" He imagines them staying at home, confined. In a projective moment the speaker thinks that the members of his family too are hungry and that they move about the way he does in the camp: "I crawl to the stable". . . / "There they crawl about, and are always hungry." Like him, his family has been reduced to an animal-like state. The third stanza contains a momentary transcendence, a fantasized escape from the camp. Importantly, this stanza constitutes an imaginative act in which a sense of community is ascertained: "und warte!" (and [I] wait!) turns into "und warten!" (and [they] wait!), becoming plural. His family waits as well, wait with and for him. He waits to get out, to see them; they wait for his return. Their lives stand still: the family sits at home and waits;

the speaker endures senseless abuse and waits. What we call "normal life" stopped for the narrator five years ago: in the poem — though also in reality — "normal life" has also been on hold for his family outside the camps. The surroundings of the family, like his own, have become threatening: they are in a city that is "large, darkened." In a sense the inmate-speaker's imagined connection to the family outside affords him a momentary escape from loneliness to a scene in which his family shares his fate. In the projective process some of the negativity of his own situation is extended beyond the limits of the concentration camps. At the same time such negativity corresponds as well to the situation of families torn apart, disenfranchised, and dispossessed by the Nazis even before all members were deported to the concentration and extermination camps. Löhner-Beda was at Buchenwald from autumn of 1938 until October of 1942. Biographers indicate that while at Buchenwald he received letters and money from his wife regularly. However the Nazis gradually dispossessed his wife and daughters (then fifteen and thirteen years old). The Nazis deported his family to the death camp Maly Trostinec near Minsk in August of 1942, where they were murdered upon arrival. Löhner-Beda never found out what happened to them (see Schwarberg, 162–63; Denscher and Peschina, 194). Biographers also cite different survivors who knew Löhner-Beda in the camps: they claim that Löhner-Beda was convinced that Franz Léhar, honored and favored by the Nazis as "the Führer's favorite composer," would rescue him from the concentration camps. Léhar did not, though he did manage to get special protection for his own Jewish wife (Denscher and Peschina, 192–94).

Through an imaginative act in "Der Häftling" the speaker emerges from the routine of camp work, the death-like and deadly lack and exhaustion. Significantly, the language makes a marked shift from the similes in the second stanza ("like a dog") and from the realistically imagined scenario in the third stanza to the realm of the fantastic in the fourth and final stanza. As the speaker defies the "order of terror," his terms become allegorical, symbolic: "tiger," "shark," "Death," "Devil," "Hell." A fantastic setting ranging from creatures out of what in Central Europe must count as an exotic zoology to less exotic but no less preternatural mythical figures makes possible defiant courage in the midst of the utmost humiliation:

> Doch mich schlägt kein Tiger, mich frißt kein Hai,
> der Tod geht täglich an mir vorbei.
> An mir beißt der Teufel die Zähne sich aus.
>
> [But no tiger will attack me, no shark'll devour me,
> Death passes me by every day.
> The devil himself will break his teeth on me.]

This kind of bravado finds expression as well in a rugged, almost rambunctious colloquial language. The fantastic setting makes it possible for the poem to avoid calling the perpetrators by their name: SS guards, Nazis, camp guards. That kind of factuality would threaten the fantastic vision — fantastic in the sense of its unrealistic coordinates, fantastic in terms of the speaker's own sense of invincibility — by exposing the futile banality of evil against which the individual inmate is rendered powerless. A personified Death and the Devil seem more agreeable counterparts in the fantasy, more acceptable enemies or obstacles. One can also say that the nouns "devil" and "hell" more accurately characterize the inmate-speaker's perception of the perpetrators and of the situation than the language of the Nazis, than the terms the Nazis used to refer to themselves and to the camp. The speaker at the end is certain that he will "get out of hell": note here that the camp in that sense is not a version or a rendition of hell, a subsidiary of hell, but "hell" itself.

The symbolic, remembered connection to another person, to a "resonating other" (in Laub and Auerhahn's phrase [1989]), brings back to the speaker confidence in the future, a cathexis to life. In the beginning, waiting connotes drudgery and despair. In the last line, "ich warte," waiting, now claimed directly by the poem's "I," evokes defiance, excitement, hope, a vision of the future, a desire to survive. In stark contrast to Grabner's "Die Häftlingsnummer" there is throughout this poem a very prominent first-person singular speaker. *Ich* opens the poem and the second stanza. In the final line of the poem, *ich* completes the sentence and rounds off the poem, replacing the *und* of the final lines of the previous three stanzas. The final *ich* thus provides closure and a reaffirmation of the speaker's personal determination to survive a world that is emotionally frozen, has stood still, symbolically, for almost "five years." The inmate-speaker seems to endure in the feeling, the hope, that he will "get out of hell" and reconnect with his family — which he symbolically and affectively achieves through this poem.

Sofsky describes the "anonymizing" environment of the camps, an environment hostile to relationships, in the following manner:

> The structure of the social world, the strata of the world of work, shared and distant world, is shattered if other people are immediately on hand yet simultaneously anonymous. They are as near, as intimately present as one's closest partners — and despite this, as alien as any distant contemporaries, an empty type, a nameless schema. It is thus mistaken to term this a forced community. The camp was not a community. The other people were not individuals whose story you knew. They were not your opposite numbers, but merely the people next to you. Physical proximity was not matched by the presence of an interpersonal "we"; there was no partnership and cooperation hand in hand with the similarity of suffering that all endured. The mass made the

other person faceless; it robbed the individual of the possibility to relate to another person, and thus also to himself or herself. In the mass, the significant other, the mirror of the self, is lacking. Violence and deprivation reduced the individual below the animal minimum for existence; the forced condition of the mass destroyed his or her self-relation as a person. (Sofsky, 155–56)

Although Sofsky's account seems to overgeneralize and is contradicted by survivor testimony such as Schnog's aforementioned description of Löhner-Beda's behavior at Buchenwald and of interpersonal relations there, his version of the camps points to some of the social and psychic effects of crowding in the camps. Poems from the camps, as means of communication, establish a relation to an "other," and thus they recreate a relation to the self.

In another poem Löhner-Beda makes the psychic importance of the connection to the world outside the camps more explicit. Unlike Grabner's political connection to a more widespread opposition to the Nazis, Löhner-Beda's imaginative act takes place in a private, familial setting. Here the speaker's family constitutes the enduring link to the external world. The following poem was originally published without a title in Schneider's *Kunst hinter Stacheldraht* (1973, 142).[8] In his biography of Löhner-Beda entitled *Dein ist mein ganzes Herz: Die Geschichte von Fritz Löhner-Beda, der die schönsten Lieder der Welt schrieb und warum Hitler ihn ermorden ließ* (Yours is My Whole Heart: The Story of Fritz Löhner-Beda, Who Wrote the Most Beautiful Songs in the World and Why Hitler Had Him Murdered), journalist Günther Schwarberg reproduces this poem giving it as a title a section of a line in the poem: "Papi, kommst du bald?" (Daddy, Are You Coming Soon? 135). Unfortunately Schwarberg provides no documentary sources in his informative though somewhat sentimental biography. With its focus on the child's question, the title Schwarberg gives to this poem highlights a sentimental pathos in the text. In this context it seems important to remember that Löhner-Beda was an expert writer of popular song lyrics with their tendency toward memorable, touching wording. The poem hovers between the sentimentality of the popular song and the lyricism of a love poem. As an untitled text written at Buchenwald by a Jewish inmate the poem acquires a certain depth since the "scene of writing" serves to constrain and give a darker, heavier weight to the wish for peace and quiet and to the longing for the family. Schwarberg claims that Löhner-Beda sent this poem to his wife and two young daughters, then still in Vienna (135). Clearly the lyrical poem addresses the narrator's family members directly:

> Wenn sich müd die Glieder senken,
> Tief ersehnen Ruh' und Traum,
> Zieht ein süßes Deingedenken,
> Liebste, durch der Seele Raum.

Große Kinderaugen schauen
Wie aus einem Märchenwald
Hold mit kindlichem Vertrauen,
Fragend: "Papi, kommst du bald?"

Und mir ist es so, als schwebe
Eure Liebe über mir,
Und ich weiß, warum ich lebe,
Und ich fühl' es tief, wofür.

[When my tired limbs sink down,
Deeply longing for rest and dreams,
A sweet remembrance of you, dearest,
Breezes through the space of my soul.

Big children's eyes look, fair,
Like out of a fairytale wood,
Asking with childlike
Trust: "Daddy, are you coming soon?"

And I feel as if your love
Were floating over me.
And I know why I am alive,
And I deeply feel, what for.]

As in the previously discussed poem by Löhner-Beda, rest and dreams bring
a memory of the family's love back to the exhausted inmate-speaker. This
phantasmatic connection to the outside world serves affectively to anchor
the speaker in a world of life-connectedness and empathy — two elements
crucially absent in the camps. At the core of trauma, according to Laub and
Auerhahn, there is a loss of faith or trust in fellow human beings — in another person's basic empathic response:

> The link between self and other is predicated on the possibility and ex-
> pectation of empathy, which are to some degree taken for granted. In
> the concentration camps, the sadistic, bureaucratic killing disproved
> this basic expectation. An empathic response was absent not only from
> the Nazis, but from fellow citizens and allies as well (i.e. from society at
> large). When people prove malignant on such a massive scale, the survi-
> vor retains the memory of a basic deficit — of a compromise in the em-
> pathic dyad. When their vital needs are neither heeded nor responded
> to by others, individuals lose the expectation that their needs will be
> met. Faith in the possibility of communication dies and intrapsychically
> there may no longer be a matrix of two people — self and resonating
> other. (1989, 378–79)

In this poem the speaker's empathic gesture establishes a bond, creates a "resonating matrix." He imagines the children's questions, their concern for him, their need for him, their father. Similarly in "Der Häftling" the speaker's wife and children wait for him. In the concentration camp love and trust seem to be childlike concepts. They are old-fashioned, as signaled by the German adjective *hold*, a markedly poetic term for "lovely," "fair." In the concentrationary world trust is something out of a fairy tale, or out of a long lost (utopian) past. The same applies to the word *Papi* (daddy) and the question that follows it, "Are you coming soon?" Such a question welcomes the person addressed instead of threatening or accusing, as might more often be the case in the camps. Like the daydream it describes, the poem functions like a fairy tale that reestablishes the family's love — the connection between the poet and the loved ones — and is a reminder of childhood innocence and trust. "Eure Liebe" (your love), as the only noun in the final stanza, is a central concept here. Its sound is acoustically connected to "ich lebe" (I live) and to the adjective "tief" (deep) that describes the speaker's sense of connectedness. Trust, love, and innocence of the type portrayed in the poem are clearly a counterpoint to the anonymous, anti-relational atmosphere in the camps. Both of these poems by Löhner-Beda constitute imaginative acts that create connections to the world outside the concentration camps and retain relationships that the Nazis were intent on destroying.

An Object as the Other

In yet another attempt to imaginatively overcome the structure of anonymous relationship in a forced crowd, the following poem performs a resignification of a material detail of life within the concentrationary universe — the striped uniform inmates had to wear. The poem makes a psychically and morally useful "other" out of a humiliating and de-individualizing object. Edgar Kupfer-Koberwitz, whose biography is discussed in the next chapter, was a non-Jewish German political prisoner without any ties to a political party. In "Gestreiftes Kleid"[9] (Striped Cloak) he concentrates on two items of external appearance in the camps — the striped uniform and the shaved head — as markers of the loss of individuality. Kupfer-Koberwitz wrote "Gestreiftes Kleid" in Dachau in the first days of February of 1944 (Kupfer-Koberwitz 1997, 249). The poem begins:

> Gestreift ist unser Kleid,
> geschoren unser Haar,
> wir stehen außerhalb des Rechts, —
> auch wer ein Individuum war,
> ein Künstler oder Denker gar,
> trägt das Gewand des Knechts. —

[Striped is our cloak,
shorn our hair,
we stand outside the law, —
even he who was an individual,
an artist or yet a thinker,
wears the garment of the slave. —]

The striped uniform and the shaved head stand in stark contrast to the idea of an individual. Not everyone was an *Individuum;* rather, "even he" (*auch wer*) who was an individual is now reduced to wearing the garments of servitude. There is a progression from individual to artist and then to thinker that evinces a humanist understanding of the world whereby the philosopher deserves the most respect and is the most individual of all. Such a humanist philosophy corresponds to the pathos evoked through Romantic notions of the Middle Ages by the use of archaic vocabulary (*Gewand des Knechts* [servant's garment]) and concepts such as the division of labor into *Künstler, Denker,* and *Knecht,* as well as an old-fashioned word order (for example, subject/predicate inversion) and a traditional rhyming pattern that weaves together the poem. In the nineteenth-century classical humanist tradition, the poet must be an individual, an artist, and a thinker. Accordingly this putatively male individual should be far removed, in his ideal world, from everyday concerns and all the more so from humiliating conditions such as those imposed on people in the Nazi camps. There is a significant political dimension, however, in the assertion that "we stand outside the law." That third line functions as an explanation for the two strange facts with which the poem opens: striped cloak, shaved hair. The rest of the poem elaborates on the three first lines. Despite its possibly hierarchical notions of individuality, the poem explicitly purports to describe the inmates' common fate, and thus continues speaking in the first-person plural:

Gestreift ist unser Kleid,
geschoren unser Haar, —
man hat uns nichts gelassen, —
und alles was uns teuer war,
das Heim, die Frau, das Kind sogar,
die haben wir verlassen. —

[Striped is our cloak,
shorn our hair, —
they left us with nothing, —
and everything that was dear to us,
the home, the wife, even the child,
all those have we left behind. —]

Home, wife, and *child* are listed together here as the most primordial relations to the outside world — the only personal, now blocked, relation to an "other" beyond the camps. In this poem, as in the preceding examples in this chapter, the perpetrators again remain unnamed: the humiliations, the dangers are described in the passive voice; the agent is an elliptical *man,* which can be translated variously as *one* or *they,* and is a grammatical device in German for writing an active sentence without naming the agent. In other camp poems Moll interprets the strategy of not naming the perpetrator directly as a way of protecting the narrative from "too much reality." As an example Moll provides the following two lines composed in Buchenwald by a Czech theater collective, the choir "Bohemia: "Als jene kamen, die uns die Freiheit nahmen / Und sie hinter Stacheldraht in Fesseln legten" (When those came who had taken our freedom, / And put it in shackles behind barbed wire). Moll writes:

> The perpetrators, tormentors and torturers are not named; that would be too realistic. Naming the perpetrators as "those," who can tendentially remain unreal, signifies the superiority of the victims. It allows them to give the perpetrators such minimal importance as not to find it necessary even to call them by name. The inmates who are being robbed of their self-identification represent themselves as those who, through a provocative failure to name them rob their direct torturers of their identification.
>
> The power relation is inverted here for a moment. Thereafter, there is a marked further self-distancing by the victims. "Those" have put freedom, not the inmates, behind barbed wired.
>
> The abstract noun is put in place of the actual sufferers, who thus at the same time become the carriers of freedom; they make themselves into freedom and thereby name their own ideal in the concentration camps. (Moll 1988, 147)

In "Gestreiftes Kleid" Kupfer-Koberwitz also refuses, as it were, to acknowledge the Nazis' power over the inmates' relationships to their home and family; the speaker does not grant the Nazis power over the inmates' most intimate personal connections. In terms of the grammar the strategy is different from the one described by Moll in the example above. There an unspecified pronominal referent to designate the perpetrators and an abstract noun in place of the inmates make the perpetrators unimportant and the inmates into metonymic representatives of freedom. In Kupfer-Koberwitz's poem it is the victims who take on the responsibility for "leaving" their loved ones: "die haben *wir* verlassen" (all those have *we* abandoned). By putting the inmates in the subject position here the poem restores agency to the victims, even if that agency is one with negative consequences. The personal pronoun "wir" is a stressed syllable in the last line of the stanza, while the pronoun "man" on the second line is not. It is not that the poem blames the victims. Rather, the poem here refuses obstinately the lack of self-determination imposed on inmates by the concentrationary system.

The following sections in particular are marked by strongly contrasting images set next to each other without further elaboration. The external threats, on the one hand, and an inner sense of pride, courage, and freedom, on the other, stand in jarring contradiction.

> Gestreift ist unser Kleid,
> geschoren unser Haar, —
> nun will man uns zerbrechen,
> doch in uns leuchtet still und klar
> der Freiheit Siegel wunderbar,
> wenn auch kein Wort wir sprechen. —

> Gestreift ist unser Kleid,
> geschoren unser Haar, —
> noch gehen wir mit stolzem Mut,
> wir leben täglich in Gefahr,
> erniedrigt, wie noch keiner war,
> bald trinkt die Erde unser Blut. —
> Dann trägt der Kamerad das Kleid,
> wohl wissend um das grosse Leid,
> das dieser Stoff umschloss. —

> [Striped is our cloak,
> shorn our hair, —
> they now want to break us,
> but the wonderful emblem of freedom
> shines in us quietly and brightly,
> even if not a word we say. —

> Striped is our cloak,
> shorn our hair, —
> still we walk about with proud courage,
> we live daily with danger,
> debased as no one has ever been,
> soon the earth will drink our blood. —
> Then the comrade will wear the cloak
> fully conscious of the great pain,
> which this cloth used to contain. —]

A power struggle ensues between, on the one hand, the overpowering reality of mortal threat and humiliation, which is described in a language whose metaphoricity the context of the poem throws into question ("debased as no one has ever been, / soon the earth will drink our blood") and, on the other hand, an idealistic (or idealized), confident self-understanding ("but the wonderful emblem of freedom / shines in us quietly and brightly," "still we walk about with proud courage"). "Siegel," translated above as emblem, is a mark or a seal. In German as in English the term connotes both a mark of authenticity, as in a "seal of assurance," and secrecy, as in "under seal." Freedom's seal in the poem shines quietly, secretly marking the inmates as belonging to freedom rather than to the SS. The poem can be read as a desperate attempt to hold on to ideals, to a positive self-representation — as in the inmates who are marked by freedom's wonderful emblem and who walk with proud courage — and to life itself while facing degradation and the imminent danger of death. As the poem progresses, each stanza brings on a more somber tone: servitude in the first stanza leads to separation from the loved ones in the second. In the third stanza the perpetrator's intention of "destroying" the inmates is contrasted by the delicate, not to say fragile, "wonderful emblem of freedom." The word *doch* (translated here as *but*), a reaffirmation to balance out the grim concreteness of *zerbrechen,* is in turn softened, or rather weakened, by the deferential confession at the end of the stanza: "wenn auch kein Wort wir sprechen." The fourth stanza then moves quickly from the temporary proud courage of the first-person-plural speaker to that speaker's utter debasement and then murder.

Silent resistance, a resigned acknowldgement of the failure of physical resistance, is apparently the only recourse available to the inmates. In the face of brutality, of physical defeat — here specifically, the physical separation from one's loved ones by internment and the personal disfiguration through the shaving and the striped uniform — this is an inward turn, a search for spiritual or moral superiority. In the fourth stanza, in the face of murder, the inmates' power is the power to know the suffering of the other: "wohl wissend um das Leid." As the rhyme suggests, this is an indirect or triangulated relation to another inmate mediated by the object, "das Kleid." The uniform conveys the knowledge of the suffering that cannot be expressed openly. In retrospect, however, Kupfer-Koberwitz's resistance is not entirely silent. By producing a text the poet contradicts his own description of the inmates' silent predicament and bears witness to both his own suffering and that of his fellow inmates. Moreover, as the following will demonstrate, in this poem the poet-speaker takes on most palpably the position of poet, thus occupying the top of the hierarchy of individuals from the first stanza and defying as well the humiliation imposed in the camps.

The first three stanzas are six lines long. The fourth stanza consists of nine lines. That stanza goes beyond the three previous ones to reveal the cycle of violence in which the death of an inmate means that that inmate's uniform will be passed on — it is as if the longer stanza itself represents the act of passing on the uniform, of extending painful knowledge. The poem's narrative ends there. The final stanza, a shorter one (four lines), does not carry the story any further. It serves instead to charge the "striped suit" with significance and to alter its meaning. The last stanza, an apostrophe, functions as an interpretative intervention on the poem and produces a topological shift from a first-person-plural speaker whose death is announced proleptically in the fourth stanza and then a third-person-singular narrative to a first-person-singular speaker who, apostrophically, addresses a second-person-singular subject and, at least in the poetic fiction of the address, achieves immortality.

Apostrophe, as Barbara Johnson writes, "involves the direct address of an absent, dead, or inanimate object by a *first-person speaker*" and "is a form of ventriloquism through which the speaker throws voice, life, and human form into the addressee, turning its silence into mute *responsiveness*" (185, my emphases). As the atrocities increase, when all there is left for the inmates is to bear witness to the suffering and death of others — a knowledge passed on like the uniform — and when even that form of witnessing is threatened by the potential death of the poem's speaker, the apostrophe in the final stanza gives new meaning to the uniform and creates another witness or literally a container for the suffering. In the poem the "striped suit" is never referred to by its prosaic and more customary names, uniform, clothing, and such. In an idealizing move the last stanza lifts the object out of the limitations of the camp environment and endows it with emotional and moral responsiveness. The first four stanzas extend the meaning of the uniform back in time through an allusion to feudal serfdom and recast its function to render it an emotional and ethical link among inmates. This prepares the way for the transformation of the uniform, in the final stanza, into an honorary cloak and, through the apostrophe, into a "thou" in an antirelational environment. The "striped suit" acquires a new dimension as it enters the field of the moral in a kind of martyrology that makes the sufferer honorable — and larger than life:

> Gestreiftes Kleid, gestreiftes Kleid,
> du bist mein höchstes Ehrenkleid,
> denn was ich litt, das viele Leid,
> macht dich unendlich gross. —

> [Striped cloak, striped cloak,
> you are my highest honor cloak,
> because what I suffered, the immense pain
> makes you infinitely large. —]

Here the uniform is "infinitely large" in a metaphorical spatial sense, in order to contain the immense pain the narrator has suffered. At the same time the uniform has grown symbolically and been elevated from a humiliating imposition to "highest" "cloak of honor." It now denotes moral stature, the moral stature of the poet-speaker. Jonathan Culler has put forward what he calls the "paradoxical fact that [apostrophe] which seems to establish relations between the self and the other can in fact be read as an act of radical interiorization and solipsism" (162), an act of, we might say, projective identification whereby in this case the empathic expansion and moral elevation of the uniform *is* the expansion and elevation of the self.

We have already seen that there is an important shift in this poem from a collective to an individual identity. Through most of the poem the speaker speaks in the first person plural, but at the end of the fourth stanza, a third-person subject, "Der Kamerad," enters the scene as someone with consciousness of the suffering ("wohl wissend um das grosse Leid"). A traumatic environment disturbs the relation between self and empathic other. In an analysis of the discourse of survivors of the Holocaust Laub and Auerhahn point out that "the word 'we' is frequently found in survivors' narratives. It is possible that its use sometimes reflects a high degree of social bonding (to both the dead and the living; Des Pres, 1976), but often 'we' is a defense against saying 'I' with any feeling. For survivors to use 'I' feelingly is to acknowledge the profoundness of their sense of abandonment and lonesomeness: It can lead to despair and surrender" (Laub and Auerhahn 1989, 383).

As was already discussed above, postwar narratives and accounts of the experience of survivors should not be conflated with those of inmates *in* the camps. There are crucial differences among literary and artistic works produced in the camps, the oral and written testimonies of survivors, and other artistic or autobiographic responses to the Shoah by survivors and others. Yet Laub and Auerhahn's interpretation here draws attention to the kinds of functions a collective identity may also be said to serve in Kupfer-Koberwitz's text. Throughout "Gestreiftes Kleid" the speaker avoids symbolic confrontation with the perpetrators by referring to them only indirectly. He also seems to shy away from close contact with other victims by speaking in a generic *we* and through a structure in which not "I" but a third-person inmate comes to know (or bear witness to) the other's pain through the intermediary of the uniform that is received from a dead inmate. Laub and Auerhahn also write of the significance of objects in a similar context: "When connectedness to other people feels too dangerous, inanimate objects may take their place" (1989, 385). Furthermore, if we follow Johnson's meditation on apostrophe, in which she writes that "if apostrophe is structured like demand, and if demand articulates the primal relation to the mother as a relation to the Other, then lyric poetry itself — summed up in the figure of the apostrophe — comes to look like the fantastically intricate history of endless elaborations and displacements of the single cry, 'Mama!'" (198–99), we may then posit for this poem the act of creation of a matrix of address or responsiveness in an environment designed to destroy even the most basic empathic response.

What the speaker finally finds or, more precisely, creates in the uniform is an "other" capable of being addressed, a literal and psychic container for his pain. Only once the apostrophic address of the final stanza establishes the relationship to the uniform can the speaker's own suffering be owned, or acknowledged, in a more direct manner: "was *ich* litt" (what *I* suffered), as if the "striped suit" provided needed boundaries to the "immense pain." Only in the last stanza do the singular personal pronouns — "du" (you, subject), "mein" (my), "ich" (I), "dich" (you, direct object) — become part of the vocabulary. Significantly, moreover, the speaker's suffering is acknowledged in the past tense: "what I *suffered*" is in the simple past, indicating a period of time that is over at the time of speaking. The simple past form of the verb "leiden" (to suffer), "litt," occupies a central position in the stanza, as it appears at the only syntactically significant mid-line caesura in the poem — a pause emphasized by the comma — and before the summative modifier that interrupts the sentence with a nominalization of the verb "leiden." It is as if the invocation of the uniform implied or produced the supersession of the situation heretofore described in the poem.

Originally the poem bore the descriptive or narrative title "Gestreift ist unser Kleid" (Striped Is Our Cloak), the first line of the poem. However, underscoring the significance of the final stanza and its direct address of the uniform, the author changed it before publication (Kupfer-Koberwitz 1997, 514). As we come to understand by the end of the poem, the new vocative title, "Gestreiftes Kleid," addresses the uniform directly. Through the relationship to the uniform a kind of resolution is found for the humiliation: "Ehre" (honor), and for the lonesomeness: "dich" (you). The abuse becomes invested with significance. This re-signification allows the poem to avoid the utter moral and psychological defeat of facing entirely gratuitous, purposeless cruelty. The "Ehrenkleid," the honorary cloak, as well as the poem, then become an idealized protective skin, a shield and a cover that may serve to ward off, to filter out at least some of the overwhelming aggression, or to transform, figuratively, suffering into honor. In the concentrationary universe there was little certainty for the inmates. At Auschwitz, Levi writes, the expression for "never" was "*morgen früh,* tomorrow morning" (1961, 121). The striped uniform that inmates were forced to wear in many of the camps would have been one stable element in that disruptive environment. In the poem the uniform appears as a second-skin; however labile, perhaps it was the only one the inmates could count on.

The apostrophe of the final stanza may also be read as the moment in the poem that serves to constitute the poet most definitely *as* poet. Culler proposes to identify "apostrophe with lyric itself," arguing with Northrop Frye that lyric is not "heard but overheard" (152), that is, in essence the lyric poet "pretends to be talking to himself or someone else" (Frye, 249). Thus, writes Culler, apostrophe as a "poetic event" "is the pure embodiment of poetic pretension: of the subject's claim that in his verse he is not merely an empirical poet, a writer of verse, but the embodiment of poetic tradition and of the spirit of poesy. Apostrophe is perhaps always an indirect invocation of the muse" (158). In Kupfer-Koberwitz's poem, the humiliated plural speaker of the first four stanzas is transformed into a singular poetic voice through the invocation in the final stanza, a poetic act that — instead of describing the situation — in the *now* of the address shifts the present of the previous stanzas into the past and achieves poetic significance by the manifest artificiality or creative freedom of the vocative.

To return briefly to the discussion about representation in the context of the Shoah: critics like Adorno and Lawrence Langer have objected to representational modes that in their aestheticism and narrative closure may cover over the distance between traumatic and "everyday" experience. Adorno has written for instance against a deceptive literature that "shows us humanity blossoming in so-called extreme situations, and in fact precisely there, and at times this becomes a dreary metaphysics that affirms the horror" (1992, 88). My analysis of the preceding poems shows that the modes of representation of the experiences of persecution that Langer and Adorno object to in postwar works, such as narrative closure and a degree of glorification of the horror, are also present in the works composed by victims of the National Socialists while they endured the trauma of the concentration camps. This in itself cannot justify such rhetorical and formal strategies of representation; nor does it mean that in this poetry "humanity blossoms." But the context of these representations should alert us to the difference between the belated and unwarranted denial or repression of extremity such critics denounce, and the restoration of form (and formality) necessary for self-expression in the face of fragmentation. These poems are not the literary equivalents of screen memories that cover over a traumatic event. "Gestreiftes Kleid" does imply that the senseless suffering makes the inmates honorable and thus extracts a positive quality from the abuse. At the same time the poem does not engage in facile optimism nor does it gratuitously invent reasons for survival. The preceding analysis shows the poetic re-signification of an oppressive element from the camps, a re-signification that makes the suffering meaningful and yet acknowledges the brutality confronted by the inmates.

In terms of theme and rhetorical strategy the poems in this chapter concern themselves with what we might bring under the general rubric of the power to name, as expressed, for example, in the imposition of the number and the uniform. Clearly this power also entails the power to separate people from one another. These poems are rhetorical strategies for defending individuality, identity, and relationships in the concentration camps through imaginative acts of connectedness. These works return the power to name to the inmate-speakers either figuratively or literally and often they leave the perpetrators unnamed.

3: "Everyday Life" in the Concentrationary Universe

A S WAS DISCUSSED IN THE INTRODUCTION, Saul Friedländer has called for attention not only to the "everyday life" of "ordinary" Germans in the Third Reich but also to the "everyday life" of the victims of the National Socialists (1994, 262). The following poems provide portrayals of daily occurrences in the concentration camps. They also show how daily atrocity alters the nature of "everydayness." They suggest in other words that everyday living with extreme physical abuse, in harmful conditions, and among corpses numbs the senses and undermines the sense of time. The poems foresee that "everyday life" in atrocity may subsequently, as an aftereffect, destroy the everydayness of ordinary life after a return to "normalcy" for those who survive.

Monotony versus Meaning

Born in Breslau (now Wroclaw, Poland) in 1906, Edgar Kupfer-Koberwitz first worked as an agricultural apprentice and then became a bank employee. During this time he wrote poetry and short essays for newspapers and magazines. He emigrated from Germany to France in 1934, and in 1937 he became a tour guide on the Italian island of Ischia. He was never directly involved in politics and did not belong to any political organization, yet in 1940 he was arrested under allegations that he had made remarks critical of the current governments in Germany and Italy. Security forces extradited him and detained him in a prison in Innsbruck. From there he was taken to Dachau on 8 November 1940, where he witnessed the liberation of the concentration camp on 29 April 1945. His long internment in Dachau was interrupted by a period of over a year that he spent under even more deleterious conditions at the concentration camp Neuengamme, near Hamburg. After liberation he spent time in the United States, not finding adequate employment, and then moved to Sardinia, where he led an isolated existence in poverty. He returned to Germany in 1984 because of health problems and died there in 1991 (see Distel).

Kupfer-Kopferwitz's writings from the camps are all from his period in Dachau after November 1942 when, following a convalescence of a few months upon his return from Neuengamme, he was given a clerical job in one of the industries on the grounds of the concentration camp, the newly created nuts-and-bolts factory "Präzifix." In that office Kupfer-Koberwitz managed to write poems, a voluminous diary (published posthumously in 1997), and a recollection of his time at Neuengamme. At Neuengamme his health deteriorated greatly: although he was only thirty-six, he came close to giving up and to becoming a Muselmann (see Distel; Kupfer-Koberwitz 1957). Back in Dachau Kupfer-Koberwitz buried his manuscripts from time to time with the help of a friend and recovered them after liberation. His case is unusual in that he managed to write and preserve over 1800 pages of text (Distel, 16). A collection of twenty of his camp poems was published with permission of the American Military Government in Stuttgart in 1946 under the title *Kette der Tage* (Chain of Days).

Kupfer-Koberwitz begins the title poem (1946, 39–40),[1] the last in the collection, with a depiction of the passing of time counted out in days: the first word of the poem, "And," implies a series that has already begun, one more element in a chain. The term "chain" also evokes the fetters that restrict the prisoner's movements both literally and figuratively. The reiteration of the first four words in the following line reinforces the sense of monotony and repetition that is the subject of the poem. In a "chain" of repetition, the same words begin the next two stanzas, with just a slight variation in the third. The sense of tedium is reflected as well in the almost complete regularity of rhyme and the slow, largely anapestic meter throughout the poem. The rhyming scheme is consistently abaab, cdccd, and so on; the "a" lines consist of ten syllables, the "b" lines of eight.

The focus at first is on the external gloominess of the days passing by:

> Und ein jeder Tag ist so grau und trüb
> und ein jeder Tag schleicht dahin —
> die Tage rinnen, wie Wasser durch Sieb,
> stehlen sich fort wie ein trauriger Dieb,
> kaum bleibt uns ein Rest noch von Sinn. —
>
> [And each and every day is gray and triste
> and each and every day creeps on —
> the days slip by like water through a sieve,
> stealing themselves away like a sad thief,
> hardly a remnant of sense remains for us. —]

The first simile ("like water through a sieve") establishes the sense that time is escaping without leaving a trace. This sense of *unlived* time anticipates the last line of the stanza: "hardly a remnant of sense remains for us." The second simile here, the days compared to a "sad thief," foreshadows a theme that will become more pronounced through the next four stanzas: a sense of agency accrues to the "day" or "days." "Trauriger" (sad) echoes acoustically and thematically the day's qualities: "grau und trüb" (gray and triste). But what causes sadness in a thief? An unsuccessful thief might be justifiably sad and would furtively retreat, as would a thief taking something unworthy of theft. The closing line of the stanza suggests that some kind of theft has been accomplished: something has been taken away from the community the speaker represents: "we" are not getting "our" full share of "sense," there are only the scant remains of meaning: "kaum bleibt uns ein Rest noch von Sinn." In German the word "Sinn" connotes not only "sense" as "meaning," as in the expression the *meaning of life* ("der Sinn des Lebens"), but also sensory perception, the senses ("die Sinne"). The next four stanzas describe the increasing loss of feeling ("Gefühle," "Fühlen"), of the very capacity to feel or perceive ("empfinden"). What the days in the shape of a thief take away from inmates in the first stanza can only be a sad booty. The thief's sadness is the inmates' sadness that has metonymically been transferred from the latter to the former.

What is only suggested in the first stanza — that the "days" may be doing something *to* the first-person plural narrator such as stealing "meaning" from them — becomes clearer in the second stanza. In the original German text the first line of the second stanza contains the pronoun "uns" (us) grammatically in the position of indirect object, from or in whom "every day" extinguishes something:

> Und ein jeder Tag löscht uns etwas aus,
> einen Funken in unsrer Brust —
>
> [And each and every day puts something out
> in us, a spark in our breast —]

In their monotony the "days" begin to affect the inmates' internal world, their feelings. The stanza continues:

> Wir sagen nur noch: "die Liebe — das Haus" —
> doch es klingt nicht echt, das Echo bleibt aus,
> wir empfinden nicht mehr die Lust. —
>
> [We merely keep saying: "our love — our home" —
> but it does not ring true, the echo is out,
> we no longer feel desire. —]

The terms "love" and "home" still form part of the inmates' vocabulary, their own speech, but they have lost their connotative function as words. They no longer have the power to evoke images, to stir memory. These linguistic signs have completely lost not the denotative meaning but their aura; the tragedy here is not the "longing" that these words might evoke in the situation but rather the lack of "echo" itself, the lack of affect related to those terms. "We" are now past longing and in a state in which, curiously, desire is absent (the German word here is "Lust" meaning both "desire" and "pleasure.")[2]

The process of loss of meaning, of sensitivity, of the auratic, of pleasure, and of desire itself continues to intensify over the next three stanzas as time becomes an increasingly violent force, molding more and more of the inmates' personalities. In the first line of the third stanza, the pronoun "uns" (us) has now shifted to direct object while "Ein jeder Tag" (Each and every day) remains the subject:

> Ein jeder Tag macht uns dumpfer und matt,
> Gefühle verdorren im Herz —
> man fühlt nur noch, ob der Magen auch satt,
> ob heut man noch Kraft zum Ertragen hat,
> und wir halten Roheit für Scherz. —
>
> So stampft jeder Tag unser Ich zur Form,
> zum nichtssagenden Dutzendstück: . . .
> jeder wird ein Häftling von gleicher Norm,
> auch die Seele trägt eine Uniform,
> nichts fühlend, nicht Leid mehr noch Glück. —
>
> Die Tage fallen, wie Hämmer so schwer
> und schmieden uns nützlich und platt —
>
> [Every day makes us more dull and weary,
> feelings wither away in our hearts —
> one just feels: has the stomach had enough,
> does one have the strength to endure today,
> and we take brutality for a joke. —
>
> Thus every day pounds our I into shape,
> into a nondescript, mass-produced item: . . .
> all become inmates of the same norm,
> even our souls wear a uniform,
> feeling nothing, no more pain nor joy. —
>
> The days fall like a hammer, as heavily,
> and forge us, useful and flat —]

By now the inmates' sensitivity is described as operating at best at a minimal physical level. The monochrome grayness of the days has produced a sensory decay. Body and psyche have been coerced, forced to adapt to inhumane and inhuman circumstances: as a consequence the ability to feel emotions, whether negative or positive ones, has altogether disappeared.

The loss of feeling and desire conjures up the image of the "Muselmann," a topos in the literature from and about the camps. Giorgio Agamben has called the "Muselmann" the "extreme figure of [the] extreme potentiality to suffer" (78). Caution is in order when making ethical or philosophical claims based on the historical figure of the "Muselmann," but Agamben's formulation points to the extremity and the complete negativity of the situation of the "Muselmänner." Primo Levi describes the kind of apathy embodied by the "Muselmänner" as fatal:

> All the mussulmans who finished in the gas chambers have the same story, or more exactly, have no story; they followed the slope down to the bottom, like streams that run down to the sea. On their entry into the camp, through basic incapacity, or by misfortune, or through some banal incident, they are overcome before they can adapt themselves; they are beaten by time, they do not begin to learn German, to disentangle the infernal knot of laws and prohibitions until their body is already in decay, and nothing can save them from selections or from death by exhaustion. Their life is short, but their number is endless; they, the *Muselmänner,* the drowned, form the backbone of the camp, an anonymous mass, continually renewed and always identical, of non-men who march and labour in silence, the divine spark dead within them, already too empty to really suffer. One hesitates to call them living: one hesitates to call their death death, in the face of which they have no fear, as they are too tired to understand. (Levi 1961, 82)

While imprisoned at Neuengamme (between 11 January 1941 and 26 April 1942), a slave-labor camp about 15 miles southeast of Hamburg, Kupfer-Koberwitz became debilitated by the atrocious lack of food and extreme working conditions there and eventually belonged as well to the category best known now as Muselmänner. In his recollection of his time at Neuengamme, written while imprisoned at Dachau, Kupfer-Koberwitz describes his own gradual physical and psychic deterioration: nearly 6 ft tall (1.8 meters), he remembers weighing 185 lb (84 kg) on the train that had brought him to Dachau. After about five months at Neuengamme preceded by two months at Dachau he drops to 90 lb (41 kg), less than half his usual weight. He is then called "Muselmann" and "Kretiner" (cretin, the term used in Dachau to refer to the phenomenon of the Muselmänner) by other inmates, who fail to recognize him if they have not seen him in a couple of months (Kupfer-Koberwitz 1957, 386). From the perspective of Neuengamme, Dachau seems like the "Schlaraffenland" (the land of milk and honey).[3] In his account of the initial stages of his increasing deterioration Kupfer-Koberwitz recalls the loss of appetite and eventually of all interest in things external and internal:

> Oh we were all much too tired. When it goes that far, one does not care about the world any more, however bad things may get, and one does not have anything do to with all that any more, one doesn't even want

to have to do with oneself. Our souls were all dead-tired and our bodies were dying. Or were our souls dying too? I don't know. (1957, 364)

Then the text of the recollection echoes the poem: "I . . . couldn't feel anything anymore, and couldn't think anything any more" (366). Kupfer-Koberwitz describes his own decline and the feeling that he is close to a state from which there is no return. Initially plain exhaustion keeps him from committing suicide, while later on an "inner voice" leads him to seek a way out of his situation. Eventually he is admitted to the camp hospital with scabies and later again with pneumonia, and thereafter given lighter work as he proves incapable of heavier physical labor. Yet despite the overwhelming lethargy that overcomes him, Kupfer-Koberwitz manages to retain some distance from the lethal condition of total apathy described by Levi.

Kupfer-Koberwitz's "inner voice" appears to be a crucial element in his narrative of his return from deterioration and total apathy. We can think of it as an "imaginative act" as Laub and Podell envision it (998). Sofsky describes the psychic state of the Muselmänner as one in which "eccentric positionality," in other words "self-distance" and an "inner voice" have been destroyed (Sofsky 101–2). Note how in the following description Sofsky seems to follow closely the topics Kupfer-Koberwitz touches on in his poem "Kette der Tage" and in his recollection: hunger, apathy, loss of memory and affect, lack of feeling, the tenuousness of the sense of time (the past, the present, and the future):

> The *Muselmänner* withdrew increasingly from the world. They lost their memory and the ability to concentrate. Memories faded and disappeared: many no longer knew their names . . . attentiveness numbed; the senses became blunted. . . . Stimulus defense and mechanisms to ward off anxiety ultimately led to total numbness and indifference toward the world and themselves. They lived neither in the society of others, nor with and by themselves . . . Eccentric positionality — that self-distance from which a person can observe himself or herself at a remove — had been deleted. They now lost the present, as they had lost the past and the future. Feelings froze and stultified. Their spirits and minds emptied, sclerosed to an inward wasteland. Just as gestures and actions forfeited their intentional goal-directedness, intentionality and consciousness withered. . . . Consciousness was no longer awareness of something, point-focused. The prisoners were unable to act, to think, to feel. In order to salvage the hulk of the body, the psyche self-destructed. In the final stage of decline, the prisoners no longer felt hunger, no longer perceived pain. . . . Anxiety and excitation reached a final stage of crystallization beyond tension; all defense mechanisms had collapsed, and the prisoners were in a condition of total apathy and subjugation. (Sofsky, 201–2)

Summarizing the accounts of various survivors, Sofsky here eloquently and perhaps imaginatively portrays the various psychic mechanisms that extreme cumulative traumatization undoes: memory and concomitantly a sense of time; self-distance or a relation to an internal other; intentionality; awareness, and even sensory perception. The poem "Kette der Tage" narrates that undoing and in the process refuses to be undone. As we shall see, this poem postulates a future without anticipating a triumph over the trauma.

Interestingly, Levi refers above to the "mussulmans" as "beaten by time" and thus parallels Kupfer-Koberwitz's metaphor of "days like a hammer" "pounding" the inmates. In the poem's fifth stanza, the speaker revises the description of the gloominess of the "days." These are still as barren and sad as in the beginning of the poem. However, rather than passing by without leaving a trace, the "days" have a great impact precisely because of their emptiness and meaninglessness. The more detailed account of the effect of the "days" on the inmates has shifted the emphasis from what was being taken away, the loss of "home," "love," "desire," "meaning," to a sense of more active brutalization of the inmates. That brutalization is carried out by means of the emptiness. The "days" are now too present in their absence, even if this can only be felt by those exceptional few (which by implication must include the poet-speaker) who have not been completely "undone" by their time in the concentration camp:

> es sind schon zuviel und werden noch mehr,
> die Tage sind grau, sind öd und sind leer
> dem, der ein Fühlen noch hat. —

> [already too many and will yet be more,
> the days are gray, are barren and empty
> to him who's still able to feel. —]

The last line here — a shorter one, seven-syllables long, like the very last line of the poem — ends the section that describes the situation in the camp. This last line of the first section contains an element of minimal hope in the "ability to feel" that in some inmates has not yet been destroyed. The speaker's attention then moves from the present condition to an explicit concern with the future, marked by a corresponding change of verb tenses:

> Und wenn diese Tage verronnen sind,
> dann wird, wer sie übersteht,
> einsam und still ragen, ein Baum im Wind,
> der Welt ganz fremd sein, ein Waisenkind,
> an dem scheu vorüber man geht. —

[And when all these days have run their course,
then will he who withstands it all
rise up lonely and still, a tree in the wind,
a total stranger to the world, an orphan,
whom shyly one hurries past. —]

"Ragen" in the original can be rendered as "rise up," implying not only a vertical position, but also the sense of "sticking out," not fitting in. The stanza continues: "der Welt ganz fremd sein": to be a total stranger to the world; to be strange in the world; to be estranged from the world. The stanza's final line then strains the grammatical structure: The poet pushes further apart than conventionally possible the grammatical subject of the sentence, the "normal" person who has never been in the camps, denoted by the (German) "man" (one), from the grammatical object, a potential "survivor" of the concentration camps who has been "orphaned" from the world. This separation foresees the type of rejection and lack of understanding survivors — Kupfer-Koberwitz among them — encountered following liberation.

Already during internment the future holds no promise of a better society:

> Denn draußen wird keiner uns ganz verstehn,
> erkennen wird niemand, warum
> wir so ganz verändert die Welt ansehn,
> warum so andere Schritte wir gehn:
> unsre Seele wurd lahm und krumm. —
>
> [Because outside no one will understand us,
> nobody will recognize why
> we look so differently on the world,
> why the paths we take are so different:
> our soul was crippled, twisted. —]

There is an awareness here that, however "empty" the "days" may be, they nonetheless create an incommensurable distance between those who experience such "empty days" — if one can use the term "experience" to refer to the annihilation of capacity to experience represented by the Muselmann — and the rest of the world, those outside, "draußen," as the poem calls the world on the other side of the barbed wire. A complete transformation takes place ("ganz verändert" [completely changed]). The speaker talks of the days as empty. The emptiness is full of monotonous labor. At one level we can understand the lack of meaningful experience as the cause of the emptiness. But in this context, the empty days, like Laub and Podell's "empty circle," describe as well the feeling of "nothingness" that results from the repeated "real failure of the empathic dyad at the time of traumatization and the resulting failure to preserve an empathic tie even with oneself" (Laub

and Podell, 992). "Emptiness" and the "days" themselves stand in symbolically for the brutalities the inmates experienced at Neuengamme and Dachau, and which Kupfer-Koberwitz describes in greater detail in his prose
and in other verses. To particularize them again here might detract from the
more general sense of a "time" that is completely out of the ordinary, a series of events that, taken together, have an insidious effect on the inmates'
psyche. Laud and Podell argue that "when the limits of representation . . .
are actually breached, the knowledge that actual atrocities occurred perhaps
eclipses and paralyzes the functions of fantasy and symbolisation" (1002). In
survivors, "a magnetic core of nothingness" then threatens to overwhelm
the psyche (1002). As was discussed earlier, many of the authors writing in
the camps never name the perpetrators directly: in this poem, "the days"
take on the role of the SS, they "beat" the prisoners and rob them of their
emotions and their future, of, as Levi puts it, their "story."

The next stanza focuses on the different temporal dimensions of the experience: the "fabric" of time is destroyed through this particular experience
in time, and in the end, no temporal dimension holds any more:

> Die Tage haben uns "Gestern" geraubt
> und die Tage nehmen uns das "Heut" —
> es war einmal, daß wir Andern geglaubt,
> daß wir Ehrfurcht hatten vor weißem Haupt
> und daß wir uns herzlich gefreut. —

> [The days have stolen our "yesterday"
> and the days take away our "today" —
> once upon a time we believed others,
> had respect for a graying head
> and were capable of true joy. —]

This, the eighth stanza, connects the current "lack" to an undoing of proper
time. The poem here harks back to the theme of the lost "echo" of intimate
words: now the past in general has become impossible, has lost its aura, its
affective content, and there is no access to the present either since this is
marked by gray monotony or nothingness. The past takes on a mythical dimension: "es war einmal" is traditionally the beginning of a fairy tale. As in
Fritz Löhner-Beda's childlike trust, what was then ordinary — to believe
someone else, to respect older people, and even to feel happiness from the
heart — has now become removed from reality and entered the realm of
fantasy.

The time spent as an inmate does not belong in the category of ordinary
time — the crisis is not only juridical and legal, nor just social, but profoundly existential. The experience of being in the concentrationary universe

undoes the past, prevents "us" from having access to the present, and alienates the inmates from their future as well:

> Da werden wir sagen: "Die Welt ist dumm,
> sie kann uns nicht mehr verstehn."
> Wir werden nicht fragen: wieso, warum? —
> werden allein sein und eben darum
> tiefer in Einsamkeit gehn. —
>
> [We will then say: "The world is stupid,
> it cannot understand us any more."
> We shall not ask: how come, why? — we
> shall be alone and just because of that
> go more deeply into loneliness.]

The final stanza closes the line of thought begun at the opening of the second section in the first line of the sixth stanza: "And when all these days have run their course." Then the isolation will be even more profound. Even though the speaker employs the first-person plural throughout the poem, whether talking about life in or outside the camps, the common experience is one of isolation and deepening loneliness. This is diametrically opposed to the image of the millions united through the number in Hasso Grabner's poem "Die Häftlingsnummer." In "Kette der Tage" there is no thought of community, of a shared destiny, just a bitter sense of loss and ruination; the empathic bond, the most basic of links between human beings, is at stake. Thought of as an imaginative act, the poem creates self-distance, a place from which to observe oneself and the voice with which to narrate that self-observation. The text as poem also represents a bond, a certain trust in intersubjective communication. As such it is one of the few and tentative safeguards against a total collapse into despair, into the impotence of words in the face of extreme physical and psychic hardship. There is narrative here but no redemption. The speaker expects a restoration of some degree of normalcy: "when all these days have run their course," and there is a cautious hope that a few will outlive the camps: "he who withstands it all." There is no utopian or triumphal vision of a complete inner liberation, of a past that one could leave behind, nor is there any mention of revenge. A heroics of survival is also absent here, of an agency seeking to master the situation. At most, if a reader is bent on extracting or critiquing a positive ending in "Kette der Tage," though this does not seem justified, this poem offers a slightly romanticized vision of melancholia: we "shall be alone and just because of that / go more deeply into loneliness." Perhaps ironically in the case of camp-survivor Kupfer-Koberwitz, as for many other survivors, this poem would prove prophetic. Barely two days after the camp's liberation at Dachau,

Kupfer-Koberwitz writes in his journal about the speeches given on the occasion of a 1 May celebration there:

> Mich machte es traurig. - Mir war es, als höre ich eine Versammlung, eine politische Versammlung von vor zwanzig Jahren, - viele Phrasen, der typische Rednerton, der keiner ist. - Oh, wie hätte mich gefreut, hätte nach all dem, was war, einer ein herzhaftes, kerniges Wort, so von Herzen kommend, packend, einfach, gefunden, - aber es waren lauter »Redner« . . . Man redete und redete, mir erschienen es leere Worte. (Kupfer-Koberwitz 1997, 454)

> [It made me sad — I felt as if I were hearing a rally, a political rally from twenty years ago — many phrases, the typical speaker's tone, which is not one. Oh, how happy it would have made me, after all that has been, if someone had found a hearty, down-to-earth word, so from the heart, gripping, simple — but they were all just a bunch of "speakers.". . . They spoke and spoke; it all seemed to me empty words.]

A year after liberation, on 6 July 1946, Kupfer-Koberwitz concludes a dedication to his sister of a typescript collection of poems written in the camps with the words: "Liebes Irmele, so verwirkt sieht vieles in mir aus, manch guter Eindruck den die Welt mir sonst machte" (dear little Irma, much looks so forfeited to me, many a good impression that the world otherwise had made on me; Kupfer-Koberwitz 1997, ill. 14). Distel reports that Kupfer-Koberwitz died isolated and disappointed by the lack of interest in his writings, writings he had risked his life to produce and to hide.

"Der Steinbruch" (The Stone Quarry), a poem written in 1944 at Buchenwald by Karl Schnog (Schnog 1947, 56),[4] uses a different set of strategies than "Kette der Tage" to describe the combination of exhausting labor and atrocious treatment that constituted the daily camp routine. The first of four stanzas reads:

> Eine Landschaft, wie am Schöpfungstage:
> Sand und Steine. Büsche. Und sonst nichts.
> Graue Gräser. Schreie wilder Klage.
> Ort des Grauens, Tal des Weltgerichts.

> [A landscape, like on the day of creation:
> Sand and stones. Bushes. And nothing else.
> Gray grasses. Screams of wild lament.
> Place of horror, valley of the Last Judgment.]

These are all sentence fragments that lack conjugated verbs. They convey a sense of elemental forces that combine into barrenness, not fruitfulness: "Sand and stones. Bushes. And nothing else." These are the minimum elements of a creation that becomes inverted in its proximity and similarity to an end-of-the-world scenario: "Place of horror, valley of the Last Judgment." Unlike the narrative portrayal of the inordinateness of concentrationary time in "Kette der Tage," this more expressionistic approach uses montage, repetition, and fragmentation to convey a sense of chaos and desolation compressed between a "day of creation" and a "Final Judgment." The poem also employs apocalyptic vocabulary and imagery to speak of a suffering that exceeds language's power to convey meaning and thus requires repetition. Through repetition the poem expresses in later stanzas the dizzying tempo and monotonous regularity that render the forced labor overwhelming: "Schleppen — Schleppen — Schleppen — Schleppen" (Carry — Carry — Carry — Carry) and "Immer, immer wieder" (Again, and again, and again). The second stanza begins with an image of tired feet and worn out stairs. This image expresses the alienation of the inmates: feet here seem connected to the ground they tread, the ground that exhausts them, rather than to the persons to whom they belong. This synecdoche juxtaposes and contrasts what is below — tired feet and worn out stairways — to what is above — a pitiless sun, a sun, one might add, quite different from Primo Levi's symbol for the positive forces of life discussed above. The mercilessness of the sun in fact forces the perspective to stay low, on the ground: "gray grasses," "feet," "sand and stones," "valley," as might befit the work in a stone quarry, but also as an expression of the exhaustion and humiliation imposed on the inmates. In the third stanza, furthermore, another natural element usually found in the sky finds itself on the ground and arises from the ground: clouds here are not made of water but rather out of dust that rises when an inmate is beaten down. Here are the second and third stanzas:

> Müde Füße, abgewetzte Treppen.
> Alles jagt und hastet, keucht und rennt.
> Schleppen — Schleppen — Schleppen — Schleppen.
> Und erbarmungslos die Sonne brennt.

> Schläge klatschen, Menschen fallen nieder.
> Wolken Staubes und dazwischen Blut.
> Fallen — Tragen. Immer, immer wieder.
> Schmerzensschreie, Schreie wilder Wut.

> [Tired feet, worn out steps.
> Everyone chases and hurries, pants and runs.
> Carry — Carry — Carry — Carry.
> And the sun burns without pity.

> Strikes resound, people fall.
> Clouds of dust and in between blood.
> Fall down — Carry away. Again, and again, and again.
> Screams of pain, screams of wild rage.]

The poem never refers to the perpetrators directly, never names them. The reference to the beating that opens the third stanza comes relatively late in the text and is, again, abstract and indirect, an auditory experience: "Strikes resound." The first three stanzas describe the present; in those stanzas, the references to the victims of the beatings are impersonal: "screams," "blood," "people fall." The scene described here is a familiar one in narratives about the camps: inmates were sadistically forced to labor faster than was possible or productive. If a prisoner survived selections, the lack of nourishment and water, the exposure to the weather, and the exhaustion, then the beatings and tricks of the overseers were designed to kill him or her. "Morgen" (Tomorrow), a wistful poem written by Hasso Grabner in Buchenwald — who like Schnog was a Communist but unlike him was not a German Jew — also depicts the fatal consequences of work in the following section (Grabner, 22):[5]

> Zu einem Tagwerk
> monotoner Schwere
> weckt uns die Pfeife
> Morgen und morgen neu.
> Und Abend für Abend
> sind von unserem Heere
> Kameraden, Freunde
> hinübergegangen ins Leere,
> Kameraden,
> von allem Leben und Leid befreit.

> [To a workday
> of monotonous hardship
> the pipe wakes us up
> morning after morning.
> And evening after evening
> comrades and friends
> leave our ranks
> to go over into the emptiness,
> comrades, freed of all
> life and sorrows.]

Again, daily monotony and the routine death of comrades are the main subjects in both poems. The concluding stanza in Schnog's "Der Steinbruch" comes unexpectedly. With its promise of a "day of freedom" the stanza appears to imply a redeeming ending or restitution. It promises freedom and justice for everyone.

> Doch der Tag der Freiheit kommt für jeden.
> Kamerad im Steinbruch, bist noch Knecht.

Einmal werden die Steine für dich reden.
Wird der Steinbruch einst an dir gerächt? . . .

[But the day of freedom will come for everyone.
Comrade in the stone quarry, you are still a slave.
One day the stones will speak for you.
Will one day the quarry be revenged? . . .]

This seemingly triumphant ending does what the rest of the poem, in its description of the abuse, degradation, and alienation, seems to avoid or to be unable to do: it addresses other inmates directly: "Kamerad" (comrade), "dich" (you). The address is abstract: a singular, representative, generic "comrade in the stone quarry" is apostrophized. A closer look at the stanza uncovers some ambiguity in this apparently positive ending. The first line proclaims defiantly and assuredly that the day of freedom will come for everyone. Already in the next line such liberation seems more attenuated: there, in the present tense, future freedom is only implied by the futurity that the word "still" (noch) connotes in the phrase "are still a slave"; for now the "comrade" is in the quarry and a slave. And what will the promised freedom bring? What is to happen then? Significantly, not "the comrade" is then to speak of the injustices he has suffered but the "stones," purportedly as his witnesses and allies in bringing the perpetrators — those who "strike" the inmates so that the latter fall in their own blood — to justice. Even the promise of justice through the speech of stones becomes questionable in the final line, as the poem comes to a close in a question very unusually followed by suspension points. Clearly the implication is that the story is not over, but the question itself is ambiguous: it mentions neither an agent of justice nor a plaintiff, nor does it name the perpetrators. The injustices the inmates suffered are rendered via a metonymic substitution: "der Steinbruch" (the stone quarry), the place where the abuse takes place, is named in the place of the abuse. "Einst" (one day) defers justice to an unspecified future. The last word of the poem, "gerächt" (revenged), a homonym of "gerecht" (just, fair), implies both vengeance and justice. We can and are expected to read the question to mean: "comrade, will all the abuse and all the sufferings you endured in the quarry be revenged on your behalf?" The question is rhetorical: the expectation anticipated in the first line of the stanza is that justice will be achieved for the comrade. But in common usage the German preposition "an" combined with "rächen" introduces the one who is the recipient of the vengeance (the perpetrator **on** whom vengeance is exacted) and not the person in whose benefit vengeance is taken, for example, as in "dieses Unrecht werde ich noch **an** *ihm* rächen," which translates as: "I intend to avenge myself **on** *him* for this injustice" (Pons). But Schnog writes: "Wird der Steinbruch einst an dir gerächt?" ([literally:] will the stone quarry some day be revenged on you?) The accused, the perpetrators, are only referred to in-directly in the last line via metalepsis or double substitution: the quarry stands in for the abuse that in turn stands in for the abusers on whom venge-ance would be taken. On closer inspection, therefore, the fourth stanza seems less distant from the other three: the assurance of freedom turns into an allusion of justice that becomes an inconclusive and ambivalently phrased question about revenge.

Like the camp songs discussed by Ruth Klüger, few of the camp poems end without offering some kind of resolution, however minimized or am-biguous one might read this to be. Both "Kette der Tage" and "Der Stein-bruch" deal with the daily exhaustion and constant brutalities of work in the camps. Both poems present a clear structure in the form of regularity of rhyme and meter and in a narrative line tending to resolution. Such structure seems to provide a frame within which these authors may describe the deso-lation without being overcome by it. Nevertheless, "Kette der Tage" envi-sions a future in which justice does not enter the scene: the inmates will not be understood. There, as we have seen, liberation brings deepening loneli-ness. Even if ambiguously "Der Steinbruch" retains a sense of justice, though even the assurance of survival is minimal since not the inmate but the stones will speak after liberation.

Hunger

That thirst, hunger, and starvation were among the most powerful and in-sidious means through which the Nazis sought to humiliate, degrade, and ultimately to "eliminate" individuals imprisoned in the camps is well known. Images of emaciated concentration camp inmates, whether alive or as corpses, have become iconic by now. Some of the writings from the concen-tration camps describe and reflect upon hunger, bringing into focus particu-lar details that a more general history or a less personalized description might overlook. In one of his diary entries from the camps Kupfer-Koberwitz offers a scene that illustrates some of the "details" concerning food at Neuen-gamme: the effect that the sale of salt has on a group of inmates. Food in the camps was not only most often murderously insufficient and monotonous, but in some camps it was also salt-free, a situation that over a longer period of time produced a desperate need for salt in the inmates, while in other camps such as Auschwitz-Birkenau the food was generally so salty that it re-duced inmates to a constant state of atrocious thirst (Klüger 2001, 100; Lewinska, 88). Some concentration camps had "canteens" run by the SS — this was yet another method by which the SS profited from and exploited its victims. The canteen at Neuengamme decided one day to sell salt to the in-mates. Kupfer-Koberwitz's diary documents the reactions and emotions caused by this event:

There was something else, and relatively cheap too, a bag of salt, half a pound. Of course I bought some too. We had done without salt for a long time already, because the food was cooked without salt, at least it tasted that way.

Otto usually ate without salt. But now he had such a salt-craving that he was spreading salt on his bread like I was doing, at least two or three teaspoons on each slice.

The eyes of those who had not been able to buy any followed us greedily and asked us for a pinch of salt. Of course we gave them some of our treasure. The Poles didn't say anything. They stared, but didn't dare to ask for any. I offered them some salt. Their eyes lit up then, and I knew that it wasn't just because of the salt, but rather because they felt treated like humans. I saw someone who ate his salt by the table-spoon. His bag was empty in two days. I must confess that I too ate a full tablespoon a few times. Even Otto did it once. Our bodies demanded it, because we had done without it for so long. (1957, 352)

In the context of extreme deprivation the exchanges in camp-money, salt, and gazes create an occasion for generosity in Kupfer-Koberwitz's text. These exchanges also illustrate the types of policies implemented to undermine solidarity among camp inmates. Poles, along with Jews, were at the lowest rank of the camp hierarchy at Neuengamme and were not allowed to receive money transfers or to purchase anything at the canteen. Jews and Jehovah's Witnesses were "housed" in separate barracks from the rest of the inmates. By implication Kupfer-Koberwitz's story also tells of the lack of generosity on the part of some inmates and of the state to which inmates had been reduced that some of them would beg for salt and some of them would not dare to do even that. The narrator does not speak here of those inmates to whom he could not have given any salt, as they were kept segregated. In all of the camps set up by the National Socialists an elaborate system of privileges and hierarchies ensured that there were always those who were "worse off" and undermined the possibility of solidarity among inmates.

As more than one poem testifies, for many inmates the most important staple of the camps' diet was the ration of bread (see also Reiter 1989). Meager as it was, it had more substance than the watery soup, the other main item on the menu. In a poem entitled "Hunger," Kupfer-Koberwitz articulates the importance of bread for the inmates (1946, 19–22).[6] In a refrain that opens the poem and occurs irregularly through this ninety-five-line-long work, bread is compared to gold:

> Das Brot ist rar, ist unser Gold,
> nehmt alles hin, habt was ihr wollt,
> wir werden alles geben,
> denn Brot ist unser Leben! —

[Bread is rare, bread is our gold,
take everything, whatever you want,
we'll give everything,
because bread is our life! —]

The speaker goes on to describe inmates begging initially for a piece of bread, only to ask later for potato skins, since it has been generally agreed upon that "bread weighs heavier than gold." The speaker's concern lies in the extreme behavior to which hunger drives people as exemplified in the following excerpts:

Und weil der Hunger zu wild and zu groß,   40
so wird aus dem Menschen ein Tier —

[And because the hunger is too wild, and too great,
so people turn into beasts —]

Essen — essen nur denkt das Hirn: —   45
der Mensch wird ein Tier, das säuft und das frisst

[the brain only thinks: Eat — Eat—
people become beasts that drink and devour]

Einmal nur satt sein, ein einzig Mal nur,   53
ganz gleich wovon, gleich auch wie! — — —

[To be sated just one, just one single time,
not matter how, no matter what from! — — —]

Der Hunger geht weiter, der bleibet nicht stehen 83
frißt unser Gedärm und Gedanken —

[Hunger goes beyond, it doesn't stay put,
devours our intestines and our thoughts —]

The poem's narrative culminates in a scene in which a "bread thief" is beaten to death, the usual punishment in the camps for such an offense. Such beating was often meted out by the inmates in charge of the barracks or by other inmates. The poem concludes:

Und der, der so elend und hungrig war,
der bat sie in seiner Not:
"Kam'raden, schlagt mich nicht tot! —
Ich stahl, weil halb irr ich vor Hunger war."
Doch sie schlugen den Brotdieb tot. —

[And he, who was so miserable and hungry,
he entreated them, in his need:

"Comrades, don't beat me dead! —
I stole, because I was half crazy with hunger."
But they did beat the bread-thief dead. —]

Kupfer-Koberwitz's poem presents a typical dilemma in the camps without attempting to resolve it: an inmate may die of hunger or may seek to avoid this by stealing bread from another inmate and thus risk death from a beating. The poem prepares the reader for the final stanza by suggesting throughout that "hunger" takes over the individual and reduces anyone to an elemental bestiality. The social order in the camps is such that the right to one's piece of bread is brutally imposed. In a "hunger" poem from Theresienstadt the poet Henri Sternberg, who survived his time there, describes how the motivation behind all the inmates' actions and desires is the one object, bread. Sternberg's poem is entitled "Das Lied vom Brot" (The Song of Bread; in Groll, 392) and it reads:

Ach, über unserm Sehnen
Und über unsrer Not
Und hinter unsren Tränen
Da steht der Schrei nach Brot.

Wir zählen unsere Tage
Berechnen, was uns droht,
Erwägen Freud und Plage
und messen unser Brot.

So hoffen wir und harren
Auf Leben oder Tod
Und drehen uns wie Narren
Um Brot, um Brot, um Brot!

[Oh, above our longing
And above our need
And behind our tears
There is the scream for bread.

We count our days
Calculate, what threatens us,
Consider joy and hardship
And measure our bread.

Thus we hope and wait
For life or death
And spin about like fools
For bread, for bread, for bread!]

Sternberg's "Schrei nach Brot" (scream for bread) brings to mind the testimony of a survivor of Auschwitz-Birkenau. He remembers the sudden mass-deportations and killings of Hungarian Jews: one morning, one large section of the camp was full of Hungarian women. They stood by the barbed wire and cried out "Chleb! Chleb!" — the Polish word for bread. The next morning, the section was empty and silent again.[7]

Despite the great differences in conditions in the various camps, some concerns, figures of speech ("hunger makes beasts of us all"), and formal elements seem available to a number of authors independently of each other and of their respective intellectual, artistic, social, or ethnic background. In Kupfer-Koberwitz's "Hunger," the (imperfect) rhyme "Not" / "Brot" / "Gold" (need / bread / gold) occurs four times before the bread-thief enters the scene. Then, in the bread-thief's voice, that rhyming pattern switches to "Not" / "tot" / "tot" (need / dead / dead) to narrate the thief's death by beating. That semantic shift, while keeping the rhyming scheme, creates a connection between "Brot" (bread) and "tot" (dead): the terms are linked by the rhyme and through the connection with the term "Not" (need). As we have seen in the poem, Kupfer-Koberwitz explains the double bind in which to steal bread means death through punishment and not to steal bread means death from starvation. Bread is necessary for life and thus precious (by the end of Kupfer-Koberwitz's poem, "more precious than gold"), but it is also connected to death: "viele Brotdiebe habe ich sterben gesehen / und viele Verhungernde wanken" (I have seen many bread-thieves die, and many starving men totter). In the first stanza of Sternberg's "Das Lied vom Brot," "Brot" rhymes with "Not." In the next stanza, the rhyme is with "droht" (threatens). Then, in the final stanza, the rhyme is "Tod" (death) / "Brot" (bread). There is an intensification: from need through threat to death, all linked to bread. As in Kupfer-Koberwitz's poem from Dachau, in Sternberg's too need, bread, and death are connected both by the narrative and by the rhyming scheme.

The beginning lines of another poem entitled "Hunger" repeat the rhyme "bread" / "death" (Boris, first poem; printed in Elling 1990, 64):

> Sechs Tage kein Brot.　　1
> Es reitet der Tod
> Durch die Reihen.
>
> [Six days without bread.
> Death rides
> Through the rows.]

The author of this poem, Georg von Boris, was imprisoned at the slave-labor camp Flossenbürg in Bavaria. While there he wrote a number of (mostly rhyming) poems between 6 July 1942 and 15 July 1945 (Boris). His poem

"Hunger" is relatively short and the language, as in most of his texts, is simple. The terse, unemotional statement of fact with which it begins ("Sechs Tage kein Brot") contains neither verb nor motion other than the implied passage of time marked by the number six. Six suggests the possibility of hope, since the tradition in Genesis establishes that something different might occur on the "seventh" day: in Genesis something has been achieved, the work of creation is completed; according to Western customs, the seventh day is the day of rest or the holy day. But the six days here set up a scene of helplessness and passive suffering. The second line of the poem introduces "Death" as the active agent in the first half of the poem's fourteen lines. "Death" wields power, moves about, makes choices. The inmates are reduced to screaming in despair and begging "Death" to relieve them of their suffering:

> Es reitet der Tod   2
> Durch die Reihen.
> Verzweifelte schreien:
> So nimm mich doch.
> Und er gelassen:
> Warte noch.
>
> [Death rides
> Through the rows.
> The desperate scream:
> Please take me, do!
> And he says calmly:
> Wait a little.]

The eighth line introduces a collective, first-person-plural speaker who is implicated in the scene just described. As discussed above, the use of "we" rather than "I" may create some distance between the speaker and the action described.

> Das können wir nicht fassen.   8
> Der Tod läßt uns leben,
> Das ist es eben.   10
>
> [We cannot grasp that.
> Death lets us live,
> That's just it.]

Indirectly these lines contain an acknowledgment of the wish to die on the part of the speaker as well. After "Death," the next active agent who does more than scream, despair, and fail to understand is "Hunger." It makes "us" into "beasts." Line 12 is a question addressed to the community that is the subject of the poem, but it may also speak to the world outside the camps. It expresses concern with crossing the line beyond properly human experience. The final rhyming couplet then reveals the source of that concern while remaining at the same linguistic register, that of a matter-of-factness, if not a given flatness or banality, as exemplified in line 10: "Das ist es eben" (That's just it):

> Doch der Hunger macht uns zum Tier.
> Sind wir noch Menschen? Wir,   12
> Es ist zum Erbleichen,
> Wir fressen an Leichen.

> [But hunger turns us into beasts.
> Are we still human? We,
> It's so disgusting,
> We are feeding on corpses.]

The term "Erbleichen" in line 13 means to "grow pale" and both acoustically and in terms of orthography contains the terms "bleichen" (to bleach) and "Leichen" (corpses); the latter association is emphasized through the rhyme of the final line. In addition, the past tense forms of "erbleichen," "erblich" and "erblichen," are now obsolete expressions that imply to die, to expire. The notion of "turning pale," with the specter of death as a possibility, brings out the incongruity in the poem between the extreme action described (feeding on corpses) and a very commonplace response to a moment of high excitability (fear, disgust, and sometimes shame). The construction of the phrase "Es ist zum Erbleichen," literally "It is to turn pale about" recalls commonplace expressions in German most often used to express disgust or distress — for example, "Es ist zum Kotzen," literally translatable as "It (would) make one puke," whereas in English we might say "It's really disgusting." The commonplace construction interrupts the sentence: "Wir, / Es ist zum Erbleichen, / Wir fressen an Leichen." This interruption, along with the repetition of the pronoun *we*, may express hesitation on the part of the speaker, vacillation about the confession about to be made. There is an incongruity or disjunction between on the one hand the colloquial language of the poem together with the controlled, rhyming language of the description and on the other hand the action described. This incongruity is a central element in the poem, the point that upholds the tension inherent in the poet's endeavor: to narrate an experience, to render it in verse form, and thus to include it in the realm of "normal" or rather "elevated" human experience and, at the same time, truthfully to give the reader a factual account of an extreme experience, one in which the speaker himself is implicated: "*We* are feeding on corpses." The anxiety this action produces is palpable: "Are we still human?" Surely one must be human in order to compose a rhyming poem. That the speaker is involved in the act of feeding on corpses permits a depiction that does not conceal or minimize the horror while at the same time it does not become moralistic. "Are we still human?" is at some level a rhetorical question, although it also raises profound, philosophical questions about "the human" after the Holocaust: in other words, had we misunderstood what it means to be human? (See Agamben). The light, fast-paced, staccato rhythm of the poem, between a song and a march, as well as the regular rhymes, heightens the disparity between the event described and the lyric form, traditionally thought of as the language of the "sweet and useful" (Forché, 42). In fact the copy of Boris's typescript archived at the Dachau Concentration Camp Memorial Site repeats that gesture of disjunction: in handwriting the author dedicates the typescript (a selection of his poems under the title *Die Lieder des Grauens* [Songs of Horror]) to the family that hosted him over vacations in the previous years, as if his "songs of horror" were still the "sweet" and beautiful object we traditionally expect poetry to be and that would make of a collection of poems a well-meaning gift.

A pathetic rendition of the event seems barred. Such rendition would overwhelm with affect an already emotionally overwhelming narrative. The author resorts to simple diction and a traditional, almost clichéd, rhyming structure. Such an approach to the topic produces alienation in the reader: What is this action doing in a mini-sonnet? The poem has recourse to a kind of gallows humor as a strategy for coping with the horror:

> Sechs Tage kein Brot.
> Es reitet der Tod
> Durch die Reihen.
> Verzweifelte schreien;
> So nimm mich doch.
> Und er gelassen:
> Warte noch.
> Das können wir nicht fassen.
> Der Tod läßt uns leben,
> Das ist es eben.
> Doch der Hunger macht uns zum Tier.
> Sind wir noch Menschen? Wir,
> Es ist zum Erbleichen,
> Wir fressen an Leichen.

> [Six days without bread.
> Death rides
> Through the rows.
> The desperate scream:
> Please take me, do!
> And he says calmly:

Wait a little.
We cannot grasp that.
Death lets us live,
That's just it.
But hunger turns us into beasts.
Are we still human? We,
It's so disgusting,
We are feeding on corpses.]

There may be a relation between such overwhelming experiences and the urge to bear witness. Hearing about an act of what we might call "survival cannibalism" is the first experience Kupfer-Koberwitz describes in his Dachau diary. He decides to write this journal "in the middle of things, in the middle of the horror, to tell of the horror, which long ago stopped shocking us":

Today is the 20th of November 1942. Yesterday something happened that shocked even those who have been most desensitized, and that is saying something, because nothing surprises us any more, nothing shocks us any more. And so it was yesterday. — It shocked only a few, maybe those who themselves had to intervene.

Yesterday 500 invalids [a designation for Muselmänner, in this case] from a camp near Danzig [Stutthof]. — Invalids are those inmates who are in the process of dying. — Later you will hear about it, when I tell you more. —

Then, of these invalids, 51 arrived dead, but their corpses had been eaten from by the others, — Two were missing entirely, just a few, unrecognizable body parts were left. — Of one, that is, of one of the corpses, the whole loin was chewed up, others were missing the genitals. — It must have been a horrible sight; I am glad that I did not see it. (1997, 31–32)

The narrator here expresses the notion "that nothing shocks us" but notices as well a further barrier crossed in the case of the cannibalism. On the next page he reassures his reader — he addresses his girlfriend in Stuttgart throughout the text — that what he writes is true. At the same time he recognizes that it will be hard to believe any one book on the topic (1997, 33).

It seems crucial to know the context of Boris's poem to become aware of the full implications of its approach to the experience, to realize the fact that the alienation produced by the poem is in proportion to the extreme experiences in the camps and not the gratuitous pursuit of an "aesthetic frisson" as Saul Friedländer calls "the opposition between the harmony of kitsch and the constant evocation of themes of death and destruction" (1993, 18). This poem moves us in the direction of a schizophrenic reading in which we read it "merely" as fiction, as an artistic endeavor, even though we know it describes a factual and outrageous experience. A rhyming couplet that ends with the sentence "we are feeding on corpses": the incommensurability of the experience is contained in the form of the poem and thus passed on to the reader.

Lawrence Langer analyzes a similarly structured moment in the video testimony of a Holocaust survivor. In Langer's description the witness presents an episode of cannibalism "so deferentially, so indifferent to its melodramatic not to say barbaric possibilities that in spite of its subject he forces us to consider it as part of the routinized response to constant hunger and oppression that typified the camp experience" (1991, 116–17).

Langer is analyzing here the workings of what he labels "humiliated memory." His primary materials are the interviews with survivors over thirty years after the liberation of the camps. He finds a "split" in the survivors' consciousness in which a "normal" and a "camp" self coexist in one mind and bring together two irreconcilable experiences of the world. The "normal" self's vocabulary provides narrative and chronology, and includes ideals. The "humiliated" self is bound neither to chronology nor to plot: "We may call [such] memory inaccessible, but what we really mean is that it is not *discussable*" (118). The process of witnessing and narrating represents for Langer a determination "to transform the unfathomable into a comprehensible way of behaving given birth by the circumstances of the Holocaust" (117). The poems from the camps rarely "explain" behavior; that is, they do not provide logical explanations. But in the portrayal of actions, experiences, circumstances, and feelings, they (as Langer puts it) "transform the unfathomable," make it part of human experience by including it in the range of topics poetry touches on. Boris's speaker similarly seems to consist of a "normal" self who goes pale, who asks himself about his own humanity in a rhyming poem, and a "camp" self that responds to intense bodily needs by breaking a most basic taboo of civilization. Vis-à-vis this forced act of cannibalism, of vulture-like anthropophagy, the self that writes the poem, we might add, thereby creates perspective, takes up an "eccentric" position from which it becomes possible to ask the question about one's humanity.

Commingling with the Dead

The encounter with death and corpses was a characteristic element of the everyday in the concentrationary universe. When individuals die or are killed at such massive rates, in such dense concentrations of people, the physical presence of dead bodies becomes part of the daily experience. At times the dead lay on the ground for days, or were stacked in piles. They never received proper burial.

> The expression "the fabrication of corpses" implies that it is no longer possible truly to speak of death, that what took place in the camps was

not death, but rather something infinitely more appalling. In Auschwitz, people did not die; rather, corpses were produced. (Agamben, 72)

Some poems from the concentration camps seek to work against the "fabri-
cation of corpses." They attempt to "bury" or memorialize a loved one who
has died and for whom the traditional rituals of mourning were not available.
The following poems deal with dead bodies on the one hand by stressing a
"routinized" relation to them or by emphasizing that the difference between
being alive and being dead is tenuous and arbitrary. At the same time the
rhetorical power of these poems relies on the unspoken acknowledgment
that the kinds of interaction with dead bodies, the attitudes and actions the
poems depict, exceed the bounds of the "ordinary" relation to the dead,
even if such "ordinary" relation to the dead and to death is traditionally ritu-
alized and in some sense mystical or magical.[8]

Ilse Weber's "Theresienstädter Kinderreim" (Theresienstadt Children's
Rhyme; Weber 1978, 71; 1991, 89[9]) brings together corpses, playing, suffering, and traveling in an energetic, upbeat-sounding, witty children's rhyme.
This rhyme enacts a gesture of incongruity similar to the one analyzed above
in Boris's poem "Hunger." Here the speaker is indifferent to and at the
same time insists on the horror. Weber's poem, written in Theresienstadt, is
an adaptation to the concentrationary universe of a traditional folk song,
"Die goldene Kutsche" (The Golden Coach). As such the poem produces a
radical and macabre transformation of a common children's song. The text
of the folksong, in Engelbert Humperdinck's version (38), is as follows:[10]

> Komm wir wollen wandern
> von einem Ort zum andern
> rirarutsch!
> Wir fahren in der Kutsch'.

> In der Kutsche fahren wir
> und auf dem Esel reiten wir;
> rirarutsch!
> Wir fahren in der Kutsch'.

> [Come, we want to travel
> from one place to another
> rirarutsch!
> We travel by coach.

> By coach we travel
> and on the donkey we ride;
> rirarutsch!
> We travel by coach.]

Weber, born Ilse Herlinger in Witkowitz, in the current Czech Republic, in 1903, published articles, poems, translations from Czech into German and vice versa, and three books for children in German between 1927 and 1930, one of which (Herlinger 1929) was translated recently into English by Ruth and Hans Fisher and published in the United States after Hans Fisher found the book again five decades after the Holocaust (Weber 2001). Weber married in 1930 and continued writing, at first sporadically, and after 1935 more regularly. Czech Jews had received full civil rights in 1918 when Czechoslovakia became independent, and the Webers were unwilling to leave Witkowitz at first. By the time Hitler occupied the area it was impossible for the Webers to find a land willing to grant them refuge. They managed to send their then eight-year-old eldest son to Sweden via England in 1939. Shortly thereafter the rest of the family was forced to move to Prague, where Weber taught in a Jewish school. In 1942 she was deported with her younger son and her husband to Theresienstadt. There she worked as head nurse in a clinic set up for children. Given the precarious conditions, one of the most readily available "medicines" at this clinic was the attention she gave to ailing children. Weber composed songs and sang to the children to the accompaniment of a guitar that had been smuggled into the camp. In October 1944 Ilse Weber and her younger son were deported to Auschwitz and killed there (see Weber 1991, 9–15, also Kahan 1997, 4–5).

As someone who wrote for children and worked with children, Weber was evidently familiar with some versions of the "Rirarutsch" children's rhyme. In her singsongy poem she creates a dynamic structure that displays the playfulness and the sense of lightness we would expect in a children's rhyme despite the dreadfulness of the scenes described. Note for example the quick "hier . . . dort / flink . . . fort" (here . . . there / quickly . . . away) in the first stanza. (The translation below was provided by David Keir Wright in a letter to the author, 25 September 2003, under the title "A Nursery Rhyme from Theresienstadt," also printed in an earlier version in Kahan 2000.)

> Rira, rirarutsch,
> wir fahren in der Leichenkutsch,
> rira, rirarutsch,
> wir fahren in der Kutsch.
> Wir stehen hier und stehen dort
> und fahren flink die Leichen fort,
> rirarutsch,
> wir fahren in der Kutsch.
>
> Rira, rirarutsch,
> was einst wir hatten ist jetzt futsch,
> rira, rirarutsch,
> ist längst schon alles futsch.

Die Freude aus, die Heimat weg,
den letzten Koffer fährt, o Schreck,
rirarutsch,
jetzt fort die Leichenkutsch.

Rira, rirarutsch,
man spannt uns vor die Leichenkutsch.
Rira, rirarutsch,
man spannt uns vor die Kutsch.
Hätt sie geladen unser Leid,
wir kämen nicht drei Schritte weit,
rirarutsch,
zu schwer wär dann die Kutsch.

[Heave! Look out ahead!
Here comes the wagon with the dead.
Heave! Look out ahead!
The wagon with the dead.
We stop right here and stop right there,
We drive dead bodies everywhere.
Look ahead!
The wagon with the dead.

Heave! Look out ahead!
Destroyed and gone – all that we had.
Heave! Look out ahead!
Destroyed and gone, I said.
The end of joy, our home's away,
Our luggage left the other day.
Look ahead!
We're coming with the dead.

Heave! Look out ahead!
They've hitched us to the cart instead.
Heave! Look out ahead!
They've hitched us up instead.
If all our pain were put on it,
We wouldn't even move one bit.
Look ahead!
A wagon full of dead.]

The text consistently alternates between iambic trimeter and tetrameter while the refrain starts in a stressed syllable. All endings are masculine, and the rhyme structure is strictly consistent in all stanzas (aaaabbaa). This creates a strong rhythmic effect. In a manner reminiscent of a fast dance or a children's game, and like in the folksong the poem transforms, the subjects ("we") move about and trade places: "We stop right here and stop right there." The fast pace allows the poem to keep going, making the transitions easy when the message is traumatic. "Was wir einst hatten, ist jetzt futsch" (literally "what we once had, is now done for") is one such apparently "light" transition; the (grammatically required) comma in the German, that short pause, is the marker of a calamitous change in the context of Theresienstadt, and in Weir's translation it is rendered with a dash. "Futsch" is a colloquialism, all the more impudent in this particular context. Another such light transition pertains to the question of who is the subject and who is the object of the action of riding the coach. In the folksong, the first-person plural speaker gleefully alternates between traveling on a golden coach and riding a donkey (Humperdinck) or between a coach and a "snail-paced" coach (Schneckenpost; Enzensberger, 71). At Theresienstadt, the variation is of a different order: "Wir fahren in der Leichenkutsch" (we travel on the corpses' cart) becomes "man spannt uns vor die Leichenkutsch" (they hitch us to the corpses' cart). "We" turns into "us" as the speaker goes from presumed agent to object: the passengers have been turned into beasts of burden. Jirí Weil also writes of "human beings harnessed to funeral carts" at Theresienstadt (1964, 61). Of course, since in Weber's poem the cargo on the carriage is corpses, there does not seem to be a good option, a good place to be in relative to the cart. Only a tacit, unnamed coach driver retains the reins: "They've hitched us up instead." The poem does not make light of the situation, but it uses gallows humor to depict the madness of the experience: the children playing on or around the cart full of corpses. This poem says lightly that "everything, home, joy" have been taken away. With a casual tone the speaker seems to overlook the shocking aspect of a scene of children playing with corpses. By treating the experience as if it were ordinary, by working against pathos, the poet confronts the reader with the unreality of daily experience in Theresienstadt. Thus Albrecht Goes writes that "this nursery rhyme from Theresienstadt is almost unbearable. But it just tells — the truth" (Goes, 7). In terms of its rhetorical strategy, the poem acknowledges the taboo that the narrative seems to overlook. What the speed and the tone of the poem disguise is that the repeated use of the verb "fahren" (to travel or to ride) gets "us" nowhere. In fact, only the corpses and the last suitcase are taken away (fort); "we" remain, and would not move even three steps if we took account of "our" suffering.

George Eisen writes that "an unemotional acceptance of death by children was evident . . . in many . . . ghettos and camps" (105). In *Children and Playing in the Holocaust* Eisen records many instances of children playing next to, around, and with corpses. Examples vary from a game "tickling a corpse" (79) to stepping over corpses to continue playing (90) to playing with the "funeral cart" at Theresienstadt: "paintings show that in Theresienstadt when the funeral hearse was not carrying corpses to the mass graves, the children played with it, inventing many games for its use" (106). He also points out that "in Auschwitz, children were seen to play with the limbs and fluttering hair of the dead as they were carted off in a pile to the crematorium" (90). Eisen writes of the emotional reactions, ranging from disbelief to horror, that such scenes evoke in adults then and now, noting divergent reactions to children's play in the populations in the ghettos and camps: those wishing to give themselves and their children some semblance of normality, thus encouraging "normal" play and distraction, and those rejecting any "playing" and entertainment as inappropriate to the circumstances. Not surprisingly Eisen claims that for the children playing was a coping mechanism, what he calls "part of an assimilation-accommodation complex," one that, in terms of adaptive behavior, was more readily available to them than to adults (113). Weber's poem is neither an expression of encouragement nor a rejection of children's play with and around corpses: rather, it enacts this type of playing, inviting the reader to participate in it through its first-person plural speaker. This enactment then leaves the critical reaction up to the reader.

Another poet from Southeastern Europe, Alfred Kittner, addresses instead the experience of being in intimate proximity to the dead in a poem that is a more self-reflexive transmutation of a love poem. Born in 1906, Kittner was a poet before and after the war. Like famous poets Paul Celan and Nelly Sachs, Kittner was a German-speaking Jewish poet from Czernowitz (now Chernivtsi in the Ukraine), in the Bukovina, a region currently divided between the Ukraine and Romania. During the Second World War Czernowitz repeatedly changed hands: the Soviet Army occupied the region in 1940 and 1941. In 1941, the Romanian army and German troops came back to the region. These forces then set up a number of smaller camps in Transnistria, in what is now the Ukraine. With other Jews from Czernowitz, Kittner was forced into long marches to those camps and from one place to the next. Kittner survived the camps, continued writing poetry in Bucharest after the war, and moved to Düsseldorf in 1981, where he died in 1991 (Kittner 1996). The title of Kittner's poem, "Unterwegs" (On the Road; Kittner 1988, 38–39[11]), refers to one of those deadly marches, and the poem, dated October 1942, develops during a stop at a stable in the vicinity of the village Tschetwertenowka (Kittner 1996, 78). This poem pivots around the notion of an accidental and inconsequential survival. The recurring line "In fact, it didn't' [or it doesn't] make any difference" takes the readers, without further ado, from an everyday event (it was raining heavily and it didn't make any difference) to a traumatic experience ("You, my beloved, died; I am still alive" and "it doesn't make any difference").

Als es in Strömen auf uns goß,
Im Grunde war es einerlei,
Trieb man mit Prügeln unseren Troß:
Nun birgt des Stalles Stroh uns zwei.
Vor mir bezogst du hier Quartier
Und liegst verwesend unter mir.
Weht Leichenruch auch durch den Raum,
Er schreckt mich nicht aus dumpfem Traum.

Den Läusen warst du bald zu kalt,
Im Grunde war es einerlei,
Du warst kein guter Aufenthalt,
Und schließlich sind wir hier doch zwei,
Drum kriechen sie zu mir herüber
Und bringen mir das schlimme Fieber,
Dem du vor Tagen hier im Mist
Des lehmigen Stalls erlegen bist.

Du, Liebste, starbst; ich lebe noch;
Im Grunde ist es einerlei.
Auch ich pfeif auf dem letzten Loch,
Und morgen schaufelt man uns zwei
Mit Hunderten ins Massengrab,
Zusammen wirft man uns hinab,
Läßt ohne vieles Federlesen
Uns bis zum Jüngsten Tag verwesen.

[It was raining heavily on us,
In fact, it didn't make any difference,
With their sticks they drove us on:
Now this barn's hay shelters the two of us.
Before me you took your place
And now you lie under me in decay.
When the smell of corpses wafts through the air,
It doesn't startle me from my dazed dream.

Soon you were too cold for the lice,
In fact, it didn't make any difference,
You were not a good place to stay,
And after all the two of us are here,
So they are crawling over to me
And bring me the bad fever,
That took your life a few days past
In the muck of this muddy barn.

You, my beloved, died; I am still alive;
In fact, it doesn't make any difference.
My life, too, hangs by a thread,
And tomorrow they will push the two of us
With hundreds of others into the mass grave,
They will throw us down together,
And, without further ado, they'll
Let us rot there until doomsday.]

"It didn't make any difference" is the thematic thread that holds the poem together. As the speaker's sense of alarm — or is it exasperation? — increases, the formulation changes to the present tense: "It doesn't make any difference." This phrase expresses the exhausted agony of the speaker and binds him to the corpse of his beloved and by extension to the "hundreds" to be thrown into the mass grave.

The first sentence establishes the unity of "you" and "me": now this "barn's hay shelters the two of us." In four short lines, the pronoun "us" appears twice and the possessive adjective "our" once. Initially the stable seems to offer protection from inclement weather ("it was raining heavily on us") and from the beatings. No sooner is the "we" divided into "you" and "me" than the illusion of comfort and community is destroyed in one short sentence: "Before me you took your place / and now lie under me in decay." In a single sentence the "beloved," the "you" addressed by the poem and apparently the speaker's only interlocutor and audience, goes from being a companion who shares the speaker's fate to being a corpse. The boundary line between "not yet dead" and "no longer alive" becomes blurred. Unlike in tragedy the point of death here is not marked, as Michael Moll points out (1988, 192). Instead, death makes itself known through one of its side effects: decomposition. Note that this is not a romantic scene of a lover's death, but the dirty, smellier, and more tangible representation of physical decomposition. The beloved is already dead and in a state of decay that can be smelled. "Vor mir" (before me) can be read spatially or temporally. In either case the preposition marks an order of sequence. "You" took your place first, died first. The implication is that "my turn" is next. The subject of the sentence undergoes a seamless transition from life to death.

In Moll's reading the depiction of the beloved's "physical decay" might be interpreted as cynical, but Moll understands this as misguided: "Where death with human dignity is no longer, what remains as a final attempt at respect is the exact description of a biological process, a process that also directly concerns the speaker as recognition of an extreme but evident reality" (1988, 193). Throughout the poem the narrator maintains the unity between himself and his beloved, he holds on to or returns to the notion of "us." The first-person-plural pronoun is crucial here. In the form of the grammatical object "us" it appears five times in the poem, prominently so in both the first and the last lines. This word establishes the enduring unity between the narrator and the dead "other": both are victims of the elements, of the beatings, the lice, and the fever, and both "will be left to rot in the mass grave" by unnamed perpetrators. In the middle of the poem, the singular pronouns "you" and "I" become more prominent. But this is a fleeting distinction that the circumstances described cancel out: "You, my beloved, died; I am still alive; / In fact, it doesn't make any difference." Tomorrow this will no longer make a difference: they will throw *us* into the mass grave and without further ado let *us* rot until doomsday. The first-person-plural pronoun is an enabling, imaginative act here that allows the speaker temporarily to overcome the ultimate difference of death through the dialogic structure of apostrophe it establishes. Although there is a "dialogue" here, verbal communication flows in one direction, from the "speaker" to the dead "beloved," but the lice, the fever, and death come from the "beloved" to the speaker. The "we" opens up the space that makes the poem possible. "You" and "I" are together, and since "you" are dead, "I" will tell "you" what is happening and will happen. Note that the number *two*, "zwei," occurs at the end of the fourth line of each stanza in this regular, rhyming poem. "Zwei" is the rhyme to the "einerlei" that ends the second line in every stanza. In German the term is etymologically and morphologically derived from the word for the number *one* (eins) — it could in fact be translated as "it's all one." The term to indicate lack of difference — it didn't or doesn't matter — is consistently echoed in the rhyme with the sign of the dyad. In this sense the initially stated lack of difference, the "oneness" or sameness of "einerlei," prevails in the end through the equalizing horror of the situation.

In the first stanza the number "two" constitutes an apparent community. The period that follows the word "two" mimics the temporary shelter of the barn. The barn protects "us" from the rain, and this first pause shelters the reader briefly from the revelation of the next sentence. There the community turns out to have been illusory or to be constituted across lines of demarcation that would normally make void the possibility of community. The pause after "zwei" diminishes in the next stanza to a comma. By the third stanza the "two" are joined relentlessly to the anonymous "hundreds" in the mass grave. Here the break is only the end of the line. In some sense the development from a couple who find refuge in a stable to first one, then two, and later hundreds of corpses is a grotesque inversion of the Nativity, where from the couple in the barn in the company of animals more agreeable than lice a triumphant third person emerges to bring "love and peace" to the world.

Upon her brother's death by asphyxiation in an overcrowded transport wagon, Helen K. vowed to survive. Upon the death of his beloved the lover-speaker here resigns himself to his own death — since his own survival is of no consequence and at best temporary: "My life, too, hangs by a thread / And tomorrow they will push the two of us / With hundreds of others into the mass grave." This unity of lover and beloved is not portrayed as the result of a heroic vow of love; it is not about a Shakespearean choice to remain with the "beloved," but rather seems like an inevitable result of the indifference, helplessness, and exhaustion that plague this situation. There is textual closure — the poem ends, and ends in a somewhat flippant rhyming couplet, "without further ado," and with an evocation of the final act in the biblical myth of the end of the world: the Last Judgment ("der Jüngste Tag"), translated above as "doomsday." The poem closes the circle, from "us" living, to "you" dead and "me" alive, and back to both of "us," now dead and soon to be rotting in a mass grave. This formal structure enables a tale, but one of despair and not one of consolation. "Im Grunde war es einerlei" (in fact it didn't make any difference). The expression "im Grunde" is translatable as "fundamentally, basically." "Grund" means ground, fundament. In the poem, then, it signifies that in essence there was no difference between "your" death and "my" (temporary) survival. Taken literally, however, the expression "im Grunde" means "in the ground" or "in the earth." In the earth (of the mass grave) it does or will not make a difference. Other terms also evoke the earth: "Mist" (muck, manure, shit), "lehmig" (clayey, muddy), "Loch" (hole), "schaufeln" (to dig). Dampness, decomposition, and the lack of differentiation of the mass grave work to absorb and undo the lovers' embrace.

Weber's "Theresienstädter Kinderreim" and Kittner's "Unterwegs" are stylistically and affectively far from one another. However, both poems minimize the distinction between being alive and being dead. The passage from one state to the next is unmarked in "Unterwegs," whose title, after reading the poem, takes on a new connotation: not only "on the road" but also "on the way" to the (mass) grave. The presence of corpses does not interfere with the children's game in Weber's text; the playing children easily move into the position reserved for the corpses: "Wir . . . fahren flink die Leichen fort / . . . / Wir fahren in der Kutsch" (We . . . quickly carry the corpses away / . . . / we travel in the cart).

Anything that happens everyday cannot continue to shock those who experience it, however out of the ordinary the events might be. By treating their experiences as "normal" experiences, as discussable events that bear narration in rhyming poems, the poets here confront readers with the unreality of their concentrationary reality. Furthermore, in the process of writing the poem, these poets simultaneously acknowledge the trauma and refuse to succumb entirely to the fragmentation of traumatic experience. Each poem finds a different "organizing principle," as one might call it, that enables a narrative. These poems demonstrate that such narrative "principle" or "imaginative act" need not be tantamount to a repression of trauma.

4: Communicating Torture

A Poem to Communicate

COMPOSING A POEM is an act of verbal communication. As a particular combination of words a poem "makes sense"; at least within its own logical system a poem is a choice, that is, it has been thought out and usually worked on. Even experimental poems that purport to defy meaning operate within a given frame of reference within which they challenge such meaning. To write poems in the concentration camps is to seek to "make sense," it is to counter the lack of sense that the perpetrators imposed on the life of inmates. As communication, whether internal (with oneself) or addressed to an actual or imaginary "other," a poem connotes a social field, creates a relation between an author and an implied audience, brings to life a narrator, a subject, and a narrative. From a psychological and even a biological perspective, a relation to an "other" is crucial for human health, howsoever different philosophies may define the "other" and the self's relationship to that "other." Thus psychiatrists José Saporta and Bessel van der Kolk write:

> Human beings have a biologically based need to form attachments with others. Children need a safe base in the form of secure attachments in order to explore their environment and develop socially, and adults continue to depend on social supports for a sense of safety, meaning, power, and control. (153)

A willful, deliberate act of giving shape, a poem draws on and confirms an author's sense of agency and autonomy. In and of itself, that is, a poem constitutes a conscious speech act and as such a creative action that counters the experience of complete loss of control over one's fate and even one's body that characterizes the experience of the concentrationary universe. The following selection of poems deals with episodes of either suffering torture or, more frequently, witnessing torture. Such experiences are particularly destructive in terms of the relationship to other people (trust) and dissociative in terms of the relation to one's own emotions. Close examination shows that these poems construct for themselves a social role and "make sense" of the experience. Thus, explicitly or not, these poems oppose the state of radical powerlessness and extreme isolation provoked by the kinds of brutality individuals experienced in the Nazi camps.

To witness torture is in itself traumatic, all the more so if the witness is explicitly at risk of becoming the next victim. Sofsky writes that in the camps "thousands were compelled to watch as their fellow prisoners, initially reduced to total defenselessness, were then forced to lie in a humiliating position and flogged. The helplessness of the victims symbolized the powerlessness of the entire prisoner society" (219). Sofsky contrasts the scenes of flogging and torture in the Nazi camps to "the historical festivals of public torture" in which the public eagerly participated. In the concentration camps inmates were forced to watch: "Anger, rage, and hatred were repressed. At its finish, the spectacle left its audience with nothing but the apathy of their absolute powerlessness" (220). In this context camp poems about torture can be understood as secret reactions to the spectacle of abuse or as private and forbidden forms of protest. Such poems give expression to emotion or imply emotion. To write a poem in the concentration camps was to "do" something, to forge an aesthetically singular narrative out of "anger, rage, and hatred" as well as despair. Thus, at a psychological level, to write a poem constituted possibly a counter-ritual, a refusal to surrender completely to the apathy of "absolute powerlessness." For example, in Kupfer-Koberwitz's "Erinnerung" (Remembrance), a poem from Dachau about witnessing psychological abuse and humiliation (rather than physical torture), the narrator clearly expresses emotion, implies indignation, and portrays or understands himself as taking action in the situation (Kupfer-Koberwitz 1946, 11[1]):

> Man gab ihm das Bild seiner toten Frau —
> stumm hat er es angeschaut —
> er schwankte, sein Antlitz wurd fahl und grau,
> tot war sein Liebstes, tot seine Frau — — —
> Stumm hat auf das Bild er geschaut. —

> "Fünf Minuten, nicht länger, verstanden, heh? —
> Saujud, hast du mich gehört?" —
> Oh, ich sehe noch alles vor mir, ich seh'
> diesen Mann, dessen Haare weiß wie der Schnee —
> und weil ich ganz dicht und ganz neben ihm steh',
> hat es mir die Seele verzehrt. —

> "Du heulst wohl, weil deine Hure verreckt? —
> Wirklich, die Judensau heult!" —
> Tief wurde mir da die Seele erschreckt,
> ich hab' vor dem Alten mich aufgereckt,
> er war hinter mir versteckt —
> fast hätte ich auch geheult. —

[They gave him the picture of his dead wife —
silently he looked at it —
he tottered, his face became ashen and gray,
dead was his beloved, dead was his wife — — —
silently he looked at the picture. —

"Five minutes, no longer, did you get that, eh?
Sow-Jew, did you hear me?" —
Oh, I still see it all in front of me, I see
this man, his hair white like snow —
and because I stood very close and right next to him,
it pierced my soul. —

"You cry because your whore kicked the bucket? —
Really, the Jewish sow is crying!" —
My soul was deeply shocked then,
I stood up in front of the old man,
he was hidden behind my back —
I almost cried myself. —]

The title "Erinnerung" (Remembrance) refers to the old man's memory of his now dead wife. Since her picture is in the possession of the SS-guards and since these guards know of her death we may safely assume that SS-guards have murdered her, or at the very least that she has died while in their custody. "Erinnerung" is also the speaker's memory of this episode of abuse that causes a deep disturbance in him: "My soul was deeply shocked then." As the memory unfolds, the speaker switches briefly to the present tense. The redundant repetition in the phrase "ganz dicht und ganz neben" (very close and very near) emphasizes that the speaker feels very, possibly too, close to the victim and to the abuse. The speaker, seeking an explanation for his own emotional reaction, attributes his shock to his uncomfortable proximity to the victim:

> und **weil** ich ganz dicht und ganz neben ihm steh',
> hat es mir die Seele verzehrt. —

> [and **because** I was standing very close and right next to him,
> it pierced my soul. —]

This rhyming poem conveys the force of the verbal and emotional mistreatment by the SS, whose abusive actions seem to increase as the victim shows an emotional reaction. The narrator refuses the "apathy of absolute powerlessness," as Sofsky calls it. Within the narrative the speaker presents himself as coming between the victim and the abusers. He provides a shield for the old man. In addition, by composing the poem the poet-narrator testifies and thus gives expression to his indignation and to his emotional response to the old man's pain. On at least two counts, then, the speaker presents himself as being in a position, not to prevent or stop the abuse, but to show concern for the victim and to attempt to offer some protection. There is an empathic, perhaps identificatory understanding of the victim that manifests itself in the protective reaction. The indignation here pertains not only to the brutal attack on someone's feelings but pointedly as well to the lack of respect for old age ("hair white like the snow") and to the anti-Semitism that takes the form of varied though repetitive insults with connotations about filth, animality, uncontrolled sexuality, and lack of masculinity: "Hure" (whore) and "verrecken" (to die, used of animals) to refer to the deceased wife; "Saujud" (swine-Jew, literally sow-Jew) and "Judensau" (Jewish sow *or* Jew's sow) to address the old man. The switch from the first to the second of these anti-Semitic insults is an intensification of the aggression: the connection between "Jews" and "swine" as bearers of impurity and dirt is made in both of them, but the second insult carries a feminization of the subject as well. Isaiah Shachar traces the history of the German medieval motif of the *Judensau* from an allegorical representation of the vices of gluttony and lust to an anti-Semitic insult in the nineteenth century and argues that although the picture of the *Judensau* disappeared, the motif, as an expression of abuse, "did persist in the German language until the present century" (1974, 64). Nicoline Hortzitz explains that composite words like "Saujud" (sow-Jew) and "Judensau" (Jew-sow) are redundant constructs since both terms in each composite noun are negatively charged and function as quasi-generic insults used to abuse Jews (Hortzitz, 34). In this poem the speaker is in touch with his own ethical standards and reacts accordingly: we find out through the words of the abusers that the "old man" is crying. The speaker's reaction, "I almost cried myself," reveals an empathic identification that threatens to unman the narrator as well.

In their derisive comments the perpetrators attribute to their Jewish victim bestiality and impurity as well as a lack of masculinity. Perhaps unwittingly, and certainly without the use of accusatory language on the side of the narrator, this poem unmasks the abusers by revealing the bestiality and cowardice of their cheap delight in the old man's suffering. The abuse is spoken in a first-person singular voice and addresses the abused man directly, but this voice also speaks of the abused man in the third person and thus addresses an implied audience who shares or is expected to share the perspective of the abuser. Whether explicitly or implicitly, the power dynamics depicted here are such that the abuse is carried out by a group while the victim of abuse is a single individual who, at most, elicits a supportive or empathic reaction in fellow inmates. The poem's depiction of the torturer's use of a photograph adds yet another dimension to the violence implicit in the "Nazi control over the technologies of production and reproduction."

Gubar writes that "most photographs taken during the Shoah constituted an action in the war against the Jews" (135). This poem makes it explicit that photographs were not only taken to "demean the victims" photographed but also purposely used to cause individual suffering.

In the concentration camps, verbal and psychological abuse, physical torture, and death, were omnipresent: any inmate could be subjected to physical violence at any moment, independently of his or her actions. In fact regulations concerning inmates were such that inmates often could not follow one rule without breaking another one. Inmates were therefore constantly liable to be punished. Moreover regulations were kept deliberately vague so that they could be "beaten into" the inmates:

> Camp power was less interested in preventing infractions than in being able to take action itself whenever it wished. It transformed calculable, concrete threats [such as might have been provided by clear, manageable regulations] into incalculable, anonymous danger." (Sofsky, 216).

Punishment in the concentration camps was arbitrary. The most common forms of punishment included being flogged in public and being made to stand outside in the heat or in freezing weather for an indeterminate amount of time, sometimes as collective punishment during roll calls, otherwise as a special punishment in the "Stehcommandos" (standing commandos). The latter consisted of prisoners who had been singled out and were made to stand without moving in one particular spot all day long, at times for days without any food. There were no limits to the extremities of abuse and violence to which the inmates in the concentration camps were exposed or subjected. In a chapter entitled "Violent Excesses," Sofsky makes a distinction between "habitual" forms of violence, such as indiscriminate beatings, and more specific torments inflicted on inmates in special prisons inside the concentration camps. In the prison bunker and interrogation cells, Sofsky writes, "torture, torment, and murder were a trade, a handicraft" (226). The main point was not to extract a confession but to inflict pain, to experiment with tormenting, to test out the physical limits of the victims. The success of the perpetrators was "evidenced not by a confession, but by the pitch of the screams of the victim" (227).

Jean Améry describes the experience of torture as a violation of one's physical and with it one's "metaphysical" being or self. Before torture, there is the assumption that "my skin surface shields me against the external world" and that another person will respect that boundary (28): the experience of torture destroys the expectation and "certainty of help," one of the "fundamental experiences of human beings." Moreover, "only in torture does the transformation of the person into flesh become complete. Frail in the face of violence, yelling out in pain, awaiting no help, capable of no resistance, the tortured person is only a body, and nothing else beside that" (Améry, 33).

As a refusal of the "most basic human recognition," torture undoes the "empathic dyad" of self and resonating other. It is therefore a dissociative experience for the victim, whereby she or he loses the proper function of basic psychic structures concerning trust in the world and intersubjective communication. The denial of the victim's needs is so radical that it amounts to a violent denial of the victim's sense of self. In the words of psychoanalysts Dori Laub and Nanette Auerhahn, "The failure of empathy not only destroys hope of communicating with others in the external world and expectation of resonance with the internal other, it also diminishes the victims' ability to be in contact and in tune with themselves, to feel that they have a self" (1989, 379–80). For witnesses of torture the experience of dissociation, the trauma, arises out of the massive need to repress spontaneous reactions of protection and care. In many cases in the concentration camps it is difficult to make clear distinctions between witnesses and victims; the basic violation of human bonds is suffered by inmates in various positions, as the following example in Sofsky's rendition of the event makes clear:

> The word was lethal. Thus many deeds of excess were carried out less on orders than through orders.
>
> A complicated variant of such deeds has been documented for a shaft Kommando at Buchenwald. The construction supervisor ordered two Jews whose strength appeared to be waning to lie down in a pit. He then commanded a Pole to fill it in and bury the two men alive. When the Polish prisoner refused, the supervisor beat him with a shovel handle, ordering him to lie down next to the two Jews in the pit. The two Jews were then commanded to cover the disobedient Pole with earth. When all that could be seen was the Pole's head, the supervisor halted the operation and had the man dug out. The Jews had to lie down once more in the pit, and the Pole was told to cover them. This time he obeyed. In the meanwhile, the other prisoners continued their work — in order to play it safe and not call any attention to themselves. When the pit was filled in, the supervisor, laughing, stamped the ground solid. Five minutes later, he called over two prisoners to dig the Jews out again. One was already dead; the other showed weak signs of life. Both were transported to the crematorium. (239)

Here the line between victim, unwilling instrument of torture, and onlooker is blurred: the prisoners around have to pretend not to notice or not to care; the prisoners covering others with earth are forced to torment and kill. In the case of the onlookers and of the inmates forced to bury fellow inmates, empathic action and ethical standards are brutally thwarted. Even though much more than empathy is squelched in scenes of the kind of brutality described, it seems important to hold on here to such a delicate notion lest the brutality of the acts make us forget the further dimensions of the violence, lest we forget that the damage perpetrated in the concentration camps is not only physical. This analysis dwells on the perhaps more subtle psychological mechanisms at work in the poems with the assumption that these destructive forces as well the defenses against them operated in a complex simultaneity of levels rather than as discrete phenomena. Extreme violence seems necessarily to produce discourse in a disparity of registers. In torture, physical and psychic boundaries are transgressed and discourse about such violations reflects that. These poems move from the banal and the bathetic to the sentimental and the tragic and try to renegotiate boundaries where they have been brutally destroyed. Note above Sofsky's reference to the lethal power of the "word." It is possible to read these poems as words that seek to counter the destructive effects of abuse and torture witnessed or experienced directly.

Witnessing Torture

A survivor of torture testifies: "I didn't mind the pain so much. It was the cries next door I couldn't bear" (Basoglu, viii). One of the mechanisms used by some individuals in the concentration camps as a way of coping with the experience of torture was to compose poems about it. Usually the perspective is that of empathic witness, not that of direct victim. In *The Body in Pain* Elaine Scarry writes about physical pain in general, not only about pain inflicted intentionally on a person by another. There she claims that a "body in pain" often needs another person in order to produce language: "Because the person in pain is ordinarily so bereft of the resources of speech, it is not surprising that the language for pain should sometimes be brought into being by those who are not themselves in pain but who speak *on behalf* of those who are" (6).

At the same time Jean Améry suggests that there is a limit to the capacity of language to express pain, that to convey truthfully the experience of torture, one would have to become a torturer:

> The pain was what it was. Beyond that there is nothing to say. Qualities of feeling are as incomparable as they are indescribable. They mark the limit of the capacity of language to communicate. If someone wanted to impart his physical pain, he would be forced to inflict it and thereby become a torturer himself. (33)

People who write about physical pain and torture in the concentration camps usually describe other people's suffering. Rarely do these writers actually develop a "language for pain," detailed descriptions of the agony. More commonly, the experience of torment and humiliation is referred to — pointed to, not rendered in its particulars — and then set in a context that gives it some kind of meaning, a particular relation to (positive) life processes. In that sense these texts seek to undo the "shattering of language" (Scarry 5) that pain entails without delving into the details of the experience of physical torture. Laub and Podell suggest that to represent "the essence of trauma from the inside, exclusively from the perspective of the victim" might create "an empty space, a 'black hole' (as some children of survivors have called it), with no outer reference-point from which to view it and take refuge" (1002). This could lead to insurmountable disorientation and paralysis. These poems retain perspective, an "outer reference-point," via a variety of distancing mechanisms.

In "Die Lieder des Grauens" (Songs of Horror; Boris, third poem; printed in Elling 1990, 63), the title poem of Georg von Boris's unpublished manuscript written in the Flossenbürg concentration camp, the author enacts the classic figuration of the poet as "messenger" who passes on or writes down what he has heard or seen. The poet-speaker recounts and interprets the experiences and words of others. These "others" are first and primarily those who have been tortured and are dying, whereby the causal relation between the torture and the dying is not made explicit: were these people already "dying" (as Muselmänner) when they were tortured, or are they now "the dying" because they have been tortured previously? Implied here is an intimate connection between torture and death. Améry writes of torture: "[the torturer] is on me and thereby destroys me" (28).

The first sentence in Boris's poem creates the impression that the "tortured" actually have told their suffering to the narrator. Only later in the poem will it become clear that the structure of communication is not as immediate as that, that "erzählen" (recount) in this section, as well as "sagen" (tell), "melden" (report), and also "wimmern" (whimper) later on, are closer to the suggestive "lassen ahnen" (let [someone] assume or guess) of the last sentence than to an ordinary verbal exchange; that is, they require an act of interpretative intervention on the part of the poet-speaker.

> Was in den Stunden,
> In denen sie gefoltert und gequält,
> Geschlagen und geschunden,
> Mir die Sterbenden erzählt,
> Bann ich im Erleben des Beschauens,
> In die Lieder meines Grauens.

> [What in the hours
> In which they were tortured and pained,
> Beaten and flayed,
> The dying have told me,
> I capture in the experience of observation,
> In the songs of my horror.]

The first word in the fifth line, "bannen," can mean to *banish* or to *exorcize* as well as to *captivate*, as in *cast a spell* and to *record* (as "ein Geschehen auf

Zelluloid *bannen*" [to *capture* an event on celluloid]). "Bannen" is the verb around which the first sentence, the length of the stanza, pivots. It describes the activity of the poet-speaker who witnesses torture and captures what he witnesses in the texts he composes. In fact, the verb instantiates the speaker as poet. The content of the message received by the speaker seems forcefully to demand an action, a creative response, both to banish and exorcize the message and to make a record of it, to pass it on.

Central here is the "experience of observation" (Erleben des Beschauens), passive receptivity as the moment of transition from "them," the "dying" to the songs. This is a temporary halt in the line of communication from the individuals suffering torture to the poet-speaker and on to the readers of the poem. This pause provides the space for the speaker's intervention. "Beschauen" (observation) evokes "Beschauer" (viewer) as well as "beschaulich" (tranquil, contemplative). Intercalated here to disrupt the sentence, the phrase "im Erleben des Beschauens" forms a grammatical and semantic caesura that opens up a gap between the experience of torture and its poetic rendition. The speaker's experience is not of the pain itself, but of witnessing, of observing someone else in pain. The tempo of the sentence reflects the transition from witnessing the torture to thinking or writing about it, a transition that parallels the shift from acoustic apprehension, what has been told to the speaker, to the visually coded witnessing of "Beschauen," the moment of internal observation. The fast-paced listing of past participles ("gefoltert," "gequält," "geschlagen," "geschunden," "erzählt") comes to a halt and a slower, weightier rhythm takes its place: "Erleben" and "Beschauen" are nominalizations. The guttural alliteration ("ge-") of the list of verbs to refer to the torture as well as the accent on the second syllable in all those past participles resembles the beatings they refer to; the repeated use of the sibilant genitive to connect nouns in the second part of the sentence reinforces the sense of stasis in that rhyming couplet: "Erleben des Beschauens," "Lieder meines Grauens."

The poem moves on then to other registers. Old age and infancy function as the framework for the torment and the dying portrayed in the first sentence. The experience of torture is not isolated as a singular, outrageous event but rather listed along with situations from everyday life, situations from beyond the confines of the camps. This provides a larger perspective within which to make sense of the suffering:

> Was mir Greise sagen,
> Die in ihren alten Tagen,
> nach dem Sensemann nicht fragen.
> Was in hellen Morgenschimmern,
> Nackte Kinder wimmern,
> Die sich um Gevatter Hein nicht kümmern.

[What old people tell me,
Who in their old days
Do not ask for the Grim Reaper.
What in the bright morning glare
Naked children whimper,
Who are not concerned with Father Death.]

The progression from "dying [people]" in the first stanza to "old people" and then "children" in the second echoes a traditional and philosophical conception of the natural cycle of life and death — a progression from birth to old age and then the grave. The cycle here is in reverse order: as a consequence of the experience of torture, death, not life, is in the foreground, comes first. New life is subsumed under questions about dying. The two situations in this stanza present a deceptive parallel. In both of them, "death" is referred to mythologically, as a fairy-tale character, the German equivalents of "the Grim Reaper," the "Angel of Death." In both cases as well "Death" appears through negation: old people who do not ask about it, naked children who are not concerned with it. Death, however, is generally closer or more obviously connected to old age than to children. The children's helplessness and patent mortality, symbolized by their nakedness, like old age, is a figure for human vulnerability. Torture exposes that vulnerability, undermines any properly adult attributes of independence, self-sufficiency, control over one's body and one's destiny.

The poem shifts from dying after torture to folkloristic allusions to death within a rhyming pattern reminiscent of doggerel ("-schimmern," "wimmern," "kümmern"). The euphemistic evocation of legends, of a pristine era of sentimental rhyme seems at odds with the reference to torture. That incongruity illustrates the disjunctive, dissociative elements inherent in the experience of torture. The narrative seeks to link the experience of torture to everyday life processes and resorts for this purpose to sentimental figures that are meant to contain such disparate elements.

From the sentimental the poem moves to elegiac language about heroes and graves to end in two rhyming couplets, the second of these essentially repeating the rhyming couplet at the end of the first stanza:

Was die Helden melden
Und die Gräber lassen ahnen,
All das Mahnen des Beschauens,
Faß ich in die Lieder meines Grauens.

[What the heroes report
And the graves let us guess,
All the warnings of observation,
I collect in the songs of my horror.]

Two opposing impulses come through in the poem. On the one hand there are notions of sublimation and communication: the poet-speaker "captures" what he hears in songs, he connects as well the experiences of victims of torture with those of common people and heroes — all in a carefully constructed rhyming pattern. This binds the poem to positive life forces and to the more "normal" rhythms of existence. On the other hand, being a witness to torture makes the poet-speaker aware of the overpowering presence of death, the isolation of torture. The different elements, his alarming observations, inspire him now to compose warning songs, songs of horror, even if the poem maintains a semblance of "normality" by sticking to the form of a rhyming song.

In the process of witnessing, the suffering is shared, communicated. There is a semantic shift from the title to the repetition of the same words in lines 6 and 16: the expression "Die Lieder des Grauens" (songs of horror) becomes through observing and reporting ("Bann ich . . ." "Faß ich . . .") "die Lieder meines Grauens" (songs of my horror). In the course of telling of the suffering, the horror that was external, something the poet-narrator observed, has become part of his consciousness. He does not compose "his" songs of horror — which, strictly speaking, would be more logical, since these are meant to be his depictions of the torment suffered by those around him —but, in an act of empathic identification, he writes the "songs of *my* horror" and thus comes to own the horror.

As discussed above, to observe torture is in itself traumatic. It is as if through contamination, situations such as babies crying in the morning, situations from "normal" life as opposed to the camp experience — a distinction that I am holding on to here, one that the poem, perhaps unwittingly, destabilizes — have become a source of "horror." "Old people," "naked children," and "heroes," placed between "the dying" who have been tortured, on the one side, and "graves" on the other, all become associated with death and suffering. Indeed the process of observation itself has become tainted as experience — "Im Erleben des Beschauens" (in the experience of observation) — turns into warning — "All das Mahnen des Beschauens" (All the warnings of observation). Almost regardless of its object, observation here translates into a warning system, into omens about the brittleness of human existence, about mortality and death.

In this poem, as in most of Georg von Boris's poetry, the perpetrators, the torturers, are neither named nor even indirectly referred to through pronouns. In "Die Lieder des Grauens," the torture is rendered exclusively via verbs in the passive voice — the agent is never designated. Interestingly, the old-fashioned or poetically licensed omission of the marker for the passive in the first sentence (here it would be "geschunden *wurden*"), with its parallel in the missing auxiliary for the active present perfect in the next line ("erzählt *haben*"), serves as a reminder or a hint of the act of elision of the agent in these lines. Bruno Bettelheim has argued that to direct anger "where it belonged: against the SS or prominent prisoners" was "tantamount to suicide" for camp inmates (216). Anger directed at the perpetrators in the poems would be meant to remain secret and as such would not necessarily be tantamount to suicide — although getting caught writing poems would likely entail punishment and possibly death. By leaving the agents of torture out of the story this poem can move from the experience of torture to other experiences of vulnerability and mortality. The text shields itself from an aspect of the traumatic reality (the torturer's lack of empathy) while at the same time it speaks about other aspects of that traumatic experience (the suffering of the victims). Again, by leaving the perpetrators unnamed, the poem refuses perhaps to acknowledge directly the power of the torturers over the victims.

In another poem, "Das Lied der unschuldigen Toten" (Song of the Innocent Dead Men; Boris, second poem; printed in Elling 1990, 65), Boris does make direct reference to the perpetrators. There he calls them "hämische Piraten" (malicious pirates). The context is a depiction of bonding between inmates against a common enemy: "Der Fremde gab dem Fremden Brot, / . . . Der Fremde schwur dem Fremden Treu, / Sie wurden Kameraden" (Stranger gave bread to stranger, / . . . Stranger swore loyalty to stranger, / They became comrades). This poem reorganizes power relations in the concentration camps and the structure of the conflict: instead of an SS-system with the power of life and death over exhausted and malnourished inmates, "malicious pirates"; not camp inmates at the mercy of an unforeseeable system of destruction but comrades fighting a noble battle against lawless riffraff. In other words the poem resorts to a romanticized description of the harsh reality of camp existence, a description in which honor and comradeship, with the help of God, are the lived values for the narrator and his allies, and the official, state-police force is described as seditious marauders. Of course one could agree with the poem about the nobility of spirit of resistors who were taken to concentration camps because of their active opposition against the regime, and one might value as well the strength and resourcefulness of inmates to hold on to life in the Nazi camps. But to depict the Nazi administration of the camps as "pirates," with the implication of rowdy types operating independently and at random, is grossly to understate the power of those forces, particularly over inmates imprisoned in the camps. From an ethical point of view, one might indeed refer to the SS as "pirates"; in the Third Reich, particularly for inmates of the camps, they were juridically and effectively in a position of unchallengeable authority. Through an "imaginative act" the poem minimizes the power of the SS. By returning power to the ideals of the victims the poem extracts a positive connotation from the experience of internment, creating an imaginary position of strength through unity for the inmates.

In the poem "Erinnerung" discussed above, Kupfer-Koberwitz never names the perpetrators. There the narrator refers to the abusers once only

through the indefinite German pronoun "man" (one or they — this pronoun, as stated above, in effect elides the agent while it retains the structure
of an active sentence) and otherwise actively avoids direct reference to the
perpetrators. The torturers enter the poem exclusively through their own
words and actions — they exist only in the form of verbal and emotional
abuse and in quotes. Their presence is limited to their own insulting language and they remain a "foreign" body, an intrusive external presence. The
perfidy of the torturers is revealed in their own speech rather than through a
narrative account of the abuse:

> "Du heulst wohl, weil deine Hure verreckt? —
> Wirklich, die Judensau heult!" —
>
> ["You cry because your whore kicked the bucket? —
> Really, the Jewish sow is crying!" —]

The *speaker's* observation of the old man, the victim, and the *speaker's* feelings for the man constitute the rest of the poem. The effect of the perpetrators is portrayed, but again the torturers are not the focus of the poem.

Kupfer-Koberwitz approaches the experience of torture from a model of
human dignity. The focus of the poem is the violation of such dignity and
the effects of such violation on the speaker: "It pierced my soul." By reporting on the torture in a lyric form, Boris anchors himself in the position of the
poet who observes and recounts experience in poetic language. Without being directly confrontational, both poets handle the perpetrators from a distance and evince a tacit disdain toward them. This attitude, specially when
contrasted to more confrontational approaches in other poems, reveals itself
as a "humanist" and possibly "well-bred" reaction to the abusers. The narrators put themselves in a position of moral superiority that almost excludes
the perpetrators from their field of vision, or, at least, from their discursive
field. In the following poems the narrators also see themselves as ethically
superior to the perpetrators, but a defiant and embattled anger directed at
the abusers, rather than superior disdain, is the dominant discursive affect in
the response to the perpetrators.

Defiance

Born in Cologne in 1897, the German actor, left-wing cabarettist, radio
speaker, and satirical poet Karl Schnog was persecuted by the Nazis as a
Communist and a Jew. He had left Germany for Switzerland in May of
1933. In 1936 the Nazis rescinded his citizenship. After the Germans in-
vaded Luxembourg, the Gestapo imprisoned Schnog there in 1940 and put
him through a number of prisons. He was then interned subsequently in the
concentration camps Dachau and Sachsenhausen, and from 1941 on in

Buchenwald, where he experienced liberation by the U.S. Army. After the war he worked as author, satirist, and editor for East Berlin Radio (Berliner Rundfunk) and for the satirical magazine "Ulenspiegel." He died in 1964 in East Berlin. (For more biographical information on Schnog, see Habel, 339; Kirsten and Kirsten, 317–18.) In 1943 at Buchenwald Schnog wrote a number of poems, among them two that describe abuse suffered by inmates: "Jedem das Seine" (To Each His Own) and "Der Häftling" (The Inmate). Unlike Kupfer-Koberwitz, Schnog confronts the perpetrators aggressively and "at their level," as it were, understanding them politically as enemies rather than as unwelcome impingements on his life.

Schnog clearly had seen the National Socialists as his enemies from the beginnings of the Nazi movement and more urgently so from the moment the Nazis came to power early in 1933. As early as 1934, in a collection of what he called "Kampfgedichte" (Battle Poems), mostly satirical, didactic, and admonitory poems written in exile and published in Luxembourg under the feistily provocative title *Kinnhaken* (Punch to the Chin), Schnog ridiculed the Nazi leadership by perverting Nazi neologisms with terms such as "Volksverführer" (seducer of the people), in a pun on "Volk" (people) and "Führer" (leader), and as "Kannibalen" (cannibals; Schnog 1934, 15), and their political program through the label: "Spezial-Verbrechertum, bewußt und arisch" (special criminality, proud and Aryan). To reports of the death of the oppositional author Erich Mühsam and of the abuses suffered by the writer and editor Karl von Ossietzky in German prisons (on Mühsam and Ossietzky, see Benz and Pehle, 1994), Schnog responded with threats and a call for justice in a poem entitled "Gelöbnis" (Vow; Schnog 1934, 36):[2]

> Keinen Seufzer werden wir vergessen,
> Keinen Striemen, den ins Fleisch ihr hiebt;
> Jede Blutspur wird Euch nachgemessen,
> Die ihr jetzt noch sauft und schreit und liebt.
>
> Einmal naht das Ende aller Qualen,
> Eher als ihr euch im Blutrausch denkt,
> Dann, ihr Mörder, müßt ihr voll bezahlen,
> Und es wird euch nicht ein Gran geschenkt.
>
> [We won't forget a single moan,
> Not a single welt that you mark on the flesh;
> Every trace of blood will be put on your bill,
> You, who now still booze and scream and love.
>
> Once the end of all torture will be near,
> Sooner than you think in your blood frenzy,
> Then, you murderers, you will have to pay in full,
> And not even an ounce will be forgiven.]

Anger and a desire for revenge are the main affects in this poem that calls the Nazis "murderers" and warns that their actions will create hundreds of "wild avengers."

Throughout this pre-interment collection of poems the tone is sardonic, embattled. The Nazis are constantly objects of ridicule. Schnog imagines the German public on his side. So too, for example, in his critique of the "Gleichschaltung" of the German press in his poem "Deutsche Freie Presse" (German Free Press), in which he wittily recasts Nazi diction (1934, 11):

> Der kleine Goebbels mit der großen Fresse,
> Einstmals entsprungen der Kloaken-Presse,
> Schroff kommandiert.
> Die deutsche Presse weit die Arme breitet
> Und wonneschauernd, gerne schriftgeleitet,
> Stramm exerziert.

> Sie kochen stets das gleiche Heldensüppchen.
> Das widerstrebt, so scheints, sogar dem Jüppchen,
> Es provoziert
> Und sagt, es wünsche Wahrheit, Buntheit, Einfall . . .
> Wer auf den Leim geht, büßt sofort den Reinfall
> Streng «konzentriert».

> Von Klügern wird auf der Terrotationsmaschine,
> — Daß man dem Aufbau und dem Umbruch diene —
> Nazisch geschmiert.
> So sieht man Führer, seitengroß, im Dutzend.
> Und Adolf: schreibend, redend, Nase putzend
> SA. marschiert . . .

> Des deutschen Schrifttums gründlicher Verweser
> Sorgt, daß von Etsch bis Belt die Zeitungsleser
> Zwangsabonniert. —
> Ob braver Landmann oder stummer Städter,
> Das deutsche Volk benutzt die Zeitungsblätter
> Nur — perforiert!

> [The little Goebbels with his big snout,
> Came once from the sewer-press,
> And commands harshly.
> The German press opens her arms wide
> And thrilling with delight, gladly pre-scripted
> Exercises in earnest.

> They always cook the same little heroes' soup.
> That annoys, it seems, even little Joey,

He provokes
And says that he wants the truth, color, inspiration . . .
Whoever falls for it, immediately pays for it
Rigorously «concentrated».

Clever heads keep the terrotation machine
— In order to serve the organization and the revolution —
Well-nazified.
Thus one sees Führers, big as the page, by the dozen.
And Adolf: writing, speaking, blowing his nose.
SA. marches by . . .

The thorough guardians of German letters
Make sure that from the Etsch to the Belt the newspaper readers
Subscribe by force. —
Whether upright country lad or silent city-dweller,
The German Volk uses the newspaper pages
Only — perforated.]

In this caustic depiction of the National Socialist leadership and the compliant German press in the Third Reich, Schnog refers to those leaders by their name, mostly in satirical forms. As we have seen, such direct naming of the perpetrators is unusual in poems written in internment. This poem speaks of the "Führer" ingloriously by his first name, countering in so doing the deifying move to give ritual power to his last name as in the alliterative salute "Heil Hitler!" The depiction of a patently "unheroic" action of Hitler's, blowing his nose, exposes the ridiculousness of such idolization. Schnog reduces as well the first name of the Minister of Propaganda, Joseph Goebbels, to a ridiculous diminutive, "Jüppchen." This makes it possible in the poem to refer to the minister by the neuter pronoun and thus to make Goebbels into an object, or, at best, into a child ("*das* Kind" [the child, a neuter noun in German]). The nickname and the use of the pronoun "es" (it) literally belittle him, make him smaller, and neuter him, castrate him. Schnog further satirizes the Nazis by parodying their language and phrases. For instance, the phrase "SA. marschiert . . ." (SA. marches by . . .) quotes the unofficial Nazi hymn, the Horst Wessel Lied: "S.A. marschiert mit ruhig, festem Schritt" (The S.A. marches with silent, solid step), but here the S.A. marches as Adolf blows his nose. Schnog's line, missing, as it does, the dot between the S and the A, is additionally a pun on the French phrase: "ça marche" (it functions), alluding to the manner in which the German press cooperates in its own Gleichschaltung. "Daß von Etsch bis Belt die Zeitungsleser, / Zwangsabonniert" (that from the Etsch to the Belt the newspaper readers / are forced to subscribe) parodies another song, one that the Nazis reinterpreted for their own purposes: *Das Lied der Deutschen* or *Deutschlandlied.* The river Etsch in

South Tyrol and the strait (Little) Belt in the Baltic Sea are two of the four bodies of water named in the song to delineate the boundaries of a then (1841) non-existent German nation. The Nazis used parts of the hymn to glorify their geopolitical aims. Schnog here uses the geographic markers to mark the reach of dictatorial control: "subscribed by force."

In "Jedem das Seine" (To Each His Own; Schnog 1947, 54),[3] written at Buchenwald in 1943, Schnog retains aspects of his pre-concentrationary rhetoric. His tone is still defiant; he addresses the perpetrators directly and disrespectfully, calls them torturers (Henker), and threatens them with revenge. His anger is directed at the SS and finds expression in the poem that, obviously, must be kept hidden from the camp guards. There is a certain gallows humor or, at least, an attention to humor and irony, for example in the word "Sprüchlein" (little proverb) to refer to the perverse motto the Nazis had inscribed on the main gate to Buchenwald: "To each his own." The depictions of the situations of the inmate (in the singular) and of the torturers (in the plural) are matter-of-fact. The poem imparts information, teaches the audience about the conditions in the concentration camps. Note, for example, that even as the speaker announces that "we," the inmates, already know what will befall "us" inside the camps, he goes on to enumerate the details of what "happens" to the prisoners and, differently, to the SS officers. In the last stanza the poem offers a solution to the inmate's suffering: power-relations will be reversed and the prisoners will have their revenge.

> Die Herren haben wirklich Humor
> In diesen bitteren Zeiten:
> "JEDEM DAS SEINE" steht höhnisch am Tor,
> Durch das die Häftlinge schreiten.
>
> So leuchtet, erhaben und arrogant,
> Was sie an das Höllentor schmieden.
> Uns ist auch ohne das Sprüchlein bekannt,
> Was jedem im Lager beschieden:
>
> Dem Häftling — das Stehen in Sonne und Sturm,
> Erfrieren und klatschende Güsse.
> Dazu vom todesdrohenden Turm
> Das ernste Versprechen der Schüsse.
>
> Den Henkern — die Ehre, der schmackhafte Schmaus,
> Das Gleiten auf federnden Felgen;
> Die Ruhe und das behagliche Haus,
> Die Wollust, die Macht und das Schwelgen.
>
> Dem Häftling — der Hunger, die Angst und die Last,
> Die Marter, die viehischen Witze;

Das Essen, das Baden, das Schlafen in Hast
Und schließlich die mordende Spritze.

Ihr Herren, die ihr heute noch grient,
Glaubt mir, was ich schwörend beteure:
Einst holt sich der Häftling, was er verdient.
Und Ihr? Ihr bekommt dann das Eure!

[Their lordships have a good sense of humor
In these bitter times:
"TO EACH HIS OWN" stands scornfully on the gate,
Through which the inmates march in.

Sublime and arrogant thus shines
What they welded onto the gate to hell,
We know even without the little saying
What everyone is fated to in the camp:

To the inmate — standing in sun and storm,
Freezing and roaring downpours.
On top of that from the mortally menacing tower
The earnest promise of bullets.

To the torturers — honor, a tasty banquet,
Gliding on well-oiled wheels;
Rest and a comfortable home,
Pleasure, power, and feasting.

To the inmate — hunger, fear, and the burden,
Torture, bestial jokes;
Eating, bathing, and sleeping in haste
And finally the murderous injection.

You lordships, who still grin today,
Believe me, what I hereby swear:
One day the inmate will claim what he deserves.
And you? You will then get your share!]

In "Der Häftling" (The Inmate; Schnog 1947, 55),[4] another poem about
torture written by Schnog in Buchenwald in 1943, the victim is a fellow
prisoner and, by implication, a political ally. The perspective of the narration
is third-person omniscience. More precisely, the speaker here is in a position
to interpret the expressions, body language, and actions of the perpetrators,
but empathetically enters only the psyche of the victim of torture. The victim, an "exemplary" inmate, any and every inmate, as the title with the definite article "Der" (the) implies, is a heroic figure, and as such he functions as

an emblem, in much the same way an "exemplary" figure might function in political inspirational literature. The poem reads:

> Sie standen um ihn, roh und wutbesessen,
> Und drohten ihm mit Knüppel, Kugel, Beil.
> Sie wollten ihn mit Schreck und Schlag erpressen,
> Und ihre Henkeraugen glänzten geil.
>
> Er sah nur stumm in ihre Mörderfressen
> Und schwieg und litt. Und dachte sich sein Teil.
> Sie schlugen zu in blutigen Exzessen
> Und gingen lachend fort und brüllten "Heil!"
>
> Er lag und überlegte unterdessen:
> Wie schweig ich nur noch eine kurze Weil'.
> Hat nie den Auftrag, nie das Ziel vergessen.
> Der Körper wund, der Wille stark und steil!
>
> [They stood around him, brutal and furious,
> And threatened him with cudgel, bullet, noose.
> They wanted to blackmail him with fear and blows,
> And their torturers' eyes glowed with lust.
>
> Without a word he watched their murderer-snouts
> And was silent and suffered. And thought his own thoughts.
> They beat him up in bloody excess
> And went away laughing and roaring "Heil!"
>
> He lay and thought in the meantime;
> How will I keep quiet for another while.
> He never forgot the duty nor the goal.
> His body in pain, his will strong and tall!]

This is a caricature-like description, particularly of the torturers. The distinction that the poem creates between the victim and the perpetrators hinges on a notion of interiority. The figure that we might call the victim but that the poem, in the title, calls "the inmate" quietly shows political integrity and personal composure while the perpetrators' cruelty is loud and rambunctious. The flatness, lack of interiority, and sadistic superficiality — or more specifically, surface-orientation — of the torturers is put in relief by the marked contrast between "their torturers' eyes" that have a cruel glow to them but are never shown to be capable of vision and the prisoner's eyesight that is connected to interior, psychic processes: "saw," "was silent," "thought his own thoughts." This contrast is further supported by the fact that the perpetrators are in the plural: they seem to lack individual identity, all act uniformly. The inmate is the center "around" whom the perpetrators have gathered. The inmate is both exemplary and individual: he has a personal conscience and an inner world. This constellation reverses the power structure in the camps, where, in the language of the SS, inmates were counted in terms of indifferent, de-individuated objects or pieces or as "human material," and where a single SS officer wielded the power of life and death over a large number of inmates.

Toward the end the poem has recourse to a topos in the religious poetry from the concentration camps and in other traditions of narratives of suffering: the separation of a strong, invincible spirit or will from a fragile, weak, defenseless, or wounded body. This separation of spheres contradicts reports by survivors about the experience of torture in which the self becomes a "body in pain," as in Améry's account. Here one may need to take into consideration that there were in fact various levels of personal and political resistance to torture, to confessing, to betraying one's fellow inmates and ideals. Furthermore, widely different methods of torture were applied with a variety of purposes. At the same time, it is important to keep in mind that with this poem we are dealing with a representation of torture by an inmate in the concentrationary universe. This inmate was himself a potential victim of torture, an empathic witness, and a Communist author, committed to a battle against the Nazis, and to a vision of victory over Nazism. For witnesses of torture in the camps, a resolution to the pain seems urgently necessary. The inmates may need narrative resolution in order to avoid succumbing to a defeatist attitude that could easily lead to letting go of the will to live, reducing inmates to the condition of Muselmänner.

In "Jedem das Seine" the speaker keeps the humiliation at a distance from himself by referring to "the" (abstract, third-person) inmate who is subjected to abuse. The speaker also ascribes power to himself, even if this manifests only in a rhetorical (perlocutionary) performance, a promise prefaced by a command (in the imperative) that is both a plea and a warning in the only section from "Jedem das Seine" in the first-person singular: "Glaubt mir, was ich schwörend beteure" (Believe me, what I hereby swear — literally: "believe me, what I avow by swearing"). This poem could not have been presented to the SS without putting the life of the author at risk. The rhetorical intensification and involution of the speaker's own speech act may point to a muted sense of the powerlessness of such speech. The threatened revenge will come from the generic inmate:

> Einst holt sich der Häftling, was er verdient.
> Und Ihr? Ihr bekommt dann das Eure!
>
> [One day the inmate will claim what he deserves.
> And you? You will then get your share!]

In "Der Häftling" the players and the action also remain external to the speaker and are referred to in the third person.

In "Jedem das Seine" the narrative voice is outspokenly defiant, even threatening. In "Der Häftling" the inmate's noble resistance implies defiance. In a short poem that Schnog wrote almost two years later, immediately after the liberation but while still on the grounds of Buchenwald, the poet-speaker admits to the horrors he himself has experienced. In "Nackte Aussage" (Naked Testimony; Schnog 1947, 62)[5] the central point is no longer a resistance of the spirit or the political will; distancing through a third-person narration no longer takes place. Here, "healing" the trauma is the focus. That process appears contingent on the act of telling: "Erst wenn ich sage, was ich sah . . ." (Only after I tell what I saw . . .). There is simplicity and humility in this short poem, and a belief in the purpose of speaking of the suffering:

> Ich habe so tief im Elend gesteckt,
> Ich schien verloren, verkommen, verdreckt.
> Gejagt ward ich und gepeinigt.
> Erst, wenn ich sage, was ich sah,
> Erst, wenn ich schreibe, was geschah,
> Bin ich vom Schmutz gereinigt.

> [I was so deep in misery,
> I seemed lost, debased, soiled.
> Persecuted was I, and tortured.
> Only after I say what I saw,
> Only after I write what happened,
> Will I be cleansed of the dirt.]

The word "Schmutz" (dirt) at the end of the single stanza is both the "dirt" of the perpetrators, their cruelties and the "dirt" of the humiliations, the abasement the speaker has undergone in the inhuman circumstances: "Ich schien . . . verdreckt" (I seemed . . . soiled). Note here the prominence of the first-person-singular pronouns: seven in six lines, of those two at the beginning of lines, including the first word of the poem. Post-liberation hindsight seems to allow for a more direct and personal relation to the degradation and pain, though there is still a cautious distance here: "I *seemed*" — instead of *was*— "soiled." Améry, with further hindsight, writes "the other person . . . destroys me" (28). Nonetheless, in this later poem by Schnog the perpetrators have become unimportant. What matters now is to overcome the contaminating effects of the brutality on the self. The function of poetry and of the act of composing has shifted. Poems may still serve as containers for the suffering, but in the case of the last poem, resistance and survival are no longer at stake. The relation to the trauma thus changes.

Here the argument is not that there are clear-cut or essential distinctions between poems composed during internment and those written after the war. Liberation does not necessarily mark a complete psychological turnabout. On the contrary, many of these poems testify to the variety of responses to the experiences, even in the concentration camps, and their concomitant changing attitudes: defiant, defeated, angry, distant, threatening, resigned, full of regret during and after traumatization, during and after internment. The poems do suggest that prewar political predispositions, such as Schnog's political and literary background, as well as individual psychological and social differences, have an important effect on the language and structures used for coming to terms with the experience. At the same time it seems important to reflect on the changes that can be observed, for example, with the operation of hindsight and the changed conditions of life for the author as marked by liberation and the relative safety implied thereby.

As was discussed above, the reception of poetry from the concentration camps also reveals changing attitudes toward the history of Nazi persecution. Defiant poems such as "Jedem das Seine" were published, for example, in Schneider's 1973 East German compilation of works from the camps. We saw in the introduction that this East German selection was intended to illustrate the heroic resistance of inmates in the battle against Fascism. The more defeated poem "Nackte Aussage" is absent in that collection but occupies a very prominent place in the two main anthologies of camp poetry published in the early 1990s. *Draußen steht eine bange Nacht* reprints "Nackte Aussage" as the only poem on its back cover as well as on page 62 and omits poems such as "Jedem das Seine" (Lau and Pampuch). Again, as was discussed in the introduction, the anthologies published in the 1990s in unified Germany are more comfortable with — one might say, more invested in — a concept of the victims of, rather than combatants against, the Third Reich. Their focus is on the suffering of the victims and on the value of telling of the suffering, the topics addressed by "Nackte Aussage."

The Experience of Torture, the Need for Revenge

Alfred Kittner's "Fünfundzwanzig" (Twenty-Five; 1988, 44–45) is one of the rare poems written in internment that describe torture experienced by the poem's speaker from a first-person perspective. Written in November 1942 in a death camp on the river Bug known as "der Steinbruch" (stone quarry) in German or "Cariera de Piatră" in Romanian, one of the many smaller camps in Transnistria (see Sternberg), this is an unusual poem on many counts. Possibly because it lacks the pathos of other poems by Kittner such as "Unterwegs" (On the Road), this poem is not included in the anthologies of camp poetry.

> Schlag zu! Schlag zu! Schon schwinden die Gedanken!
> Willkommen, Ohnmacht! noch die letzten zehn.
> Bald ists vorbei. Des Lebens Bilder schwanken,
> Schauer des Schweigens fühl ich um mich wehn.

Die Zähne beißen täglich wir zusammen,
An eure Schläge habt ihr uns gewöhnt.
Wir tragens leichter, wenn wir still den Namen
Des Schurken fluchen, der uns so verhöhnt.

Daß du mich schlägst, und ich die Schläge dulde,
Es scheint dem Geiste dieser Zeit gemäß,
Und was ich, Deutschland, dir bis heute schulde,
Dein schlimmster Bube bleut mirs aufs Gesäß.

Um meine Schenkel läßt er seinen Riemen
Elastisch tanzen und er haut mit Wucht
Mir auf die nackte Haut ein Netz von Striemen,
Gelassen, wie man eine Rechnung bucht.

Ihr könnt mich, Schweinehunde, massakrieren,
Rutsch ich gebunden jetzt auch auf dem Bauch,
Ich werd euch diese Rechnung präsentieren
Zur rechten Zeit, und eurem Führer auch!

[Strike on! Strike on! My thoughts already vanish!
Welcome, blackout! Just the last ten.
Soon it will be over. The pictures of life wobble,
I feel showers of silence go around me.

Every day we grit our teeth,
You have got us used to your beatings.
We bear it more lightly when we silently curse
The name of the rogue who thus derides us.

It seems to accord with the spirit of the times,
That you beat me and I endure the beatings,
And what I owe you, Germany, until today,
Your worst villain thrashes on my behind.

Elastically he lets his whip dance
Around my thighs and with force he strikes
On my naked skin a web of welts,
Calmly, like one calculating a bill.

You pigs can massacre me,
As now I, tied up, slide on my belly,
I will present this bill to you
At the right time, and to your Führer too!]

The title of the poem, "Twenty-Five," refers to the twenty-five lashings an inmate would be given as a punishment. In Sternberg's account of the Transnistrian camps, this was the usual punishment if a guard found a louse on an inmate, or claimed he had. The whippings would be performed in the open: the inmate's pants would be taken down and all other inmates were forced to watch (Sternberg, 2:76). The poem opens with a command, a verb in the imperative. This verbal feat is an imaginative act of taking control over the humiliating situation. The victim tells the perpetrator what to do, puts himself in the position of initiator of the "exchange." In a marked reversal of roles, the inmate gives orders; the guard "obeys."

The speaker here is unusually direct in confronting the perpetrators. He addresses the camp guards in particular and the "Germans" in general with invective — "Schweinehunde" (pigs, literally pig-dogs), "Schurke" (rogue, scoundrel), "schlimmster Bube" (worst villain). Inmates were forced to use the polite form when addressing SS and other camp guards, even though the latter would not normally use the polite form to talk to an inmate. Poems like Schnog's and Kittner's are fictions in which the inmate gets a chance to use the informal form of address to speak to the perpetrators, again reconfiguring in poetry the power relations in the concentration camps. Kittner switches in his address here between the singular and plural pronouns, but the first-person speaker is clearly central here. The torturers are spoken to in the plural, sometimes in the second-person singular as well as in the third person, but the positions are clearly delineated here: "That you beat me and I endure the beatings."

As the poem would have it, the physical abuse has lost some of its power because it has become routine: "täglich" (every day): "An eure Schläge habt ihr uns gewöhnt" (You have got us used to your beatings). The speaker now knows what to expect, "remembers" that the loss of consciousness will bring relief, "Willkommen, Ohnmacht!" (Welcome, blackout!), and that the beating will eventually end: "noch die letzten zehn" (just the last ten [lashings]).

The poem reflects on the uses of language. To insult the perpetrators, however quietly, the poem claims, makes the abuse more bearable; psychologically, it makes the wounds less serious: "Wir tragen es leichter, wenn wir still den Namen / Des Schurken fluchen, der uns so verhöhnt" (We bear it more lightly when we silently curse / The name of the scoundrel who thus derides us).

Taking imaginary control over the situation, insulting the abusers, and a fantasy of revenge: these imaginative acts make it easier for the speaker to withstand the ignominy. A strong connection to a temporal dimension sustains the anger and the hope: "Bald ists vorbei" (soon it will be over). The poem is essentially concerned with turning the tables on the abusers. What happens now is only temporary; it corresponds to the "spirit of the times" and as such will pass by: "Ihr könnt mich, Schweinehunde, massakrieren, /

Rutsch ich gebunden *jetzt* auf dem Bauch" (You pigs can massacre me, / As *now* I, tied up, slide on my belly). What the inmate-speaker is made to "pay" to Germany now, the "Rechnung" (bill) being counted out on his body at this wrongful time, will be presented to the Germans and their Führer, "Zur rechten Zeit" (at the right time).

Kittner's poem contains an imaginative act of justice that will come "at the right time." In the face of the current state of powerlessness, the poem is a fantasy that takes stock of the situation and promises to subvert it. The "aestheticized," alliterative and rhyming account of the whipping constitutes at the same time a *prise de parole* that reveals the inmate's power to distance himself from the situation and speak of it in controlled verses. The "I" confronts the suffering directly but not without mediation. The form of the poem seems to provide the structure to defy the brutal force of the perpetrators, whose power is depicted as limited, contingent. This contrasts for example with testimonies that speak of the incredulousness of some survivors at the time of liberation: how could the all-powerful Germans have been defeated?

Narratives about abuse and torture seem to require an evident structure that allows the narrator to stand at some distance from the pain, a structure that prevents the pain from becoming an all-encompassing or overwhelming element or the sole frame of reference. Poetry, with its relatively stringent strictures, seems particularly suited to provide such structure. The form and language of these poems also tell us of individual differences in reactions and attitudes to the experiences of abuse in the concentration camps. Thus the poems by Kupfer-Koberwitz and Boris center on acts of witnessing on the part of their respective poet-speakers. The roles of poet-speaker and that of witness are joined in the empathic response to the abuse suffered by others. Ultimately their poems hold on to the humanity of the victims and witnesses. The poems of Schnog and Kittner defend from the abuse through an attack on the abusers and thus retain an imaginary sense of power for the victims and for the speakers aligned with them. Victimhood there is represented as a temporary aberration. Schnog's poems contrast a noble inmate to brutal SS men and, like Kittner's, rescue from the experience of torture a sense of revenge, of a time when things will change and the abusers will be confronted with their crimes.

5: Contemporaneous Poetry in the Third Reich

WHILE EVERY POEM HAS A cultural and a social history that includes the biography of its author, poems from the Third Reich present critics with a number of peculiar historical and social issues. Poems written by Nazis and their sympathizers are tainted with the cataclysmic history of the National Socialist regime and its genocidal campaigns. This is particularly the case for poems that praise Hitler and his regime, but it is true as well of poems whose concern does not seem directly related to Nazi ideology. Such poems are morally bankrupt, but this does not mean that they should not be analyzed. We read them necessarily from a perspective of hindsight that precludes a sympathetic reading. However, an analysis of Nazi poetry gives us insight into stylistic and thematic tendencies of the time and shows that the particular combination of aesthetics and politics promoted by the Nazis had multiple effects on the literature of the time. This includes the fact that seemingly harmless poems are permeated by Nazi ideology, for example, insofar as they subscribe to the notion, useful to the Nazi regime, that the "private" was a realm detached from politics. Read in conjunction with poetry written in the concentration camps, such poems make problematic any theoretical stance that draws an absolute separation between Nazi society and the concentrationary universe that this society had created. At the same time a comparison between these sets of poems brings to the foreground the difference in individual experience signified by the "barbed wire" and an author's position relative to it. While certain stylistic, lexical, and thematic concerns are shared by both sets of poems, the historical position of the author makes a difference in terms of how the poets handle the shared heritage and in terms of how we now read the valence of a particular style or topic. No attempt will be made here to determine whether or not the historical position of the authors could be established solely on the basis of the text. The answer to that is that this would be the case in many, but certainly not all, cases. The concern here is neither to prove that ideology always shows through a text nor to show that biography determines what gets written. The point rather is to provide a fuller perspective on the literary activity of the period than the one afforded by the more usual studies on either the literature of the Third Reich or the literature of the victims of the Nazis.

Poems written by Jews within the Third Reich offer yet another perspective on the cultural upheavals of the period. Unlike poems from the concentration camps, poetry published for example under the auspices of the "Kulturbund deutscher Juden" (Cultural Association of German Jews) confronts cultural discrimination, not expulsion from the human community. Poems by Jews living in the Third Reich are sites of contestation of the racial definitions of cultural identity that were brutally imposed by the National Socialists.

Within the German-speaking realm under Nazi rule, then, literary production must be considered under a number of distinct but not mutually exclusive rubrics: the published literature promoted by the National Socialists and the published literature tolerated by them; the literature of the separate German-Jewish sphere that was either published and promoted in the context of the "Kulturbund" or went unpublished; unpublished, oppositional political poetry; and the cultural production by inmates in the ghettos and concentration camps. Additionally, one could consider the literature written by German-speaking exiles again as a body of texts that responds to the same configuration of political developments from yet another vantage point. All of these broadly defined sets of texts share or react to a similar cultural heritage and arise, contemporaneously, in the face of very different but not unrelated attacks on a humanist individualism in the Third Reich and, in the concentration camps, attacks on the most basic physical and psychic needs of individuals. Uwe Ketelsen also argues against what he calls the "synchronic drawing of boundaries" among "literature of the Third Reich," "Inner Emigration," and "Exile literature" by pointing out that these literatures, for example in poetry, shared the same heritage (1985, 301). While a crucial boundary is crossed when we add literature from the concentration camps to Ketelsen's list, it must be recognized that this inclusion is necessary from a historical perspective that considers the concentration camps an essential component in the history of the Third Reich.

Literature in the Third Reich: Historical Considerations

In the years leading up to 1933 and during the first years of their regime the National Socialists were intent on asserting their revolutionary character and their potential for bringing about change to a country in dire economic straits and political turmoil. They boasted about the differences between their cultural program and that of the Weimar Republic. The Nazis regarded the Weimar Republic as a period of "juification" of the Volk and of German culture through the introduction of "foreign" and "superficial" "Bolshevist" and "Americanist" styles and concepts. A title such as Wilhelm Stapel's 1937 *Die literarische Vorherrschaft der Juden in Deutschland 1918 bis 1933* (The Literary Dominance of the Jews in Germany, 1918 to 1933) speaks for itself here. However, this identification of the modernist "extreme distortion of form" of Weimar arts and letters with the social crisis itself was in no way exclusive to the Nazis (Schäfer 1983, 85). For the National Socialists, 1933 marked a break not only with the parliamentary form of government: well beyond that, it was intended as a revolution in the "total conception of life," "a re-forming of the totality of public life" (Bley 1934, 96) — a change in which cultural productions were meant to play an essential role. Thus, for example, Hitler declared in a speech at the Nuremberg party convention in 1933 that art had a "mission to compel to fanaticism." Art was to work hard to "safeguard" "the Weltanschauung of the community of the people" (cited in Strothmann, 5). As far as literature is concerned, the National Socialist government promoted and achieved a climate in which the experimental forms of narrative that had been eagerly pursued in the 1910s and 1920s practically disappeared and were replaced by what the National Socialists in their speeches and slogans insisted was a new literary style and the rebirth of a "great" literature. This purportedly more closely reflected the spirit of the "community of the people" as well as Germany's role as a racial world leader: ". . . the pseudo-culture of the liberal epoch was determined by the high-handedness of the individual . . . thus the new German culture, whose growth is in step with the progress of National Socialist thought, derives from the community of the people" (Bley 1935, 38).

This new order was not simply a spontaneous occurrence stimulated by a change in government: in literature the change involved violence, both public (book burning, expatriation, imprisonment) and secret (black lists, politically-motivated paper shortages, threats), and acts of censorship. All this was glossed over by literary commentators sympathetic to the regime in the biologistic terms of a scientific "selection":

> Because we have awoken from the lethargy and have become "agents" in Goethe's sense of the word, we must apparently forget much. But this forgetting and this putting away is not an act of arbitrariness, but rather a very consciously made selection; and a selection that can distinguish ill from healthy just as much in the literary realm . . . (Heinz Kindermann 1939, cited in Gilman 1971, 35)

The National Socialists promised an escape from the "unhealthy" modern experiences of mass anonymity, industrial routine, social stratification, and urban poverty. They promised a return to the "traditional" values of family, national unity, and racial pride. It remains an entirely different set of questions whether or not and in what ways they delivered on these promises, but the promises were certainly part of a successful strategy to set themselves apart from the problems of the Weimar Republic.

A definite silencing of voices, particularly those of Jewish (in the Nazi definition of the term), modernist, and Communist authors did take place, but the intended renewal of literature along "racial" principles was not en-

tirely successful, partly due to the rivalries between the more opportunis-
tic, public-oriented Head of the Ministry of Propaganda, Joseph Goebbels,
and the dogmatically "völkisch" Führer's Delegate for the Entire Intellectual
and Philosophical Instruction of the National Socialist Party, Alfred Rosenberg
(see Bollmus). This limited success was also due to the widespread preference for a literature that seemed to present an alternative to the cultural
sphere provided by the party: a literature geared toward "Innerlichkeit" (interiority) and at least in appearance free of political issues. Popular taste was
important in the decisions taken by the different control organs; Goebbels
realized that an excess of explicitly political, "völkisch" products would likely
be counterproductive: "The instant that propaganda is recognized it loses its
effect" (Goebbels cited in Reichel, 180). With Goebbels's increasing power
and the government's attempt to overcome the "revolutionary" image of the
initial stages of the movement, starting in 1935 the literature of a "politi-
cally-detached interiority" came to dominate the literary scene, much to the
chagrin of the authors who had identified with the political movement and
were producing nationalist, "Blut und Boden" (blood and soil) literature.

  After the defeat of Hitler's Germany, a number of approaches to the
Third Reich developed in literary criticism, initially to a large extent conditioned by the cultural and political contingencies after the war: the need to
rebuild as quickly as possible, the onset of the Cold War, and the fact that,
for a number of critics and authors, the military defeat and political rupture
did not entail a disruption of their literary activity, notwithstanding the
rhetoric about the "Stunde Null" (Zero Hour) in West Germany and about
a historical, thoroughgoing, and principled alternative to fascism in East
Germany. Some literary critics followed the Nazi narrative about its monolithic cultural singularity only in order to attach to it the contrary valuation.
Now all literature published in Germany between 1933 and 1945 was dismissed as "völkisch," "Blut und Boden Kitsch" unworthy of study. In 1945
Thomas Mann declared that "books that could be printed at all in Germany
between 1933 and 1945 are less than worthless and they are not good to
touch with one's hands. They are enveloped in a smell of blood and shame.
They should all be destroyed" (Mann, 31). Variations of this position are
not uncommon today. In a standard introduction to the history of German
literature used in universities in Germany, the heading under National
Socialism opens with the following words: "Even though a good number of
important authors accommodated themselves to the National Socialist theory of Volk and salvation, not a single significant piece of literature came
from it" (Fricke and Schreiber, 351). Or, as literary critic Joseph Wulf put it:
"The origin and result of this literature are clearly failure and degeneration"
(5). Very often literature from the Third Reich was taken to be pure propaganda aimed at covering up the crimes of the regime, a product created by a

calculating government. In some accounts this has meant implicitly or explicitly that the population at large was excused from complicity.

In some conservative and liberal circles the Third Reich was understood as a historical aberration spanning the years 1933–1945, with no connection to either the Weimar Republic or the postwar states. An important consequence of the wholesale dismissal of the works published in that period was a widespread "amnesia" that allowed a number of authors who had been neither silent nor oppositional during the Third Reich to become central figures in postwar literature. Wulf reports, for example, that after the war Wilhelm Stapel simply excluded from the list of his works the aforementioned anti-Semitic title (Wulf, 7). Other critics saw a connection between literary and cultural products of the Nazi era and the period that preceded it, but found in National Socialism the expression of a centuries-long tradition of etatism and authoritarianism, a predictable development: "The Nazi triumph in that country [Germany] is little more than 'seeing the chickens come home to roost'" (McGovern, 597). This long-range perspective of a particularly German "way" had little interest in the specifics of literary production in the Third Reich. It concentrated rather on tracing notions of absolute leadership or anti-Semitic theories through centuries of writing.

Another strand of literary criticism that admitted to the literary activities of some of its canonical figures during the Third Reich differentiated between Nazi literature and "inner emigration." In this view some authors who had not gone into exile had suffered under the tyranny but had been able to preserve or create a space for a private withdrawal from the National Socialist public sphere. This withdrawal from official Nazi politics and culture was seen as oppositional, as having refused to serve as foils for the Nazi crimes. Critique of the regime, it was argued, was exercised through a highly coded language, a "slave's language" heavily reliant on allegory, one that was accessible only to those who would have sympathized with the author's views. A number of problems arise here, prominently among them the fact that multiple meanings often make it impossible to extract a clearly oppositional message from a text. Frequently, to the contrary, these ambiguous works produce the impression of disingenuous complicity with the dictatorship.[1]

To a large extent, and not surprisingly, literary histories of the period depend on the overall historiographic conceptions with which they align themselves. Two major strands that were prevalent in the 1960s and 1970s are important here. One of these, following Hanna Arendt's arguments in *The Origins of Totalitarianism* (1958), sees the Nazi regime as a clear manifestation of the phenomenon of totalitarian rule that comes into existence any time a deviation from liberal, representative democracy occurs, whether this results in a government of extreme right or of extreme left. In this theory the central players are charismatic leaders who manipulate a particular ideology to their own means and control virtually every sphere of public life, from economics to entertainment. According to this view the arts play a role to the extent that they propagate the all-powerful ideology and they are strictly controlled by the state. As far as literary history is concerned, this theory leads to an emphasis on the regulatory mechanisms, legislative measures, and official directives rather than on the actual literary activity. Such concern with control mechanisms is exemplified in Dietrich Strothmann's detailed study of National Socialist publishing policies, *Nationalsozialistische Literaturpolitik* (National Socialist Literary Policies).

A contending line of historical research explains National Socialism as a logical development of late capitalism. This theory views the basis for the Nazi regime as being in big-business interests, private property, and capitalistic imperialism and exploitation; the state's propaganda machinery and the whole theatricalization of ideological notions such as the "Volk" are all part of a powerful cover-up for capitalism's real structures for the oppression of the working class. Under this thesis, known sometimes as Dimitrov's formula or the Fascism theory, studies concentrate on the economic policies of the regime, and literature plays only a marginal role, primarily as another means through which the state apparatus creates a "false consciousness" about the workers' real situation. In this view there are continuities between the Weimar Republic, the Third Reich, and the Federal Republic of Germany, but these are of consequence at the level of class relations from an economic perspective. A related cluster of thinkers, however, takes for granted the primacy of economic relations as the basis for National Socialism but focuses on Nazi aesthetics as the central component of the cultural practices that made it possible for the regime to create a powerful, almost hermetic "schöner Schein" (beautiful surface) that almost inevitably would lead to war. Only explicitly anti-capitalistic literature, then, could be seen as in opposition to the Nazi regime (see Emmerich 1977).

Other scholars, such as Uwe-K. Ketelsen, but also George Mosse, find in the literature of the 1930s and 1940s the continuation and coming to center stage of a bourgeois tradition of reaction against modernism, a longing for a utopian past of community and unity, of responsibility in the private realm, and of sublime interiority. This entails a uniquely bourgeois admixture of Classicism and Romanticism whose roots lay in the 1790s and in the nineteenth-century tradition of realism. As we have seen, for instance, Ruth Klüger, who was born in Vienna in 1931, characterizes her own aesthetic and literary background critically in this manner (Klüger 1994, 127).

More contemporary approaches to the history of the Third Reich consider a multiplicity of factors, cultural, political, and economic, that contributed to a complex interaction of state control and private entrepreneurship. This complexity is reflected in cultural productions that often responded to both modernist and "völkisch" impulses. Following inspiration from the recent historical interest in *Alltagsgeschichte,* cultural and literary historians such as Hans-Dieter Schäfer and Peter Reichel pay close attention to the details of cultural life in the period and point to significant differences between the kinds of writings National Socialist cultural policies intended to foster and the literature that was actually published. Schäfer finds that the most prominent literary current within a "many-sided literary life" (1983, 56) is a shift to a certain formalism and a withdrawal from political engagement, both of which he sees as related to a cultural climate prevalent in Europe from 1930 to 1960: a return to classicism, a traditional formalism, existentialism. Schäfer is careful not to connect this retreat from the sphere of political rhetoric to what he calls the "meaningless slogan 'inner emigration'" (60). Indeed, Anson Rabinbach has shown the deeply problematic nature of the distinction between a public realm that is markedly political and a private realm of interiority that is, by implication, free from the political: "To construct the history of National Socialism in terms of the polarity between the "official/political" and the "everyday/private" uncritically recapitulates the "divided consciousness" that many Germans experienced during the Nazi era" (9). A critique such as Rabinbach's is important in order to avoid a facile "normalization" of the everyday and to counter a comfortable valorization of "interiority" as oppositional. As Rabinbach puts it: "The sharp distinction between public and private, between inner reality and outer experience, was itself a major theme in Nazi ideology and politics" (10).

Since the 1980s it has become increasingly clear that the notion of a monolithic, thoroughly-controlled cultural sphere is problematically one-sided: it leads one to concentrate solely or primarily on the directives, laws, and assessments of the National Socialists, and to neglect the actual cultural products and events. Attention to the actual range of literature created in the Third Reich has led to the notion of a "restricted cultural pluralism" (Reichel, 321). Here it seems important to consider the idea of pluralism in context. It is necessary to pay close attention to the variety of stylistic and thematic elements and to the diversity of political, social, and religious visions inside the Third Reich, to acknowledge, for instance, the differences between works explicitly intent on inciting political fervor by recycling Nazi slogans and those cultural products that strongly defend against any intrusion of openly political concerns. However, it is at least as crucial to study the more subtle ways in which even the latter can become complicit with the discourse of the National Socialists. As Mary Nolan has argued: "If *Alltagsgeschichte* has shown that many remained immune to the regime's ideological appeals and even opposed some of its policies, it has not paid sufficient attention to how people's lives and consciousness were subtly transformed" (75).

In terms of the history of literature, one can argue along similar lines that it is historically correct to attend to the differences manifested in this creative medium and to recognize the pluralism that existed within National Socialist Germany, but also that it is imperative to keep in mind the constraints imposed on that pluralism by the cultural climate created by the government and the Nazi party. It is essential to consider the "limits" that were internalized, so to speak, the more subtle discursive practices that permeated public life and cultural productions. When we also consider the literature produced in the concentration camps, moreover, we are reminded of the very limited sense in which it is possible to think of "cultural pluralism" within the Third Reich, given the brutality with which the Nazis sought to eradicate any cultural manifestation that they considered politically questionable or racially tainted.

As far as the issue of authoritarian control is concerned, it may be useful to remember here that literature, unlike film, radio, and architecture, could play only a minor role in the theatricalization of the state. Film, radio, and architecture were considered essential by a government concerned with mobilizing and entertaining the masses. Hitler's architect, Albert Speer, speculated on Hitler's lack of interest in literature thus:

> Perhaps the chief reason was that Hitler took everything as an instrument, and that of all the arts literature lends itself the least to the uses of power politics. Its effects are always unpredictable, and the mere fact that books are meant for private consumption must have made him suspicious. The audience for every other art could be swayed by showmanship — but not the solitary reader within his four walls. (313)

Even if this view, with its assumption of the minimal political power of literature, might appear simplistic, Speer's remarks highlight the private nature of most literary consumption and the elusiveness of literature in terms of the theatricalization of state power.

State control was neither all-pervasive nor particularly invested in tightly managing literary production. What can be said about literature's relatively lesser importance for the Nazi regime applies especially well to poetry. Poetry in particular lends itself even more readily than genres such as the historical novel or theater to a literary current that tended to an "apolitical, romantic-religious interiority" (Reichel, 329) and looked for "escape and safety from the chaos" (Schäfer 1983, 41) in bourgeois, traditional aestheticism. In this context Schäfer argues that "no genre is more accommodating of the tendency to subjectivity than poetry" (41) and Reichel correlates the widespread "preference for subjective, allegorical modes of expression" during the Third Reich to poetry in particular (334).

In her critique of cultural histories of the Third Reich that minimize the Holocaust, Nolan argues:

> Complicity is minimized by those approaches that argue for indifference or even opposition to the regime's racial policies . . . [such approaches] ignore the pervasiveness of complicity, in however differential form. An examination of the appeal of eugenics, if not pursued at the expense of anti-Semitism, offers one way of studying involvement and

responsibility. The work of Claudia Koonz, which shows the mainte-
nance of normality in every day life . . . suggests another. Such analyses
do not represent a return to crude theories of collective guilt. Rather,
they offer a way to link normality and terror, supporter/resister and victim, everyday life and Auschwitz. (80)

Studying the diverse literature in National Socialist Germany in conjunction
with the literature written by the victims of the National Socialists offers another register on which the history of "everyday life" in the Third Reich and
"life in the camps" may throw light on each other.

A comparison between poems written in the concentration camps and
poems published under National Socialism raises questions about how different contexts affect the function of poetry, a genre in which "the educated
German bourgeoisie . . . had seen a medium for their hopes since Classicism
and Romanticism" (Ketelsen 1983, 478); such comparison also unsettles
easy distinctions between the "personal" and the "political." It further necessitates a differentiated analysis of the return to formalism, as aesthetic es-
capism on the one hand, and, on the other, as a viable and perhaps necessary
form of expression when language threatens to fail in the face of extremity
and personal disintegration.

Comparisons

In the category of poetry published in the Third Reich we find the crudely
propagandistic, as in the "Horst Wessel Song," which in practice became the
most well known Nazi hymn ("Die Fahne hoch" [Raise the Banner High]
by Horst Wessel, cited in Ketelsen 1992, 342[2]):

> Es schau'n aufs Hakenkreuz voll Hoffnung schon Millionen
> Der Tag für Freiheit und für Brot bricht an;
>
> [Millions filled with hope already look up to the swastika
> The day for freedom and for bread begins;]

the inflammatory, full of exclamatory and violent excitement (from Hermann
Burte's "Entscheidung" (Decision), printed in Schumann, 436):

> Mord hält am Leben!
> Schaue Natur an
> Fraß oder Fresser,
> Volk, mußt du sein!
>
> [Murder keeps you alive!
> Look at nature,
> My people, you must be
> devoured or devourer!]

as well as what appears more subdued because of its focus on an interior realm rather than an explicit political movement. As even a cursory reading makes clear, this is not necessarily less insidious than crudely propagandistic pronouncements. For example, Will Vesper's poem "Dem Führer" (To the Führer; Vesper, 377 and Schumann, 508) begins with an invocation of "ancestral customs" according to which "Es steigt der Führer / aus Volkes Mitte" (The Führer rises / from the middle of the Volk). The final stanza of this poem reads as follows:

> Herzog des Reiches
> wie wir es meinen
> bist du schon lange
> im Herzen der deinen.

> [Duke of our Kingdom
> as we see it
> you have already long
> been in the hearts of your people.]

Here Vesper elevates a political declaration, "to the Führer," into a collective religious confession and doubly inscribes a political figure in terms of nobility (Herzog) and of religion. He does this as well by activating both secular and divine connotations for the word "Reich" (kingdom), as in "das Reich Gottes" (the Kingdom of God) and "das deutsche Reich" (the German empire), thus elevating the Third Reich, and by connecting these notions with the trope of something lodged in one's heart, much like doctrinal concepts of Christian faith. The religiosity is reinforced by a rhythmic regularity and metric simplicity that evoke church prayers. Furthermore, he creates a sense of a community that seems to actively seek its own submission, looking for a "Herzog" "wie *wir* es meinen" (a leader, as *we* conceive of it) though, as it turns out in the end, the community is only defined in relation to the Führer, that is, it has already been tautologically established: "You are in the hearts of all those who are yours." Effectively, then, the tautology makes the connection to the Führer a spiritual, internal one, howsoever "those who are yours" be defined.

As Reichel, Ketelsen (1992), and Schäfer (1983) have shown, however, such politically focused lyric was not the main form of literary production, in part because of the preferences of a number of intellectuals and the public, but also because of intervention on the part of the regime. This becomes clear from the fact that members of the government, in particular Goebbels in his role of Reich Minister of Public Enlightenment and Propaganda, eventually came to oppose and suppress a movement like the "Thingtheaterbewegung," a form of monumental open-air theater with claims to old Germanic antecedents (see Ritchie, 101–2). In its very concern with politics, this

type of politically engaged literature, even if of clearly National Socialist confession, also could open up the possibility for other political ideas and needs
to be expressed, a danger that was non-existent in the more specialized, private, literary self-referentiality of "interiority" or in a more romanticist orientation toward nature (Reichel, 336–45). As an example of literary
detachment from the political, a poem like "Heimat ist gut" (Home is
Good; published by Albrecht Goes as the title poem in a collection printed
in 1935, reprinted in Schäfer 1983, 45) illustrates the concern with the intimate and the familial. At the same time it mobilizes a term of crucial significance and high frequency in Nazi ideology, "Heimat" (home or homeland):

> Regen und Regenwind
> Singen mich wach,
> Schwarz ist das Fensterkreuz,
> Still das Gemach.
> Decke sich sacht bewegt,
> Weib atmet rein,
> Mägdlein weint leise auf,
> Schläft wieder ein —
> Turmuhr sagt Mitternacht,
> Lebenstag ruht.
> Alles ist heimatnah,
> Heimat ist gut.

> [Rain and wind of rain
> Sing me into waking,
> Black is the window's cross-beam,
> Quiet is the chamber.
> The cover moves lightly,
> My wife breathes in,
> My little girl whines softly,
> Falls asleep again —
> The tower's clock says midnight,
> The day's life rests.
> Everything is close to home,
> Home is good.]

Here the romanticist personification of the natural elements (rain and wind
sing) is carried over to objects of life in the village: the "tower's clock" does
not represent the hectic rhythms of industrial life. On the contrary, the clock
says that it is midnight and therewith becomes part of the reining familial in-
timacy. Outdated terms like "Gemach" (chamber) and "Weib" (woman or
wife) and the use of alliteration seek to ground the poem in an aestheticist,
pastoral tradition. There is a political quietism here that reaffirms the

"goodness" of "home" defined as a self-sufficient private realm and absorbs into the domestic chamber all external elements, both natural (wind, rain) and artificial (clock). Specifically, proximity is a crucial element here: everything is close to home. "Home is good." By implication, as we know from Nazi ideology more generally, what is imagined as not belonging to the home runs the danger of being declared evil. Other poems as well focus on everyday objects as loci of familiar coziness (Gemütlichkeit) and a feeling of home (Heimatgefühl). Schäfer cites Elisabeth Langgässer's sharp critique of this type of lyric in the Third Reich: "It did not have the 'smell of blood,' this anacreontic dallying with flowers and blossoms over the atrocious abyss of mass graves, wide-open but covered with these flowers" (Schäfer 1983, 46).

One obvious result of the turn to "Innerlichkeit" or interiority is self-referentiality: the poem often speaks about itself and thus avoids the political. In the case of poems published in Germany between 1933 and 1945, this does not mean the kind of critical self-ironization of the modern and perhaps postmodern projects; rather, it is usually in the form of an unironic celebration of the poetic endeavor. In the anthology *Die Ernte der Gegenwart* (Harvest of the Present Time; Vesper) a large number of poems praise the "book" and the "poet." Indeed the anthology is introduced by editor Will Vesper's poem "Anruf des Herzens" (Call of the Heart):

> Einsamer Wanderer im Gitter der Brust,
> mit festem Schritt wanderst du stet
> durch Wachen und Schlaf, durch Leid und Lust.
> — Weißt du, wohin es geht?
> Wann
> kommst du an?
> Wo?
> Wohin treibt es dich so?
> Siehst du Licht?
> Siehst du Land?
> Aber es antwortet nicht
> unter der zuckenden Hand,
> geht seinen Gang,
> herkommend weit,
> durch mich, durch die Zeit,
> in Ewigkeit,
> und kürzt sich den Weg mit Gesang.

> [Lonely wanderer in the breast chamber,
> with steady step you wander always
> through waking and sleeping, through pain and joy.
> — Do you know where the path leads?

When
will you arrive?
Where?
Where are you going to?
Do you see light?
Do you see land?
But it does not answer
under the shaky hand
it goes on its path,
coming from afar,
through me, through the times,
in eternity,
and shortens its way with songs.]

The depths of the heart and an uncertain yet present death — the final destination of the heart, the unknown place where the heart will "arrive" — create a mystical atmosphere in this rhyming poem. Here poetry ("Gesang" [songs]) functions as a vital element that corresponds to the heart's function. Thus poetry is an expression of the heart, the heart's own way of passing time. It is also the heart's response to the poet's query: there are no direct answers to the questions, just the last word of the poem: "Gesang" (songs). On its mystical path the heart "shortens its way" with rhymes. Poetry is regarded here as the fitting accompaniment on the way through life for the poet and by extension for the reader who also has a "heart."

Poems such as those by Goes and Vesper cited above, or in Schäfer's "Die nichtnationalsozialistische Literatur der jungen Generation im Dritten Reich" (The Non-National Socialist Literature of the Young Generation in the Third Reich; 1976), give the impression that German-language poetry in the period between 1933 and 1945 was an epigonic reaction, a turn against the experimentation and political engagement of the 1910s and 1920s. In these poems the narrowly political plays no role. With its anacreontic formalism, this poetry is a return to "outdated" lyric models and reflects a larger phenomenon in the literature of the industrialized Western world during the 1930s and 1940s:

> In terms of the history of form, one can speak of a "classicist turn" within European-American literature, a turn which to some extent brought to an end the vehement "breakthrough to the modern" since the second half of the nineteenth century. (Ketelsen 1983, 476)

Ketelsen casts a wide net here when he writes of a "classicist turn" in "European-American literature," but his work has shown that a number of literary tendencies that are sometimes ascribed to the cultural climate created by the Nazis need to be rethought in a wider cultural context that is not exclusive to societies under fascism. Assumptions about the National Socialist cultural sphere also need reconsideration when the literature from the Third Reich is analyzed in conjunction with the literature created in Germany either in the small, separate sphere originally provided for and by Jews (most prominently in the "Kulturbund"), as well as the literature written illegally. A look beyond the poetry that was published legally allows us to consider the complex context of the "normality" of the works promoted or tolerated in the Third Reich and to ponder the apparent singularity of the poetry written at this time in German in ghettos and detention, concentration, and extermination camps. This poetry — which had minimal, if any, circulation — as well as the partisan, oppositional, illegal pamphlet poetry (Emmerich 1976, 431–36), when placed next to the poetry that circulated in published form, expands and complicates the framework for literary analysis and changes our understanding of the "normality" and apparent "pluralism" evident in the published works. At the same time this kind of comparative approach renders porous, retrospectively, the cultural border enforced by the "barbed wire," not in order to unduly confuse significant categories such as perpetrator, collaborator, bystander, persecuted, and victim, but rather so as to make it possible to consider the overall cultural context of these works and their specificity within such general framework.

In response to the successive waves of "Aryanizations" of cultural institutions that started in 1933, most public cultural activity in the Third Reich that involved Jews in one form or another took place under the auspices of the "Kulturbund." This organization was called into life by Jewish initiative in order to provide employment to Jewish musicians and artists who had lost their jobs as well as to offer an alternative to the mainstream cultural programming that, under the Nazis, became increasingly intolerable (Jäger, 100–101). The "Kulturbund" provided an autonomous cultural sphere and thus a much-needed outlet for the creative energies of Jewish artists and for the cultural needs of the Jewish public.[3] Founded in 1933, the "Kulturbund deutscher Juden" (Cultural Association of German Jews) was forced to change its name to "Jüdischer Kulturbund" (Jewish Cultural Association) in 1935 because Nazi ideology dictated that there were no "German Jews" (Schlenstedt, 729). These cultural associations, originally in Berlin and soon thereafter in other cities, were allowed to create cultural programming by Jews exclusively for a Jewish public under the supervision of the Reich Chamber of Culture. Alan Steinweis has written of the particular importance of SS Commandant Hans Hinkel regarding Jewish cultural affairs: he was in charge of the "Entjudung" (de-Judification) of culture and eventually earned for himself the title of "Special Commissioner for the Supervision and Monitoring of the Cultural and Intellectual Activity of All Non-Aryans Living in the Territory of the German Reich" (Steinweis 1993a, 211–13). The various Jewish cultural organizations were unified and eventually centralized by the

Nazis. From the perspective of the Nazis, this system helped to ensure that Jews in the Reich were more easily controlled and completely isolated from the general culture. These Jewish cultural organizations were forbidden in 1941, their property confiscated, and the remaining members arrested (Schlenstedt, 729; Steinweis 1993b, 121 and 123–26). As Saul Friedländer has argued, the "Kulturbund" "fitted Nazi needs" and "it foreshadowed the Nazi ghetto, in which a pretense of internal autonomy camouflaged the total subordination of an appointed Jewish leadership to the dictates of its masters" (1997, 65–66).

Sonja Hilzinger has written about how German-Jewish authors in the Third Reich responded to their incremental but rapid exclusion from the cultural sphere. "German-Jewish authors were not only persecuted and expelled," she argues, "but also, through their exclusion from German-speaking culture, they were denied their identity" (72). Hilzinger provides a summary of the many different ways in which German-Jewish writers living in the Third Reich reacted to the experience of exclusion from the public sphere in their works:

- They affirmed their own perception by portraying the persecution and threat in a realistic form and thus created a "true" counter-world to official Nazi public life; in this respect German-Jewish poetry was part of anti-fascist art.

- They held onto German-language culture and traditions, which was evident not only in their use of Christian metaphors but also with respect to literary models from Goethe to Rilke; in this respect German-Jewish poetry remained, according to its own self-understanding, a part of precisely that culture from which they were being brutally excluded by that culture's self-appointed wardens.

- By reaching back to Jewish themes and traditions they developed a Jewish identification that contributed individually to the stabilization of identity and collectively to the constitution of a Jewish community.

- They became silent. (72–73)

Hilzinger's summary of the cultural possibilities available to German-Jewish authors in the 1930s in Nazi Germany makes it clear that a consideration of context is crucial for interpretation. For example, the persistence of or return to traditional lyric forms played a number of different roles during the period. In what the Nazis might label "Aryan" poetry published in the Third Reich, traditional forms would likely imply a formalism that refused political engagement and in some sense thus quietly complied with the National Socialist project to exclude from discourse alternative political and social visions. For German-Jewish poetry a return to traditional forms would signify more likely a political defiance of Nazi racial exclusion. As we have seen, the Nazis considered traditional lyric to be an art form not available to Jews. In addition, as Kerstin Schoor (123) points out, the

> external coercion to create a "Jewish culture" had its reverse application in a process that Arnold Zweig . . . described as a "reflection on Jewish roots and Jewish future," and that even within Germany implied the search for a positively formulated self-definition, the attempt to maintain and find an identity in a moment in which it was completely being brought into question from the outside.

Both Schlenstedt and Schoor describe the debates within the "Kulturbund' around the definition of a "Jewish culture in German." Schoor discusses this on the basis of an anthology of contemporary poetry published in 1936 by Kurt Pinthus in the literary supplement of the newspaper of the "Central-Verein deutscher Staatsbürger jüdischen Glaubens" (Central Association of German Citizens of the Jewish Faith). As Schoor puts it, there was consensus only about what "did not necessarily constitute Jewish art" (128). Schoor further cites another text by Pinthus that implicitly describes the task of the literary critic of the period as two-pronged. The literary critic would seek to establish a Jewish specificity (albeit without defining it) on the one hand while, on the other hand, avoiding the kind of isolation imposed by the National Socialists by making explicit references to the connection of an author to said author's national literature and to "world" literature:

> To find in each Jewish author the conscious and unconscious relations to Jewishness (not only with regard to theme but also in the intellectual construction and in the ethic content) and at the same time to identify the artistic and ideological connections to the thinkers and poets of the land in whose language the author writes, and also to world literature . . . (Pinthus, cited in Schoor, 128).

Schoor's essay calls for the inclusion of the "literary life of German Jews after 1933 in Germany" in comparative discussions of antifascist literature in Exile and the literature of the "so-called Inner Emigration," arguing that while German-Jewish literature from the period may not have found new forms of expression, it had to contend with the pressures from the Nazis to create a "Jewish culture" (140).

In the context of German-Jewish poetry written in the Third Reich, Gertrud Kolmar's work serves as an apposite example.[4] Born in 1894 into an assimilated, affluent family in Berlin, Kolmar grew up as a member of the German-Jewish bourgeoisie. Peter Gay characterizes the German-Jewish bourgeoisie as having had a "passionate affection for high German culture" (154).[5] Although reclusive and usually secretive about her writings, Kolmar had published poetry before 1933 and continued thereafter to write and publish. Her last collection to be published before her deportation, *Die Frau und die Tiere* (The Woman and the Animals; 1938), was received with glowing reviews in the German-Jewish press in the fall of 1938, but following the pogrom of November of 1938 unsold copies of her collection were destroyed and the newspapers publishing the reviews were forced to close. *Die Frau und die Tiere* had appeared under Kolmar's birth name, Chodziesner, because at the beginning of 1936 an ordinance from the Reich Chamber of Culture forbade Jews from using pseudonyms (Schlenstedt, 727). Furthermore, Kolmar and her father were forced out of their large home in the suburbs and moved to overcrowded "Jewish Housing," also in November of 1938. Kolmar remained in Berlin and performed forced labor in a factory until her deportation to Auschwitz in 1943. She did not survive.[6] Monika Shafi argues that Kolmar's work is "wedged uneasily between tradition and modernity" (2003, 692). My contention here is that much of the literature produced in the 1930s and 1940s fits this description, and that the historical and political contexts of these texts condition their aesthetic relations to "tradition and modernity."

Perhaps surprisingly for a poet whose work is otherwise concerned with the "transcendental" and the "essential" and avoids the more mundane "distractions" of social and political events (Jäger, 49–52) Kolmar responded to the Nazis' repressive measures quickly: between August and October of 1933 she wrote a poem cycle entitled "Das Wort der Stummen" (The Word of the Silenced) that was first published in 1978 in East Berlin. Shafi argues that the cycle "Das Wort der Stummen" can be connected to the rest of Kolmar's oeuvre through the introductory set of poems, which at first appears to be "far away from the daily reality of the year 1933" and deals with the central topics of Kolmar's poetry: woman, animals, and images of nature. However, Shafi argues, all these poems deal with loss and death and, like the rest of the cycle, portray "victims" and "outsiders" (1995, 125–27). The tripartite cycle of twenty-two poems contains texts such as "Im Lager" (In the Camp), a poem that describes "how the prisoners . . . are dehumanized, losing their bodies, minds, and souls" (Shafi 2003, 690). In 1933 the system of concentration camps existed only in rudimentary form. Given the paucity of information about conditions in the then new concentration camps this poem seems prophetic or at least perceptively foresighted in its depiction of conditions there. All the poems in the cycle, as is the case with a good number of poems she wrote during her internment, are precisely dated. Shafi points out that Kolmar's cycle of poems hardly mentions the perpetrators and their motives. Thus the "exact historical context" is provided not by the poems themselves but by their precise dating:

> The dates of the poems expose the perpetrators as they point to the chronology of events of 1933: Hitler's seizure of power, the dissolution of the Reichstag, the Reichstag fire and first wave of arrests, the estab-

lishment of the first concentration camps, the Enabling Act, the organized boycott of Jewish businesses. This is the political context, and Kolmar is able to focus on it through the dating of her texts without having to refer to the political events directly in the poems. The poems concentrate on individual stories. The historical anchoring of the poems achieved through the dating functions as a frame that expands, intensifies, and also radicalizes the poetic message. (Shafi 1995, 127–28)

We have already seen the ways in which poems written in internment tend to avoid direct mention of the perpetrators. In the case of poems from the concentration camps, the historical context is often provided by indications of the date and place of the creation of the poem. In Berlin in the last half of September of 1933 Kolmar composed poems with titles that make clear her concern with the political developments: "Wir Juden" (We Jews), 15 September; "Ewiger Jude" (Eternal Jew), 20 September; "Die Gefangenen" (The Imprisoned Ones), 30 September. Kolmar's poem "Im Lager" (In the Camp), dated 17 September 1933, opens with a description of the psychological and physical state of inmates (Kolmar 1978, 21[7]). This poem speaks empathically about the inmates of the concentration camps. The third-person-plural narration serves possibly a different function here than it does in poems about inmates in the concentration camps written in the third-person by fellow inmates. In both cases the third-person serves as a distancing mechanism, but outside the concentration camps the threat directed against the lyric voice is not as radical or direct as it is in the concentration-ary universe. In the camps a self-distancing mechanism such as Klüger's lines about "men" marching toward their death seems necessary in order to create a narrative perspective that does not succumb to despair. In Kolmar's case we may safely assume that the incremental discrimination she faced in Nazi Germany as a Jewish woman and poet would have inspired some of her concern for inmates in the camps, but she does not attempt to arrogate to herself their plight.

> Die hier umhergehn, sind nur Leiber
> Und haben keine Seele mehr,
> Sind Namen nur im Buch der Schreiber,
> Gefangne: Männer. Knaben. Weiber.
> Und ihre Augen starren leer
>
> Mit bröckelndem, zerfallnem Schauen
> Auf Stunden, da in düsterm Loch
> Gewürgt, zertrampelt, blindgehauen
> Ihr Qualgeächz, ihr Wahnsinnsgrauen,
> Ein Tier, auf Händ und Füßen kroch . . .

[Those walking around here are only bodies
And no longer have souls,
Are names only in the book of the accountant,
Prisoners: Men. Boys. Women.
And their eyes stare emptily

With fragmented, broken gazes
At hours, there, in the dark hole
Strangled, trampled, beaten blind
Their tortured scream, their insane horror,
An animal crept on hands and feet . . .]

Kolmar describes in the first two of five stanzas the kind of "brokenness" of existence in the concentration camps that we have come to know from the writings of survivors. Without first-hand experience, and possibly before the use of numbers to identify inmates was systematically imposed in the camps, she writes of the inmates as reduced to a physical, animal existence, and to names consigned to a book for record-keeping. Significantly at this early date in the history of the camps she specifies that the imprisoned ones are "Men. Boys. Women." She does not seem to participate in the bourgeois expectation that the Nazis would direct their aggression at Jewish men and that Jewish women and children would be "civilly" spared. Kolmar seems keenly aware that the political developments taking place in Nazi Germany were not an affair that concerned only men. The poem goes on with a depiction of the brutalization experienced by inmates:

Sie tragen Ohren noch und hören
Doch nimmermehr den eignen Schrei.
Die Kerker drücken ein, zerstören:
Kein Herz, kein Herz mehr zum Empören!
Der leise Wecker schrillt entzwei.

Sie mühn sich wie blöde, grau entartet,
Vom bunten Menschensein getrennt,
Starr, abgestempelt und zerschartet,
Wie Schlachtvieh auf den Metzger wartet
Und dumpf noch Trog und Hürde kennt.

[They still have ears and hear
No longer their own screams.
The prison walls press in, destroy:
No heart, no heart remains to rage!
The quiet alarm clock shrills until it breaks.

> They toil themselves senseless, degenerate grey,
> Separated from the colorful existence of people,
> Stiff, branded, and scraped aground,
> Like slaughter cattle waiting for the butcher
> And dimly recognizing still trough and holding pen.]

Kolmar continues here her image from the second stanza of the inmates' existence as animal-like. She also seems to point to a state of dissociation: the inmates still have ears but no longer hear their own cries. Even though they are still alive, they have been cut off from the "colorful" side of human existence, and their hearts have been broken. The metaphor of the heart as a quiet alarm clock ringing itself to pieces suggests that the "heart" is trying to wake up from the nightmare of the situation, but since there is no escape it continues ringing until past its breaking point. Even as early as 1933 Kolmar used the simile of cattle being led to their slaughter to refer to the inmates, a figure that would become commonplace years later in talking about the plight of Jews persecuted by the Nazis. The final stanza reads:

> Nur Angst, nur Schauder in den Mienen,
> Wenn nachts ein Schuß das Opfer greift . . .
> Und keinem ist der Mann erschienen,
> Der schweigend mitten ihnen
> Sein kahles Kreuz zur Richtstatt schleift.—

> [Only fear, only terror on their faces,
> When at night a bullet reaches its victim . . .
> And to no one has the man appeared
> Who silently in their midst
> Drags his barren cross to the place of execution.—]

The implied reference to Jesus ("the man" with the "barren cross") creates a connection between the inmates' imprisonment and Christ's Calvary. At the same time, the fact that Jesus with his cross has not shown himself speaks of the utter abandonment of the inmates, reinforcing the impression that they are cut off from the world, and possibly from salvation. It is unlikely that one would be able to derive from Kolmar's oeuvre a traditional theological vision, be it Christian or Jewish. The appearance of the Christ figure at the end of this poem and in the other two poems about the "imprisoned ones" in this cycle is likely the poet's attempt to provide closure to the scene of humiliation with an image of the silent acceptance of suffering. As in the case of Christ, the suffering is thereby imbued with significance.[8] A Christ who does not show himself, however, both evokes and occludes salvation. The missing appearance declares either the inability or non-existence of this "man," his lack of concern or validity for the plight of those imprisoned by the Nazis.

The rhyming scheme here (abaab, and so on) follows a traditional conception of poetry. In terms of style the "controlled rhythms" of Kolmar's secret cycle about persecution seem closely related to the rhymes and rhythms of poetry from the concentration camps. Kolmar's "Wort der Stummen," like concentration-camp poetry, constitutes an attempt to render intelligible and to bear witness to senseless brutality and, as the title of the cycle proclaims, to give a voice to individuals who were violently denied self-representation. The traditional lyric form of this cycle is a continuation of Kolmar's earlier poetic work. It may also be a strategy for safeguarding a sense of normalcy through traditions that preceded the Nazi movement. Interestingly in this context, Lawrence Langer has argued that in her last lyrical cycle, *Welten* (Worlds), written in the latter half of 1937 and only published posthumously, Kolmar "adopted an uncharacteristic free-verse style virtually absent from her early work, as if the mounting threats to the self in the Hitler era required an assertion beyond the rhyme and controlled rhythms of those earlier poems" (Langer 1982, 211).

Nevertheless, the traditional form that most of Kolmar's poetry shares with much poetry published in the Third Reich can be read as an indication of Kolmar's desire not to be excluded from the German literary heritage that was her own. Again, such classicism performed a different function for poets tolerated or promoted by the Nazi regime. For them such a classicist turn created an appearance of freedom from the political. These different sets of texts show formal and thematic connections that work themselves out differently in each case.

For a comparison between poetry published in Nazi Germany and poetry written in the camps, we can turn, for instance, to the idealization of comradeship, an attitude shared by National Socialists in the Third Reich and by Communists underground and in the concentration camps. This was inherited in both cases from the socialist workers' movement as well as from representations of the experience of the trenches of the First World War. The notion of comradeship functions differently in each of the following two poems. Moreover, the historical position of each particular poem leads us to give them different empathic and critical readings.

In "Der Kamerad" by Herybert Menzel, published in Munich in 1944 (in Schumann, 455), we find the commonplace of a reciprocal relation in which hardship is shared equally by the two comrades, and what benefits one of them will benefit the other one as well. The poem begins with reciprocity and mutual encouragement in the face of difficulty. In fact, the two members of the dyad are undistinguishable and hardly separable. This is an idea of complete reciprocity, but it is generic and therefore abstract. Since comradeship remains confined to the couple, this is a model of love; without the title one might read the first stanza as a panegyric on lasting romantic unions. The second stanza resolves the fear of death via military idealism and a model of incorporation that avoids the pain of loss. Interestingly, like the poetry of "Innerlichkeit" in general, this poem avoids any outspoken political positions other than to support the soldier or "Kämpfer" (fighter). Neither patriotism nor National Socialism is explicitly invoked. What is to keep the soldiers fighting is a loosely defined faith with religious overtones. The second half of the first stanza implies that there could be doubt, less about victory than about the soldier's own safety; the invocation of "a God" in the second stanza introduces a religious element that makes the anxiety a moot point:

> Wenn einer von uns müde wird,
> der andre für ihn wacht.
> Wenn einer von uns zweifeln will,
> der andre gläubig lacht.
>
> Wenn einer von uns fallen sollt,
> der andre steht für zwei;
> denn jedem Kämpfer gibt ein Gott
> den Kameraden bei.
>
> [If one of us becomes tired,
> the other one watches out for him.
> If one of us wants to doubt,
> the other one laughs with faith.
>
> If one of us should fall,
> the other one is there for two;
> because to each fighter a God
> gives his comrade.]

The intent of this poem is to praise and encourage the "fighter"; it does so from a specifically private and intimate perspective: the first-person speaker and the addressee are both "the comrade" of the title. As the last two lines make clear, being a "fighter" is a precondition for partaking in this comradeship designed by divine providence, for both being and having "the comrade." The prospect of death seems to require the introduction of a third term, "a God," as the guarantor of the continuance of the comradeship after death. As long as one fights, the poem promises, one will have a comrade, or a God to provide one.

In "Gelungene Flucht" (Successful Escape) written by imprisoned resistance-fighter Heinz Hentschke in the Emslandlager some time between 1942 and 1944 (printed in Perk 1979, 134–35),[9] the situation of comradeship is more complex. There is a narrative development, and it is not clear until the end what the outcome will be: whether the status of the comradeship will hold up or not. The second section of the poem begins with the switch, instated by the vocative "Kamerad" (comrade), from detached third-person narration to a singular, second-person address by a communal, plural first-person voice. That section expresses a loss of the sense of reciprocity and of solidarity so grave that it threatens to undo the relation, but the rhetorical force of the word "Kamerad" is reaffirmed in the last stanza through repetition of that word, and, more significantly, through a performative declaration that gives priority to the affective bonding of comradeship over the needs of the group. The harshness of the situation, then, requires the rescue — through linguistic affirmation and through a shift in the terms of the relationship — of a value that momentarily threatens to lose its meaning:

"Hei geiht . . ."
Schrieb Fichte auf seinem Kaffeepott und dann,
Dann war er im dichten Nebel verschwunden,
Spurlos verschwunden im Gelände.

Häscher suchten ihn,
Durchstöberten das Lager;
Das gesamte Moor wurde abgesucht,
Auch das übrige Deutschland.

Sie haben ihn nie gefunden.
Er blieb verschwunden.

Kamerad,
Wir indessen,
Stehen wegen deiner Flucht
Zum Dauer-Appell angetreten:
Einen Tag, eine Nacht
Und bis zum anderen Morgen . . .

Zur Strafe dafür,
Daß du erfolgreich
Durch den Draht
Und durch den Nebel bist entkommen!

Nein,
Wir sind dir nicht böse,
Kamerad!

["He's going . . ."
Wrote Fichte on his coffee pot and then,
Then he disappeared in the thick fog,
Disappeared without a trace in the field.

Bloodhounds looked for him,
They scoured the camp;

The whole moor was searched
And also the rest of Germany.

They never found him.
He disappeared for good.

Comrade,
We, in the meantime,
Because of your escape,
Are standing in permanent roll call:
A day, a night
And until the next morning . . .

As punishment,
Because you, successfully
Through the wire
Through the fog, got out!

No,
We are not angry with you,
Comrade!]

In "Der Kamerad," published under National Socialism, the notion of comradeship serves to render military duty romantic and to idealize military sacrifice as a matter of fraternal love and divine grace. In "Gelungene Flucht," a concentration-camp inmate admonishes another inmate for the harsh collective punishment received on the latter's account: "wegen deiner Flucht" (because of your escape). At the same time this poem empathically celebrates the inmate's successful flight, his escape into individual freedom that contrasts with the collective punishment suffered by the remaining inmates and necessitates the individual "comrade's" separation from the group. The poem thus serves to put the inflicted punishment in context, to give it a positive connotation. An implicit, almost vicarious victory can be celebrated by the speaker. The word "disappeared" is repeated in the third and fourth lines as if in incredulity. The term appears again, now triumphantly, in the third stanza: "He disappeared for good." Both poems derive their rhetoric from received valuations of comradeship, but the historical "scene of writing" gives them very different connotations. The dream of escaping into freedom and an individual's implicit superiority over the persecutors inspires hope in "Gelungene Flucht." The looming possibility of death binds the comrades to each other in "Der Kamerad" and provokes a shift to a quasi-religious faith that seems mechanical in its reciprocal automaticity.

More generally, a study of modern concentration-camp poetry makes evident a particular relation to death and mortality in the concentration camps that differs significantly from the relation to death promoted by a public sphere saturated with the language of nationalist heroism and kitsch representations of sublime military death, or by a romanticist sentimentality, as in "Anruf des Herzens" discussed above. A regular rhyme scheme and strict meter mark both the poem "Totenehrung" (Honoring the Dead) by Kurt Eggers, a prolific poet, a soldier, and an SS-leader, and the poem "Friedhof Obodowka" (Obodowka Cemetery), written by Alfred Kittner in the concentration camp Obodowka in Transnistria in October of 1943. Eggers's "Totenehrung," anthologized in 1944 in Munich (in Schumann, 447–48), reads:

> Fragt nicht!
> Klagt nicht!
> Die gefallen,
> sind uns allen
> neu verbunden,
> denn ein Volk
> hat heimgefunden.
>
> Höret!
> Schwöret
> heilge Eide,
> daß ich scheide
> gut von böse.
> Daß das Blut
> das Volk erlöse.
>
> Bangt nicht!
> Wankt nicht!
> Seht von Norden,
> hell geworden,
> unser Zeichen!
> Und die Nacht
> muß von uns weichen.
>
> Neigt euch!
> Beugt euch!
> Vor den Geistern,
> die uns meistern!
> Wir sind Freie.
> Uns umfängt
> des Lichtes Weihe.
>
> Fragt nicht!
> Klagt nicht!
> Die gefallen

sind uns allen
neu verbunden,
denn ein Volk
hat heimgefunden.

[Ask not!
Complain not!
The fallen
are newly united
to us all
because a people
has come home.

Listen!
Swear
holy oaths,
that I may separate
good from bad.
That blood
may save the people.

Fear not!
Falter not!
See from the North,
shining bright,
our sign!
And the night
must yield to us.

Bow down!
Submit!
To the ghosts
who master us!
We are free!
We are surrounded
by the light of consecration.

Ask not!
Complain not!
The fallen
are newly united
to us all
because a people
has come home.]

In "Honoring the Dead," the dead are distant and de-individuated, even if they constitute part of the title and provide the occasion for the poem. The dead remain incorporeal and are incorporated and reincorporated ("neu verbunden") into the community of the living, the "Volk" who has "come home." The dead are linked anew to "all of us" because we have found our racial home. A rhetoric of light, freedom, racial community, and home is invoked in order to dispel any darkness the deadness of the fallen ones might cast: the "night must yield" as the "light from the North" increases, a reference most likely to mythical notions of racial renewal. Note that the speaking voice in the poem is communal and triumphant as it addresses the reader in the second-person plural: we "have come home," "are free," "are surrounded by the light of consecration." This poem to honor the dead is concerned, rather, with the rhetorical validation of the living. The emotional force it has derives from its communal exhilaration in a compulsorily imposed denial of death: "Fragt nicht! / Klagt nicht!"

Kittner's "Friedhof Obodowka" reads at times like an inversion of Eggers's poem. In Kittner's poem the dead have bodies with feet and other body parts that dogs threaten to bite and tear apart. The dead are individuals connected to other individuals both dead (sister, son) and alive (speaker). The poem consists of the speaker's apostrophic address of one such dead individual. The orientation of the poem is rather towards death, as the dead are more numerous and possess a power of attraction that pulls the poet-speaker towards joining the many in the mass grave. There is no validation here, only a frustrated desire to bury the dead person in the winter ice with bare hands. Narrative resolution is achieved through the speaker's concession to biological and historical reality: "But tomorrow in the mass grave you / must rot with the others." As was the case in Kittner's "On the Road," analyzed earlier, death is portrayed as an organic process of decomposition. The desire to provide burial seems an almost banal piety and an unfulfillable habit, a remnant from a former world, one that used to be mindful of the traditional rituals accorded to the dead. Such narrative resolution does not lead to closure: the poem ends with a rhetorical question that reinforces the power of attraction of those who are dead. "Friedhof Obodowka" reads (Kittner 1991, 53–54[10]):

> Dies ist ein finstrer Zeitvertrieb,
> Die Hunde abzuwehren.
> Sie balgen sich um deinen Leib
> Und wollen ihn verzehren.
>
> Sie haben deiner Schwester schon
> Die Füße angebissen
> Und deinen nackten toten Sohn
> In Stücke bald gerissen.

Wie du im Frost liegst, just und weiß,
Scheinst du dich noch zu regen.
Mit eigner Hand im Wintereis
Wollt ich zu Grab dich legen!

Doch morgen musst im Massengrab
Du modern mit den andern.
Wer käm nicht gern zu dir hinab,
Statt von hier fortzuwandern?

[This is a dark way of passing time,
Fending off the dogs,
They scuffle for your body
And want to eat it up.

They have already bitten into
Your sister's feet
And your naked dead son
Almost torn to pieces.

The way you lie in the frost, young and white,
You still seem to move.
With my own hand in the ice of winter
I wanted to give you burial!

But tomorrow in the mass grave must
You rot with the others.
Who wouldn't like to go down to you
Instead of wandering on from here?]

Both poems have regular rhyme and rhythm. Eggers's declaration of a meta-physical union with the dead takes place in very short verses with a staccato rhythm that creates the impression of military discipline and harshness: "Fragt nicht! / Klagt nicht!" These curt imperatives have a mechanical sound that reflects the message the imperatives convey: deny your questions and doubts, deny your mourning, and act in concert with a community of the "Volk." Eggers's poem gives the impression of a disciplined, militarized modernity. Kittner's style, with its longer lines, is more conventionally traditional in terms of form, but the poem's narrative open-endedness and its matter-of-factness in its handling of the dead place it squarely in the twentieth century.

Both of these poems are concerned with honoring and showing respect for the dead, but their rhetorical resources and their development of theme differ widely. Certainly we can justifiably attribute some of this divergence to individual differences among authors, to their divergent sensibilities. Beyond this, however, as documents from the time these poems also convey moods and mentalities that are inextricably linked to their position relative to the "barbed wire." This is not to say that Eggers's poem represents all poetry published under the ægis of the National Socialists, nor that Kittner's poetry is a direct reflection of a general sensibility with respect to death in the concentrationary universe. Rather, each of these poems, like the poems examined earlier by Kolmar, Menzel, and Hentschke, uses the classical lyric heritage in German in a response to events and ideas that correspond to the period and to the author's situation during the period, a time that was characterized by the sense of exception it created for all those involved. The goal of working with these different sets of lyric texts is not to compile a set of comparisons that in any case would be weighed heavily by moral considerations, but rather, based on textual analysis, to examine details of the emotional and mental landscape instantiated there and to explore the differing relations to a common cultural heritage as conditioned by the material and cultural positions of the particular poet.

Conclusion

IN THIS BOOK I HAVE SOUGHt to open a number of poems to scrutiny. My hope is that these poems will continue to reverberate and to do cultural work. As I stated in the introduction, other poems also deserve careful attention. The readings constitute an attempt, however humble, to bring some of these poems into wider circulation and to understand the cultural work with words that these poems perform, the work they did then and the work they can do now. By excavating what Susan Gubar has called "eccentric or trivial details from the calamity" one can hope — like the English-language poets she studies — to "counter not only cultural amnesia but also collective memories that lose their potency when they get recycled as packaged commodities" (146).

As Adorno made clear, literature about the Holocaust must contend with the inadequacy of language to confront or express the extreme, with the speechlessness produced by that historical trauma, and with the inhumanly euphemistic and bureaucratic distortions to which the Nazis subjected language, though the focus on language must not distract from the physical acts of atrocity committed by the Nazis. Carolyn Forché has claimed that "extremity . . . demands new forms and alters older modes of poetic thought" and that "it also breaks forms and creates new forms from these breaks" (42). Paul Celan, "the most important poet of the German language since 1945" (Emmerich 1999, 7), is perhaps exemplary in his acute awareness of the problems poetry faces after the Shoah. Peter Szondi reformulates Adorno while praising Celan's poem "Engführung" (Stretto): "After Auschwitz, one can no longer write poetry, except with respect to Auschwitz" (74), and Theo Buck writes that Celan's "Todesfuge" (Death Fugue) "is and remains for us an exemplary case of possible lyric — after Auschwitz and with Auschwitz." (92). While it is profoundly innovative, Celan's "Todesfuge" participates in conventional notions of melodious, lyric beauty. On the other hand, the following excerpt from "Stretto" shows Celan's avoidance of conventional narrative and form (Celan 1:199). "Stretto" goes beyond that as well: words become fragmented and even syntax fails. There is a mutation of expression and a "de-poetization," but also, down to the typography, a "conscious rejection of every regularity. Out of this practice result verses that in a conventional sense are no longer such. The alienating versification produces anti-verses," claims Buck (108).

Kam, kam.
Kam ein Wort, kam,
kam durch die Nacht,
wollt leuchten, wollt leuchten.

Asche.
Asche, Asche.
Nacht.
Nacht-und-Nacht.—Zum
Aug geh, zum feuchten.

In John Felstiner's translation, this excerpt reads (1995, 121–22):

Came, came.
Came a word, came.
Came through the night,
would lighten, would lighten.

Ashes.
Ashes, Ashes.
Night.
Night-and-Night.—Find
that eye, the moist one.

Felstiner comments on this section thus:

> At its nadir "Stretto" ["Engführung"] has no "I," "you," "they," or
> "we," but a single word: "Ashes." And then, both expanding and emp-
> tying the sense: "Ashes, Ashes." A decade earlier, Celan had felt the
> struggle for "ashes of burnt-out meanings and not only that!" (3:157).
> "Stretto" enacts that struggle. When actuality dumbfounds speech, one
> repeats, with no hope or with hope in this word only: "Night. / Night-
> and-Night." (122)

A reading of poetry from the National Socialist concentration camps suggests that writers there felt compelled to defy the confounding of their
speech and that, in extremity, old forms became useful, or even necessary, as
readily available shapes to constrain in some sense, and to serve as container
for experiences that overwhelm the psyche. Indeed, Celan's early poetry,
some of which was written in internment and under the fresh impression of
the news of the murder of his parents by the Nazis, is more conventional
(Emmerich 1999, 46). Crucially, this difference cannot be traced back simply to differences in experience and temporal perspectives — literary influences as well as intellectual and literary expectations play a role here. In order
to tell their story, to make sense of the senseless violence, authors in the
camps resorted to traditional form, classic versification, and conventional

narrative. Their poetry from the camps offers the concreteness of lived events that finds expression in conventional verse and easily discernible narratives. Later works often use a fragmentary style and figurative language to render concrete the despair, the violence, the tear in the imaginary fabric that holds civilization together. However, as Gubar has shown, other later poets "dealing with the rigid constraints imposed by historical calamity seem drawn to the rigor of structured forms" (258). Of course, by making obscenely violent metaphors actuality, the Nazis rendered the question of metaphoricity itself problematic. The word *Night* is symbolic in Celan's poems as well as in the titles of a number of anthologies of poetry from the camps. The term *Ashes,* however, both operates as a metaphor for inhumanity and refers to the actual human remains produced in the crematoria.

Considered from the perspective of a critique of aesthetic ideology, the camp-poets' use of traditional forms may reproduce structures of consciousness and textual cultures that were part of aesthetic ideology in the 1930s and 1940s in Europe as well as in Nazi Germany. We tend, as Baetens notes, to associate traditionally written poetry with "reactionary or elderly authors" (2), or to think of traditional, canonical forms as "authoritarian and elitist" (Zeiger, 166). Yet poems from the concentration camps can help us reconsider the political valence we assign to lyric forms. These poems demonstrate that traditional rhyme and meter are of use to others besides the agents of hegemonic or oppressive systems and that anti-conventional, avant-gardist lyric is one part, but not the totality, of the poetic response to the Holocaust. To judge the poems analyzed in this book as verses about the Holocaust would be to commit an anachronism. On the contrary, the perspective in the poems is marked by the violently imposed isolation of the writers. But in their particularity these poems convey the work with words that some individuals turned to in order to retain a voice of their own, in order to leave a trace. The challenge for us is to keep their traces from being erased by oblivion.

Appendix of Complete Poems

T HE POEMS ANALYZED IN THIS BOOK are reprinted on the following pages under the author's name. In all cases permission was either obtained or our best efforts to determine copyright holders were unsuccessful.

Georg von Boris
(Flossenbürg, 1942–45)

Hunger

Sechs Tage kein Brot.
Es reitet der Tod
Durch die Reihen.
Verzweifelte schreien;
So nimm mich doch.
Und er gelassen:
Warte noch.
Das können wir nicht fassen.
Der Tod läßt uns leben,
Das ist es eben.
Doch der Hunger macht uns zum Tier.
Sind wir noch Menschen? Wir,
Es ist zum Erbleichen,
Wir fressen an Leichen.

[**Hunger**

Six days without bread.
Death rides
Through the rows.
The desperate scream:
Please take me, do!
And he says calmly:
Wait a little.
We cannot grasp that.
Death lets us live,
That's just it.
But hunger turns us into beasts.
Are we still human? We,
It's so disgusting,
We are feeding on corpses.]

Georg von Boris (continued)

Die Lieder des Grauens

Was in den Stunden,
In denen sie gefoltert und gequält,
Geschlagen und geschunden,
Mir die Sterbenden erzählt,
Bann ich im Erleben des Beschauens,
In die Lieder meines Grauens.

Was mir Greise sagen,
Die in ihren alten Tagen,
nach dem Sensemann nicht fragen.
Was in hellen Morgenschimmern,
Nackte Kinder wimmern,
Die sich um Gevatter Hein nicht kümmern.

Was die Helden melden
Und die Gräber lassen ahnen,
All das Mahnen des Beschauens,
Faß ich in die Lieder meines Grauens.

[**The Songs of Horror**

What in the hours
In which they were tortured and pained,
Beaten and flayed,
The dying have told me,
I capture in the experience of observation,
In the songs of my horror.

What old people tell me,
Who in their old days
Do not ask for the Grim Reaper.
What in the bright morning glare
Naked children whimper,
Who are not concerned with Father Death.

What the heroes report
And the graves let us guess,
All the warnings of observation,
I collect in the songs of my horror.]

Hasso Grabner (1911–76)
(Buchenwald, 1938–40)
© Aufbau-Verlag 1959

Die Häftlingsnummer

Sie möchten gern, daß sie den Menschen lösche
und seinen Namen ins Vergessen trägt,
verlorner Ruf, der keinen Hall erregt,
ein grauer Strich auf einer grauen Fläche.

Ein windverwehtes Nichts in seiner Schwäche,
vom Leben als Karteiblatt abgelegt,
ein Schatten, wo sich sonst ein Herz bewegt,
damit das Herz an dieser Zahl zerbreche.

Nichts kann dem dunklen Wollen Sieg verleihn.
Es nimmt die Nummer jeden an die Hand,
als einer großen Kette dienend Glied,

als voller Ton in unserm hohen Lied,
das Millionen unzertrennbar band,
das Lied: Ich war, ich bin, ich werde sein.

[The Prisoner's Number

They would like it to extinguish the person
and to carry his name into oblivion,
a lost call that evokes no response,
a gray line on a gray surface.

A wind-blown nothing in its weakness,
discarded from life like an index-card,
a shadow, where otherwise a heart would move,
so that the heart will break over that cipher.

Nothing can give victory to that dark will.
The number takes each one by the hand,
as a link beholden to a great chain,

as full sound in our high song
that united millions inseparably,
the song: I was, I am, I will be.]

Heinz Hentschke (1904–70)
(Emlandslager 1942–44)

Gelungene Flucht

"Hei geiht . . ."
Schrieb Fichte auf seinem Kaffeepott und dann,
Dann war er im dichten Nebel verschwunden,
Spurlos verschwunden im Gelände.

Häscher suchten ihn,
Durchstöberten das Lager;
Das gesamte Moor wurde abgesucht,
Auch das übrige Deutschland.

Sie haben ihn nie gefunden.
Er blieb verschwunden.

Kamerad,
Wir indessen,
Stehen wegen deiner Flucht
Zum Dauer-Appell angetreten:
Einen Tag, eine Nacht
Und bis zum anderen Morgen . . .

Zur Strafe dafür,
Daß du erfolgreich
Durch den Draht
Und durch den Nebel bist entkommen!

Nein,
Wir sind dir nicht böse,
Kamerad!

[**Successful Escape**

"He's going . . ."
Wrote Fichte on his coffee pot and then,
Then he disappeared in the thick fog,
Disappeared without a trace in the field.

Bloodhounds looked for him,
They scoured the camp;
The whole moor was searched
And also the rest of Germany.

They never found him.
He disappeared for good.

Comrade,
We, in the meantime,
Because of your escape,
Are standing in permanent roll call:
A day, a night
And until the next morning . . .

As punishment,
Because you, successfully
Through the wire
Through the fog, got out!

No,
We are not angry with you,
Comrade!]

Alfred Kittner (1906–91)
(Steinbruch am Bug and Obodowka
in Transnistria, 1942–44)

Unterwegs

Als es in Strömen auf uns goß,
Im Grunde war es einerlei,
Trieb man mit Prügeln unseren Troß:
Nun birgt des Stalles Stroh uns zwei.
Vor mir bezogst du hier Quartier
Und liegst verwesend unter mir.
Weht Leichenruch auch durch den Raum,
Er schreckt mich nicht aus dumpfem Traum.

Den Läusen warst du bald zu kalt,
Im Grunde war es einerlei,
Du warst kein guter Aufenthalt,
Und schließlich sind wir hier doch zwei,
Drum kriechen sie zu mir herüber
Und bringen mir das schlimme Fieber,
Dem du vor Tagen hier im Mist
Des Lehmigen Stalls erlegen bist.

Du, Liebste, starbst; ich lebe noch;
Im Grunde ist es einerlei.
Auch ich pfeif auf dem letzten Loch,
Und morgen schaufelt man uns zwei
Mit Hunderten ins Massengrab,
Zusammen wirft man uns hinab,
Läßt ohne vieles Federlesen
Uns bis zum Jüngsten Tag verwesen.

[On the Road

It was raining heavily on us,
In fact, it didn't make any difference,
With their sticks they drove us on:
Now this barn's hay shelters the two of us.
Before me you took your place
And now you lie under me in decay.
When the smell of corpses wafts through the air,
It doesn't startle me from my dazed dream.

Soon you were too cold for the lice,
In fact, it didn't make any difference,
You were not a good place to stay,
And after all the two of us are here,
So they are crawling over to me
And bring me the bad fever,
That took your life a few days past
In the muck of this muddy barn.

You, my beloved, died; I am still alive;
In fact, it doesn't make any difference.
My life, too, hangs by a thread,
And tomorrow they will push the two of us
With hundreds of others into the mass grave,
They will throw us down together,
And, without further ado, they'll
Let us rot there until doomsday.]

Alfred Kittner (continued)

Fünfundzwanzig

Schlag zu! Schlag zu! Schon schwinden die Gedanken!
Willkommen, Ohnmacht! noch die letzten zehn.
Bald ists vorbei. Des Lebens Bilder schwanken,
Schauer des Schweigens fühl ich um mich wehn.

Die Zähne beißen täglich wir zusammen,
An eure Schläge habt ihr uns gewöhnt.
Wir tragens leichter, wenn wir still den Namen
Des Schurken fluchen, der uns so verhöhnt.

Daß du mich schlägst, und ich die Schläge dulde,
Es scheint dem Geiste dieser Zeit gemäß,
Und was ich, Deutschland, dir bis heute schulde,
Dein schlimmster Bube bleut mirs aufs Gesäß.

Um meine Schenkel läßt er seinen Riemen
Elastisch tanzen und er haut mit Wucht
Mir auf die nackte Haut ein Netz von Striemen,
Gelassen, wie man eine Rechnung bucht.

Ihr könnt mich, Schweinehunde, massakrieren,
Rutsch ich gebunden jetzt auch auf dem Bauch,
Ich werd euch diese Rechnung präsentieren
Zur rechten Zeit, und eurem Führer auch!

[**Twenty-Five**

Strike on! Strike on! My thoughts already vanish!
Welcome, blackout! Just the last ten.
Soon it will be over. The pictures of life wobble,
I feel showers of silence go around me.

Every day we grit our teeth,
You have got us used to your beatings.
We bear it more lightly when we silently curse
The name of the rogue who thus derides us.

It seems to accord with the spirit of the times,
That you beat me and I endure the beatings,
And what I owe you, Germany, until today,
Your worst villain thrashes on my behind.

Elastically he lets his whip dance
Around my thighs and with force he strikes
On my naked skin a web of welts,
Calmly, like one calculating a bill.

You pigs can massacre me,
As now I, tied up, slide on my belly,
I will present this bill to you
At the right time, and to your Führer too!]

Alfred Kittner (continued)

Friedhof Obodowka

Dies ist ein finstrer Zeitvertrieb
Die Hunde abzuwehren.
Sie balgen sich um deinen Leib
Und wollen ihn verzehren.

Sie haben deiner Schwester schon
Die Füße angebissen
Und deinen nackten toten Sohn
In Stücke bald gerissen.

Wie du im Frost liegst, just und weiß,
Scheinst du dich noch zu regen.
Mit eigner Hand im Wintereis
Wollt ich zu Grab dich legen!

Doch morgen musst im Massengrab
Du modern mit den andern.
Wer käm nicht gern zu dir hinab,
Statt von hier fortzu wandern?

Alfred Kittner (continued)

[**Obodowka Cemetery**

This is a dark way of passing time,
Fending off the dogs,
They scuffle for your body
And want to eat it up.

They have already bitten into
Your sister's feet
And your naked dead son
Almost torn to pieces.

The way you lie in the frost, young and white,
You still seem to move.
With my own hand in the ice of winter
I wanted to give you burial!

But tomorrow in the mass grave must
You rot with the others.
Who wouldn't like to go down to you
Instead of wandering on from here?]

Ruth Klüger (1931–)
(Theresienstadt, Auschwitz and Christianstadt, 1942–45)

Der Kamin

Täglich hinter den Baracken
Seh ich Rauch und Feuer stehn.
Jude, beuge deinen Nacken,
Keiner hier kann *dem* entgehn.
Siehst du in dem Rauche nicht
Ein verzerrtes Angesicht?
Ruft es nicht voll Spott und Hohn:
Fünf Millionen berg' ich schon!
Auschwitz liegt in meiner Hand,
Alles, alles wird verbrannt.

Täglich hinterm Stacheldraht
Steigt die Sonne purpurn auf,
Doch ihr Licht wirkt öd und fad,
Bricht die andere Flamme auf.
Denn das warme Lebenslicht
Gilt in Auschwitz längst schon nicht.
Blick zur roten Flamme hin:
Einzig wahr ist der Kamin.
Auschwitz liegt in seiner Hand,
Alles, alles wird verbrannt.

Mancher lebte einst voll Grauen
Vor der drohenden Gefahr.
Heut kann er gelassen schauen,
Bietet ruhig sein Leben dar.
Jeder ist zermürbt von Leiden,
Keine Schönheit, keine Freuden.
Leben, Sonne, sie sind hin.
Und es lodert der Kamin.
Auschwitz liegt in seiner Hand,
Alles, alles wird verbrannt.

[**The Chimney**[1]

Daily behind the barracks
I see smoke and fire.
Jew, bend your back,
No one can escape *that*.
Do you not see in the smoke
A distorted face?
Does it not call out, full of mockery and sarcasm:
Five million I now contain!
Auschwitz lies in my hand,
Everything, everything will be consumed.

Daily behind the barbed wire
The sun rises purple,
But its light seems empty and hollow
When the other flame appears.
For the warm light of life
Has had no meaning in Auschwitz.
Look into the red flame:
The only truth is the chimney.
Auschwitz lies in its hand,
Everything, everything will be consumed.

Some have lived full of horror
Faced with threatening danger.
Today they look with equanimity,
Offering up their life.
Everyone is depressed by suffering,
No beauty, no joy,
Life, sun are gone,
And the chimney glows.
Auschwitz lies in its hand,
Everything, everything will be consumed.

Ruth Kluger's "Der Kamin" [The Chimney] (continued)

> Hört ihr Ächzen nicht und Stöhnen,
> Wie von einem, der verschied?
> Und dazwischen bittres Höhnen,
> Des Kamines schaurig Lied:
> Keiner ist mir noch entronnen,
> Keinen, keinen werd ich schonen.
> Und die mich gebaut als Grab
> Schling ich selbst zuletzt hinab.
> Auschwitz liegt in meiner Hand,
> Alles, alles wird verbrannt.

Don't you hear the moans and groaning
As from someone who is dying?
And between them bitter mockery,
The chimney's horrid song:
No one has yet outrun me.
No one, no one will I spare.
And those who built me as a grave
I will consume at last.
Auschwitz lies in my hand,
Everything, everything will be consumed.]

Ruth Kluger (continued)

Auschwitz

Kalt und trüb ist noch der Morgen,
Männer gehn zur Arbeit hin,
Schwer von Leid, gedrückt von Sorgen,
Fern der Zeit, da sie geborgen,
Langsam wandern sie dahin.

Aber jene Männer dort
Bald nicht mehr die Sonne sehn.
Freiheit nahm man ihnen fort.
Welch ein grauenvoller Mord,
Dem sie still entgegengehn.

Gott, du allein darfst's doch nur geben,
Das große, heilige Menschenleben,
Du gibst das Dasein und Du gibst den Tod.
Und du, du siehst dieses endlose Morden,
Du siehst die blutigen, grausamen Horden,
Und Menschen verachten dein höchstes Gebot!

Wir haben die herrliche Heimat verlassen,
Bleiben wir ewig in Elend und Not?
Willst Du, daß alle Menschen uns hassen,
Daß wir im Staube der schmutzigen Gassen
Leiden den elendsten, niedrigsten Tod?

Hinter den Baracken brennt
Feuer, Feuer Tag und Nacht.
Jeder Jude es hier kennt,
Jeder weiß, für wen es brennt,
Und kein Aug, das uns bewacht?

Sag, wofür muß ich hier büßen?
Nenn mir eines Unrechts Spur.
Darf ich nicht das Leben grüßen?
Darf mich nicht der Morgen küssen
Und die Schönheit der Natur?

[Auschwitz

Cold and gray is still the morning,
Men go to work,
Heavy with sorrow, depressed with worries,
Far away is the time when they were safe,
Slowly they walk away.

But those men there
Will soon no longer see the sun.
Freedom was taken away from them.
What a horrible murder
Are they quietly approaching.

God, only you alone can give it,
The great, holy human life,
You give existence and You give death.
And you, you see this endless murder,
You see the bloody, brutal hordes,
And people despise your highest law!

We have left behind our lovely homeland,
Will we remain forever in misery and need?
Do You want all people to hate us,
want us, in the dust of the dirty alleys,
To suffer the most miserable, despicable death?

Behind the barracks fire
Burns, fire day and night.
Every Jew here knows it,
Every one knows for whom it burns,
And no eye watches over us?

Say, what must I expiate here?
Tell me of one trace of wrongdoing.
May I not greet life?
May not the morning and the beauty
Of nature kiss me?

Ruth Kluger's "Auschwitz" [Auschwitz] (continued)

Fressen unsere Leichen Raben?
Müssen wir vernichtet sein?
Sag, wo werd ich einst begraben?
Herr, ich will nur Freiheit haben
und der Heimat Sonnenschein!

Fern im Osten liegt ein Dunst,
Und Natur zeigt ihre Kunst:
Sieh, die Sonne bricht hervor.
Zeigt mir diese Strahlensonne
eine neue Lebenswonne,
Zieht die Freiheit still empor?

Will ravens devour our corpses?
Must we be destroyed?
— Say, where will I be buried —
Lord, all I want is to have freedom,
And the sunshine from home.

Far in the East there is a mist
And nature shows her art:
Look, the sun comes through.
Does the sparkling sun show me
a new joy of life,
Is freedom quietly rising?]

Edgar Kupfer-Koberwitz (1906–91)
(Dachau and Neuengamme, 1940–45)

Gestreiftes Kleid

Gestreift ist unser Kleid,
geschoren unser Haar,
wir stehen außerhalb des Rechts, —
auch wer ein Individuum war,
ein Künstler oder Denker gar,
trägt das Gewand des Knechts. —

Gestreift ist unser Kleid,
geschoren unser Haar, —
man hat uns nichts gelassen, —
und alles was uns teuer war,
das Heim, die Frau, das Kind sogar,
die haben wir verlassen. —

Gestreift ist unser Kleid,
geschoren unser Haar, —
nun will man uns zerbrechen,
doch in uns leuchtet still und klar
der Freiheit Siegel wunderbar,
wenn auch kein Wort wir sprechen.—

Gestreift ist unser Kleid,
geschoren unser Haar, —
noch gehen wir mit stolzem Mut,
wie leben täglich in Gefahr,
erniedrigt, wie noch keiner war,
bald trinkt die Erde unser Blut. —
Dann trägt der Kamerad das Kleid,
wohl wissend um das grosse Leid,
das dieser Stoff umschloss. —

Gestreiftes Kleid, gestreiftes Kleid,
du bist mein höchstes Ehrenkleid,
denn was ich litt, das viele Leid,
macht dich unendlich gross. —

[**Striped Cloak**

Striped is our cloak,
shorn our hair,
we stand outside the law, —
even he who as an individual,
an artist or yet a thinker,
wears the gown of the slave. —

Striped is our cloak,
shorn our hair, —
they left us with nothing, —
and everything that was dear to us,
the home, the wife, even the child,
all those have we left behind. —

Striped is our cloak,
shorn our hair, —
they now want to break us,
but the wonderful emblem of freedom
shines in us quietly and brightly,
even if not a word we say.—

Striped is our cloak,
shorn our hair, —
still we walk about with proud courage,
we live daily with danger,
debased as no one has ever been,
soon the earth will drink our blood. —
Then the comrade will wear the cloak
fully conscious of the great pain,
which this cloth used to contain. —

Striped cloak, striped cloak,
you are my highest honor cloak,
because what I suffered, the immense pain
makes you infinitely large. —]

Edgar Kupfer-Koberwitz (continued)

Kette der Tage

Und ein jeder Tag ist so grau und trüb
und ein jeder Tag schleicht dahin —
die Tage rinnen, wie Wasser durch Sieb,
stehlen sich fort wie ein trauriger Dieb,
kaum bleibt uns ein Rest noch von Sinn. —

Und ein jeder Tag löscht uns etwas aus,
einen Funken in unsrer Brust —
Wir sagen nur noch: "die Liebe — das Haus" —
doch es klingt nicht echt, das Echo bleibt aus,
wir empfinden nicht mehr die Lust. —

Ein jeder Tag macht uns dumpfer und matt,
Gefühle verdorren im Herz —
man fühlt nur noch, ob der Magen auch satt,
ob heut man noch Kraft zum Ertragen hat,
und wir halten Roheit für Scherz. —

So stampft jeder Tag unser Ich zur Form,
zum nichtssagenden Dutzendstück: . . .
jeder wird ein Häftling von gleicher Norm,
auch die Seele trägt eine Uniform,
nichts fühlend, nicht Leid mehr noch Glück. —

Die Tage fallen, wie Hämmer so schwer
und schmieden uns nützlich und platt —
es sind schon zuviel und werden noch mehr,
die Tage sind grau, sind öd und sind leer
dem, der ein Fühlen noch hat. —

Und wenn diese Tage verronnen sind,
dann wird, wer sie übersteht,
einsam und still ragen, ein Baum im Wind,
der Welt ganz fremd sein, ein Waisenkind,
an dem scheu vorüber man geht. —

[Chain of Days

And each and every day is gray and triste
and each and every day creeps on —
the days slip by like water through a sieve,
stealing themselves away like a sad thief,
hardly a remnant of sense remains for us. —

And each and every day puts something out
in us, a spark in our breast —
We merely keep saying: "our love — our home" —
but it does not ring true, the echo is out,
we no longer feel desire. —

Every day makes us more dull and weary,
feelings wither away in our hearts —
one just feels: has the stomach had enough,
does one have the strength to endure today,
and we take brutality for a joke. —

Thus every day pounds our I into shape,
into an nondescript, mass-produced item: . . .
all become inmates of the same norm,
even our souls wear a uniform,
feeling nothing, no more pain nor joy. —

The days fall like a hammer, as heavily,
and forge us, useful and flat —
already too many and will yet be more,
the days are gray, are barren and empty
to him who's still able to feel.

And when all these days have run their course,
then will he who withstands it all,
rise up lonely and still, a tree in the wind,
a total stranger to the world, an orphan,
whom shyly one hurries past. —

Kupfer-Koberwitz' "Kette der Tage" [Chain of Days] (continued)

Denn draußen wird keiner uns ganz verstehn,
erkennen wird niemand, warum
wir so ganz verändert die Welt ansehn,
warum so andere Schritte wir gehn:
unsre Seele wurd lahm und krumm. —

Die Tage haben uns "Gestern" geraubt
und die Tage nehmen uns das "Heut" —
es war einmal, daß wir Andern geglaubt,
daß wir Ehrfurcht hatten vor weißem Haupt
und daß wir uns herzlich gefreut. —

Da werden wir sagen: "Die Welt ist dumm,
sie kann uns nicht mehr verstehn."
Wir werden nicht fragen: wieso, warum? —
werden allein sein und eben darum
tiefer in Einsamkeit gehn. —

Because outside no one will understand us,
nobody will recognize why
we look so differently on the world,
why the paths we take are so different:
our soul was crippled, twisted. —

The days have stolen our "yesterday"
and the days take away our "today" —
once upon a time we believed others,
had respect for a graying head
and were capable of true joy. —

We will then say: "The world is stupid,
it cannot understand us any more."
We shall not ask: how come, why? — we
shall be alone and just because of that
go more deeply into loneliness.]

Edgar Kupfer-Koberwitz (continued)

Erinnerung

Man gab ihm das Bild seiner toten Frau —
stumm hat er es angeschaut —
er schwankte, sein Antlitz wurd fahl und grau,
tot war sein Liebstes, tot seine Frau — — —
Stumm hat auf das Bild er geschaut. —

"Fünf Minuten, nicht länger, verstanden, heh? —
Saujud, hast du mich gehört?" —
Oh, ich sehe noch alles vor mir, ich seh'
diesen Mann, dessen Haare weiß wie der Schnee —
und weil ich ganz dicht und ganz neben ihm steh',
hat es mir die Seele verzehrt. —

"Du heulst wohl, weil deine Hure verreckt? —
Wirklich, die Judensau heult!" —
Tief wurde mir da die Seele erschreckt,
ich hab' vor dem Alten mich aufgereckt,
er war hinter mir versteckt —
fast hätte ich auch geheult. —

[**Remembrance**

They gave him the picture of his dead wife —
silently he looked at it —
he tottered, his face became ashen and gray,
dead was his beloved, dead was his wife — — —
silently he looked at the picture. —

"Five minutes, no longer, did you get that, ah?
Sow-Jew, did you hear me?" —
Oh, I still see it all in front of me, I see
this man, his hair white like snow —
and because I stood very close and right next to him,
it pierced my soul. —

"You cry because your whore kicked the bucket? —
Really, the Jewish sow is crying!" —
My soul was deeply shocked then,
I stood up in front of the old man,
he was hidden behind my back —
I almost cried myself. —]

Fritz Löhner-Beda (1883–1942 in Auschwitz)
(Dachau, Buchenwald, and Auschwitz, 1938–42)

Der Häftling

Ich bin ein Häftling, sonst bin ich nix,
hab' keinen Namen, die Nummer X.
Gestreift ist mein Rock, die Hose auch,
Ich schnüre den Riemen um gar keinen Bauch —
und warte!

Ich schaffe am Tag an die vierzehn Stund',
ich kriech' in den Stall und bin müd' wie ein Hund.
Dann ess' ich die Handvoll verkrümeltes Brot
und fall' auf den Strohsack und schlafe wie tot —
und warte!

Das Weib und die Kinder, die sitzen zu Haus'.
Bald sind es fünf Jahre! Wie seh'n sie wohl aus?
Ich sehe die große verdunkelte Stadt,
da sind sie verkrochen und werden nicht satt —
und warten!

Doch mich schlägt kein Tiger, mich frißt kein Hai,
der Tod geht täglich an mir vorbei.
An mir beißt der Teufel die Zähne sich aus.
Ich fühl' es: Ich komm' aus der Hölle heraus!
Ich warte!

[The Inmate

I'm an inmate, nothing else,
I've got no name, the number X.
Striped is my jacket and so are my pants,
I tighten my belt around no belly at all —
and wait!

I labor for fourteen hours a day,
I crawl to the stable, tired like a dog.
Then I eat my handful of breadcrumbs
and fall onto the straw sack and sleep like I'm dead —
and wait!

The wife and the children are sitting at home.
Soon it will be five years. What do they look like?
I see the city, big and darkened,
there they crawl about, always hungry —
and they wait!

But no tiger will attack me, no shark'll devour me,
Death passes me by every day.
The devil himself will break his teeth on me.
I feel it: I will get out of hell!
I'm waiting!]

Fritz Löhner-Beda (continued)

Untitled

Wenn sich müd die Glieder senken,
Tief ersehnen Ruh' und Traum,
Zieht ein süßes Deingedenken,
Liebste, durch der Seele Raum.

Große Kinderaugen schauen
Wie aus einem Märchenwald
Hold mit kindlichem Vertrauen,
Fragend: "Papi, kommst du bald?"

Und mir ist es so, als schwebe
Eure Liebe über mir,
Und ich weiß, warum ich lebe,
Und ich fühl' es tief, wofür.

[**Untitled**

When my tired limbs sink down,
Deeply longing for rest and dreams,
A sweet remembrance of you, dearest,
Breezes through the space of my soul.

Big children's eyes look, fair,
Like out of a fairytale wood,
Asking with childlike
Trust: "Daddy, are you coming soon?"

And I feel as if your love
Were floating over me.
And I know why I am alive,
And I deeply feel, what for.]

Karl Schnog (1897–1964)
(Dachau, Sachsenhausen, and
Buchenwald, 1941–45)

Der Steinbruch

Eine Landschaft, wie am Schöpfungstage:
Sand und Steine. Büsche. Und sonst nichts.
Graue Gräser. Schreie wilder Klage.
Ort des Grauens, Tal des Weltgerichts.

Müde Füße, abgewetzte Treppen.
Alles jagt und hastet, keucht und rennt.
Schleppen — Schleppen — Schleppen — Schleppen.
Und erbarmungslos die Sonne brennt.

Schläge klatschen, Menschen fallen nieder.
Wolken Staubes und dazwischen Blut.
Fallen — Tragen. Immer, immer wieder.
Schmerzensschreie, Schreie wilder Wut.

Doch der Tag der Freiheit kommt für jeden.
Kamerad im Steinbruch, bist noch Knecht.
Einmal werden die Steine für dich reden.
Wird der Steinbruch einst an dir gerächt? . . .

[The Stone Quarry

A landscape, like on the day of creation:
Sand and stones. Bushes. And nothing else.
Gray grasses. Screams of wild lament.
Place of horror, valley of the Last Judgment.

Tired feet, worn out steps.
Everyone chases and hurries, pants and runs.
Carry — Carry — Carry — Carry.
And the sun burns without pity.

Strikes resound, people fall.
Clouds of dust and in between blood.
Fall down — Carry away. Again, and again, and again.
Screams of pain, screams of wild rage.

But the day of freedom will come for everyone.
Comrade in the stone quarry, you are still a slave.
One day the stones will speak for you.
Will one day the quarry be revenged? . . .]

Karl Schnog (continued)

Jedem das Seine

Die Herren haben wirklich Humor
In diesen bitteren Zeiten:
"JEDEM DAS SEINE" steht höhnisch am Tor,
Durch das die Häftlinge schreiten.

So leuchtet, erhaben und arrogant,
Was sie an das Höllentor schmieden.
Uns ist auch ohne das Sprüchlein bekannt,
Was jedem im Lager beschieden:

Dem Häftling — das Stehen in Sonne und Sturm,
Erfrieren und klatschende Güsse.
Dazu vom todesdrohenden Turm
Das ernste Versprechen der Schüsse.

Den Henkern — die Ehre, der schmackhafte Schmaus,
Das Gleiten auf federnden Felgen;
Die Ruhe und das behagliche Haus,
Die Wollust, die Macht und das Schwelgen.

Dem Häftling — der Hunger, die Angst und die Last,
Die Marter, die viehischen Witze;
Das Essen, das Baden, das Schlafen in Hast
Und schließlich die mordende Spritze.

Ihr Herren, die ihr heute noch grient,
Glaubt mir, was ich schwörend beteure:
Einst holt sich der Häftling, was er verdient.
Und Ihr? Ihr bekommt dann das Eure!

[To Each His Own

Their lordships have a good sense of humor
In these bitter times:
"TO EACH HIS OWN" stands scornfully on the gate,
Through which the inmates march in.

Sublime and arrogant thus shines
What they welded onto the gate to hell,
We know even without the little saying
What everyone is fated to in the camp:

To the inmate — standing in sun and storm,
Freezing and roaring downpours.
On top of that from the mortally menacing tower
The earnest promise of bullets.

To the torturers — honor, a tasty banquet,
Gliding on well-oiled wheels;
Rest and a comfortable home,
Pleasure, power, and feasting.

To the inmate — hunger, fear, and the burden,
Torture, bestial jokes;
Eating, bathing, and sleeping in haste
And finally the murderous injection.

You lordships, who still grin today,
Believe me, what I hereby swear:
One day the inmate will claim what he deserves.
And you? You will then get your share!]

Karl Schnog (continued)

Der Häftling

Sie standen um ihn, roh und wutbesessen,
Und drohten ihm mit Knüppel, Kugel, Beil.
Sie wollten ihn mit Schreck und Schlag erpressen,
Und ihre Henkeraugen glänzten geil.

Er sah nur stumm in ihre Mörderfressen
Und schwieg und litt. Und dachte sich sein Teil.
Sie schlugen zu in blutigen Exzessen
Und gingen lachend fort und brüllten "Heil!"

Er lag und überlegte unterdessen:
Wie schweig ich nur noch eine kurze Weil'.
Hat nie den Auftrag, nie das Ziel vergessen.
Der Körper wund, der Wille stark und steil!

Nackte Aussage

Ich habe so tief im Elend gesteckt,
Ich schien verloren, verkommen, verdreckt.
Gejagt ward ich und gepeinigt.
Erst, wenn ich sage, was ich sah,
Erst, wenn ich schreibe, was geschah,
Bin ich vom Schmutz gereinigt.

[The Inmate

They stood around him, brutal and furious,
And threatened him with cudgel, bullet, noose.
They wanted to blackmail him with fear and blows,
And their torturers' eyes glowed with lust.

Without a word he watched their murderer-snouts
And was silent and suffered. And thought his own thoughts.
They beat him up in bloody excess
And went away laughing and roaring "Heil!"

He lay and thought in the meantime;
How will I keep quiet for another while.
He never forgot the duty nor the goal.
His body in pain, his will strong and tall!]

[Naked Testimony

I was so deep in misery,
I seemed lost, debased, soiled.
Persecuted was I, and tortured.
Only after I say what I saw,
Only after I write what happened,
Will I be cleansed of the dirt.]

Ilse Weber (1903–44 in Auschwitz) (Theresienstadt 1942–44)

Theresienstädter Kinderreim

Rira, rirarutsch,
wir fahren in der Leichenkutsch,
rira, rirarutsch,
wir fahren in der Kutsch.
Wir stehen hier und stehen dort
und fahren flink die Leichen fort,
rirarutsch,
wir fahren in der Kutsch.

Rira, rirarutsch,
was einst wir hatten ist jetzt futsch,
rira, rirarutsch,
ist längst schon alles futsch.
Die Freude aus, die Heimat weg,
den letzten Koffer fährt, o Schreck,
rirarutsch,
jetzt fort die Leichenkutsch.

Rira, rirarutsch,
man spannt uns vor die Leichenkutsch.
Rira, rirarutsch,
man spannt uns vor die Kutsch.
Hätt sie geladen unser Leid,
wir kämen nicht drei Schritte weit,
rirarutsch,
zu schwer wär dann die Kutsch.

[A Nursery Rhyme from Theresienstadt[2]

Heave! Look out ahead!
Here comes the wagon with the dead.
Heave! Look out ahead!
The wagon with the dead.
We stop right here and stop right there,
We drive dead bodies everywhere.
Look ahead!
The wagon with the dead.

Heave! Look out ahead!
Destroyed and gone — all that we had.
Heave! Look out ahead!
Destroyed and gone, I said.
The end of joy, our home's away,
Our luggage left the other day.
Look ahead!
We're coming with the dead.

Heave! Look out ahead!
They've hitched us to the cart instead.
Heave! Look out ahead!
They've hitched us up instead.
If all our pain were put on it,
We wouldn't even move one bit.
Look ahead!
A wagon full of dead.]

Notes

Introduction

[1] Hélène Cixous, "Poetry is/and (the) Political" (1980, 16). In the original French version of this text, Cixous more forcefully suggests a varied relation between poetry and silence, while she understands poetry both as a subject "Could poetry still whisper at Auschwitz?" and as an action "Who poeticizes in Cambodia?": "Que voulait dire la poésie dans le ghetto de Varsovie? La poésie murmurait-elle encore à Auschwitz? Qui poème au Cambodge? Quand commence le silence? Quand échappons-nous au silence? Quand le silence est-il de pierre, de sable, d'or? De souffle? A partir de quand perdons-nous la possibilité de poésie?" (1979, 29).

[2] "About the composition of literature and in particular the production of verse," Susan Gubar writes, "the 1949 judgment of Theodor Adorno was taken to be as axiomatic as the biblical commandment against graven images: 'To write poetry after Auschwitz is barbaric'" (3–4). For an enlightening account of the reception of Adorno's formulations on writing "poetry after Auschwitz" see Michael Rothberg 2000, especially chapter 1. For a recent example of the reception of Adorno in German see Günther Bonheim. As an anonymous reader of this book in its manuscript form candidly suggested, Adorno's sentence has been overreferenced, if not overanalyzed. Though reference to it will be made in this book, the bulk of attention will be given to the poems themselves.

[3] Poems from the ghettos and camps in other languages have been studied: for example, poetry in Polish and Yiddish by Frieda Aaron; poetry in Yiddish by Rachel Ertel, Christina Pareigis, and Florian Freund et al.; and writings in Yiddish by David Roskies (1984, 1986), as have other writings from the camps such as diaries (Andrea Reiter 2000; Renata Laqueur). Artistic and personal expressions from the ghettos and camps in a variety of media, from painting (Mickenberg, Granof, and Hayes), music (Fackler), religion (Rahe), cabaret (Kühn), and theater (Rovit and Goldfarb), to recipes (Silva; Goldenberg) have also been researched.

[4] The formulation dates from earlier; see Arendt 1948; 1950.

[5] When the original text cited is in a language other than English, the translation, unless otherwise noted, is my own.

[6] The German word "Reich" is also contained in the first word from Celan's speech cited here, "Erreichbar," suggesting that the (German) language remains *reachable* only through the "Reich." In addition the term "enriched" connotes the enrichment of minerals that makes them radioactive and thus suggests that the language is more gravely affected than is at first obvious from the speech. I thank Thomas A. Pepper for pointing this out to me.

[7] Given the "transnational, trangeneric nature of art after the Shoah," Susan Gubar writes of poets who view "not a single national idiom but language itself as the only homeland" (247).

[8] Michael Rothberg has argued for careful periodization in this context, pointing out that "the temporal break that we retroactively infer in the phrase "after Auschwitz" had not yet taken place in 1940s' public consciousness. The response to, and the form of, some of the texts of the late 1940s (including Adorno's) confirm that the afterlife of an event needs to be periodized as carefully as the event itself. An event alone does not always rupture history; rather, the constellation that that event forms with later events creates the conditions in which epochal discontinuity can be thought" (38).

[9] Poetry therapy, like psychotherapy more generally, was a traditionally gendered field: hence the prototypically male therapist reads here to the typically female patient — in quasi-pedagogical fashion.

[10] The notion of "emergency poetry" comes from an essay on poetry therapy by Joost Meerloo (1969).

[11] For a synopsis of Meerloo's life, see Coleman Nelson.

[12] Meerloo's "personal anecdote" is a case in point for the kinds of distancing structures often evident in poems from the camps. There is no specific information about chronology or location. The narrator begins with the announcement that what will follow was a personal experience: "I had a personal encounter," and then proceeds to recount: "I remember how three prisoners lay crowded . . ." At first it is not entirely clear whether or not the narrator is one of the three prisoners or not. From that point on, the personal narrator becomes a first person plural narrator: "we were from different lands." With the grammatical structure "one of us," it is no longer possible to identify the subject of the action, and later on Meerloo will refer to "the emergency poets" in the third person, as if his deference to "more creative talents" preempted any personal claim to "war poetry by non-poets," other than knowledge: "my repeated experience" that people in extreme anxiety "would suddenly find a rhythmic voice inside themselves."

[13] On the transferential relation to texts, see Ihanus.

[14] Work with Holocaust survivors and their children has proved fertile ground for the exploration of questions such as: What do survivors remember? How does memory work? How is affect repressed or displaced? How does the traumatic experience affect the survivor's personality and behavior in the present? Is there a "survivor syndrome"? What are the intergenerational effects of trauma? What possibilities are there for a creative elaboration of trauma?

[15] Elsewhere LaCapra writes "Empathy is, I think, a virtual but not a vicarious experience in that the historian puts him- or herself in the other's position without taking the other's place or becoming a substitute or surrogate for the other who is authorized to speak in the other's voice. Empathy involves affective response to the other, and affective response interacts with difference as well as critical distancing and analysis in historiography. It implies what I am terming empathic unsettlement in the secondary witness . . . This unsettlement should, I think, have nonformulaic stylistic effects in representation, for example, in placing in jeopardy harmonizing or fetishis-

tic accounts that bring unearned spiritual uplift or meaning . . . At the very least the empathic unsettlement of the secondary witness with respect to trauma brings out the dubiousness of a quest for closure or full dialectical synthesis" (2004, 65).

[16] Crucially, Gubar allows for the risks of imaginative identification while insisting, however, that "perverted forms of empathy do not delegitimize efforts to conceptualize the empathic imagination within frameworks that take into account and defuse its potential for symbolic violence amid those disparate power relations it seeks to traverse" (255).

[17] Bakhtin writes in 1970: "There exists a very strong, but one-sided and thus untrustworthy, idea that in order better to understand a foreign culture, one must enter into it, forgetting one's own, and view the world through the eyes of this foreign culture. This idea, as I said, is one-sided. Of course, a certain entry into a foreign culture, the possibility of seeing the world through its eyes, is a necessary part of the process of understanding it; but if this were the only aspect of this understanding, it would merely be a duplication and would not entail anything new. *Creative understanding* does not renounce itself, its own place in time, its own culture; and it forgets nothing. In order to understand, it is immensely important for the person who understands to be *located outside* the object of his or her creative understanding — in time, in space, in culture" (Bakhtin, 7). See also Todorov (1984), especially pp. 94–112. Todorov describes three kinds of interpretation: "The first consists in unifying in the name of the self: the critic projects himself in the work he reads, and all authors illustrate or exemplify his thought. The second kind corresponds to the 'criticism of identification' . . . The critic has no proper identity, there is but one identity, that of the author under examination, and the critic becomes his mouthpiece . . . The third kind would be the dialogue advocated by Bakhtin, where each of the two identities remains affirmed (there is neither integration nor identification), where knowledge takes the form of a dialogue with a 'thou' equal to the 'I' and yet different from it" (1984, 107–8).

[18] Dominick LaCapra writes: "Recognizing transferential tendencies should ideally enable one to resist uncritical identification with the other and the derivation of one's identity from others in ways that deny their otherness . . . Recognizing the force of, or trying to come to terms with, transference also enables one to appreciate both the insistence of tendencies toward identification and the limitations of objectification that ignores such tendencies, forecloses the problem of the investigator's subject positions, and denies the other's voice and the questions it poses for oneself and one's approach. Here a crucial issue is the extent to which one comes to terms with transference through acting-out and working-through" (2004, 83).

[19] Gubar continues: "Because fascist rhetoric turned Jews into parasites, vermin or germs or poisoners to be exterminated, perhaps we will evade too vacuous or lurid, too theatrical or too theoretical, too glib or too sanctimonious a tone by keeping steadily before our eyes the sinister potential of our own rhetoric to imperil the humanity of its subjects" (7).

[20] Garland emphasizes the *individual* nature of the response to trauma: "However precisely we might be able to identify and quantify the nature of the stressor, it is not sufficient as a way of understanding the impact on the individual. The individual has a constitution and a history which have shaped his internal world; hence a character

and personality. *He also has a culture.* He is someone who is more or less vulnerable to that particular event at that particular moment in his developmental history. That vulnerability is a function of the inevitable interplay between objective and subjective, external and internal reality" (23, my emphasis).

[21] Langer argues that "It is virtually useless . . . to approach the experience [of Nazi persecution] from the reservoir of normal values, armed with questions like 'Why didn't they resist?' and 'Why didn't they help each other?' The first answer is that they did; the second is that sometimes it made no difference; and the third is that, under those circumstances, more often than not they couldn't. All are true, just as each testimony is true, even when the testimonies contradict one another" (1991, 20–21).

[22] In the *Dictionnaire des genres et notions littéraires,* Jean-Marie Schaeffer distinguishes between genres as "historically specific texts" and more abstract, transhistoric categories (354). He also emphasizes that considerations are relative, that different classifications in terms of genre bring about different aspects of a text into focus, and that "une œuvre littéraire n'est jamais uniquement une réalité textuelle (qu'elle soit écrite ou orale), mais aussi un acte, une interaction verbale socialement réglée entre un auteur et un public. Quel que soit le contenu ou la forme de l'œuvre que l'auteur veut communiquer à ses lecteurs ou à son auditoire, il faut d'abord qu'il réussisse à faire reconnaître son œuvre comme acte communicationnel spécifique" (355; a work of literature is never just a textual reality (whether written or oral), it is also an act that accords to social rules, a verbal interation between an author and a public. Whatever the content or form of the work that the author wants to communicate to the readers or listeners: to begin with the author must have the literary work recognized as a specific act of communication). Through their form, poems from the camps seem to insist on their own status as poems.

[23] Poetry from the ghettos and concentration camps has been used in official ceremonies of commemoration. For instance, in a special session of the German Bundestag to mark the sixtieth anniversary of the liberation of Auschwitz, Wolf Biermann read from his translation of Yitzhak Katzenelson's Yiddish epic poem written in internment. See Jule Luteroth, "Holocaust-Gedenkstunde im Bundestag: 'Weh mir. Es weint keiner mehr,'" *Spiegel Online,* 27 January 2005, http://www.spiegel.de/politik/deutschland/0,1518,338818,00.html (accessed 27 January 2005).

[24] Emmerich's call to study these poems does not seem to have inspired Moll's work; Emmerich's essay (1976) does not appear in Moll's bibliography.

[25] Though not dedicated to the Holocaust, the Jewish Museum in Berlin, in particular in its architecture, bears witness to the centrality of the Holocaust in German-Jewish history and in Germany's relationship to history and to Jewish communities at home and abroad.

[26] For a detailed and incisive history of the concept of trauma, see Leys.

[27] In this context it seems worth noting that this publishing house, founded by Samuel Fischer, was the publisher for such prominent authors as Thomas Mann, Franz Kafka, and Sigmund Freud. In 1955 Fischer Verlag brought out *Anne Frank's Diary* in German and in 1984 the writings and letters of the Scholl siblings (see the history of the publishing house on its website: http://www.fischerverlage.de/sixcms/detail.

php?template=fv_default_wrapper&_navi_area=fv_vert2&_navi_item=01.01.00.00&_
content_template=fv_verlag_geschichte_detail&id=39699).

[28] 1993 saw the publication of *Mein Schatten in Dachau: Gedichte und Biographien
der Überlebenden und Toten des Konzentrationslagers* (My Shadow in Dachau: Poems
and Biographies of the Survivors and the Deceased of the Concentration Camp),
compiled by Dorothea Heiser and sponsored by the Comité International de Dachau. A thin volume edited by Katja Klein, *Kazett-Lyrik: Untersuchungen zu
Gedichten und Liedern aus dem Konzentrationslager Sachsenhausen* (Concentration-
Camp Poetry: Analyses of Poems and Songs from the Sachsenhausen Concentration
Camp), appeared in 1995, as did a reprint of a notebook of songs illegally created
collaboratively by a number of inmates in Sachsenhausen under the title: *Sachsenhausen-Liederbuch* (Sachsenhausen Songbook; Morsch). *Stimmen aus Buchenwald:
Ein Lesebuch* (Voices from Buchenwald: A Reader) contains a few poems from that
camp (Kirsten and Kirsten).

[29] Books of poetry from the camps by individual authors include Hermann Adler,
Gesänge aus der Stadt des Todes: Todeslagergedichte aus dem Wilnaer Ghetto, 1941/42
(Song from the City of Death: Death-Camp Poems from the Vilna Ghetto,
1941/42; 1994); Selma Meerbaum-Eisinger, *Ich bin in Sehnsucht eingehüllt: Gedichte*
(I am Shrouded in Yearning: Poems); Alfred Kittner, *Schattenschrift: Gedichte*
(Shadow-Writing: Poems; 1988); as well as two books of poems by Ilse Weber, one
published in Sweden as *Ilse Weber — Theresienstadt* (1978), and one published in
Germany as *In deinen Mauern wohnt das Leid: Gedichte aus dem KZ Theresienstadt*
(Sorrow Dwells within Your Walls: Poems from the Concentration Camp Theresienstadt; 1991). Curiously, and perhaps symptomatic for the history of publication of
these types of writings, although a number of works were published shortly after the
war and then republished in the 1990s, publishers of the later editions were often
unaware of the earlier printings. For example, Yitzhak (or Jizchak) Katzenelson's
Yiddish epic, which was written in internment and translated into Hebrew and English in Israel as *The Song of the Murdered Jewish People* (1980), had appeared in a free
translation into German by Hermann Adler in Switzerland in 1951 as *Dos lid funm
ojsgehargetn jidischen folk: Das Lied vom letzten Juden in der Nachdichtung von
Hermann Adler* (The Song of the Exterminated Jewish People: The Song of the Last
Jew in Hermann Adler's Adaptation). The publisher Hentrich in Berlin put out a reprint of Adler's translation in 1992. In 1994, Wolf Biermann published a new (the
book claims first) translation into German of Katzenelson's epic under the title
Großer Gesang vom ausgerotteten jüdischen Volk (The Great Song of the Exterminated
Jewish People).

Chapter 1

[1] Rothberg continues: "In [Klüger's] text, the extreme and the everyday are neither
opposed, collapsed, nor transcended through a dialectical synthesis — instead, they
are at once held together and kept forever apart in a mode of representation I call
traumatic realism" (129–30).

[2] "Going on Living" is Lore Segal's title for her foreword to Ruth Klüger's *Still Alive*
(2001). She writes: "The English title *Still Alive* thumbs its nose at those who

wanted Ruth Kluger dead, but loses perhaps a small nuance in the German *weiter le-ben:* "going on living" suggests it's a bit of a chore" (Segal 2001, 12). (The English-language edition writes Kluger instead of Klüger, even though the copyright page uses the diacritical mark over the letter *u*, as does Klüger's own text when she refers to her father's name plate [2001, 31].)

[3] For a discussion of a problematic and somewhat unsympathetic popular reception of Klüger's book in the US press, see Linda Schulte-Sasse. Schulte-Sasse argues that Klüger's critiques of voyeurism and sentimentality in the relation to Holocaust survivors combined with her refusal to offer a seamless surface for identification have scandalized some of her US readers. Schulte-Sasse claims that Klüger "frustrates our redemptive Holocaust paradigm with two oppositional strategies, the intermingling of a Holocaust story with personal recollections that are too close, and with a narrative attitude that's too far away" (474). On the other hand, Nancy K. Miller's nuanced essay on *Still Alive* explores some significant and significantly "familiar" aspects of the book as a mother-daughter memoir and as a tale of immigration and Americanization (2004).

[4] Rothberg writes: "The exclusionary gesture of focusing on experience at the expense of history and representation ultimately leads Langer to exclude as well all experiential evidence that does not fit his thesis about the radical rupture of extremity. Any testimony that might support the idea of a continuity between the experience of the concentrationary universe and the values of the outside world is dismissed, as are any accounts that deny the ultimate contamination of the survivor's post-Holocaust world by the death-world of mass murder" (120–21).

[5] Here, too, one may point out that oral testimonies can only take place against the background of survival, thus possibly also providing a "reassuring appearance of" the triumph of life over death. In addition, Rothberg has argued that "Langer's stress on immediacy is problematic first because of the indefensible position that oral testimony is not inflected by rhetoric, the social context of the interview's production, and intervening historical factors. Equally odd, however, for a literary critic, is Langer's situating of the immediacy of experience on the side of the interviewers and viewers" (120).

[6] See, for example, Rosenfeld's discussion of Elie Wiesel's and Michael Wyschogrod's positions in Rosenfeld, chapter 1.

[7] Ironically the transcendental is precisely what the second half of Hölderlin's poem seems to avoid.

[8] In this context see also Rothberg's notion of differentiation: "Differentiation, on the other hand, can be seen as a nontotalizing process of distinction whereby differences are held together, while simultaneously a "displacement of the clear borderlines of thought" takes place" (132).

[9] For the concept of "imagined communities," see Anderson.

[10] I discuss the issue of the Muselmänner in greater detail in chapter 3.

[11] The dedication, with its apparent inspiration to sentimentalism, seems to have a life of its own. It is announced in the sub-headline for the article, and after the newspaper publication, the name adds on an *h*, it become "Hannah Ungar" in Schlösser, where it is included with the main text (1960, 121). Thereafter, the dedication

moves to the authors' information section in the back in Seydel (549), and then returns to be printed after the title of the poem in Moll and Weiler (132) and in Lau and Pampuch (56). The dedication is not mentioned in Klüger (1994).

[12] "Flamme" (flame) in the original; "name" in Gilman's translation, which I assume is a typographical error.

[13] Text by Fritz Löhner-Beda, music by Hermann Leopoldi (see Denscher and Peschina, 188–89).

[14] Text by Johann Esser and Wolfgang Langhoff, music by Rudi Goguel (Fackler, 245–65).

[15] For a compelling and detailed study of concentration-camp songs and of the use of music in the concentration camps, see Guido Fackler's *"Des Lagers Stimme": Musik im KZ* ("The Camp's Voice: Music in the Concentration Camps).

Chapter 2

[1] For a detailed description and analysis of the humiliation and dehumanization in these conditions, see Des Pres, particularly chapter 3: "The Excremental Assault" (51–72).

[2] From Jean Samuel, "Primo Levi: A Companion, a Friend, a Witness." Lecture delivered at Cornell University, Fall 1997.

[3] Levi comments on the tattooing of the number thus: "The operation was not very painful and lasted no more than a minute, but it was traumatic. Its symbolic meaning was clear to everyone: this is an indelible mark, you will never leave here; this is a mark with which slaves are branded and cattle sent to the slaughter, and that is what you have become. You no longer have a name; this is your new name. The violence of the tattoo was gratuitous, an end in itself, pure offense: were the three canvas numbers sewed to pants, jackets, and winter coat not enough? No, they were not enough: something more was needed, a non-verbal message, so that the innocent would feel his sentence written on his flesh. It was also a return to barbarism, all the more perturbing for Orthodox Jews: in fact, precisely in order to distinguish Jews from the barbarians, the tattoo is forbidden by Mosaic law (Leviticus 19:28)" (1988, 119). For a different reaction to the tattooing of the number, consider Ruth Klüger's recollection, which speaks of the projections into the future elicited by the experience and an ambiguous sense of self-importance attached to it too: "The tattoo produced a new alertness in me. Thanks to the dog tag under my skin, I was suddenly so aware of the enormity, the monstrosity, really, of my situation that I felt a kind of glee about it. I was living through something that was worth witnessing. Perhaps I would write a book with a title like *A Hundred Days in a Concentration Camp.* (Books and pamphlets with such titles did crop up after the war.) No one would be able to deny that I was one of the persecuted who had to be respected for their unusual and dangerous experiences, unlike those who had been simply neglected or pushed aside. I would have to be taken seriously with my tattooed number. . . . It tells you something about how beaten down and stripped of a sense of self I already was that I thus invented for myself a future based on the experience of the most abysmal humiliation yet, a future where precisely that abyss would appear honorable" (2001, 98).

[4] In Grabner, 21, © Aufbau-Verlag Berlin 1959. Reprinted in Schneider 1973 and 1976, 168; Moll 1983, 109; Elling 1990, 42; Kirsten and Kirsten, 24.

[5] For a compelling analysis of the bureaucratic order in the camps, see Sofsky, 111–12.

[6] For an account of this military unit, see for example Deutscher Militärverlag, 1965

[7] Printed in Schneider 1973 and 1976, 167–68. Reprinted in Moll 1983, 229; Elling 1990, 34; Schwarberg, 139–40.

[8] Reprinted in Schneider 1976, 142; Moll 1983, 424; Elling 1990, 36; Schwarberg, 135.

[9] In Kupfer-Koberwitz n.d. Reprinted in Heiser, 62–63; Kupfer-Koberwitz 1997, 516–17.

Chapter 3

[1] Also printed in Kupfer-Koberwitz 1997, 537–38. According to the diary, this poem was written in July of 1944 (Kupfer-Koberwitz 1997, 329).

[2] Gubar, for example, writes of the cancellation of eroticism and of the damage to masculinity in and through the Holocaust (244–45, 253).

[3] The rumor started going around at Neuengamme that the weak and the ill would be "transported" to Dachau, Kupfer-Koberwitz among them. He describes the reaction to the rumor thus: "People spoke of Dachau. To many it sounded like fairytales: everyone his own bed with linen, pillow, and blankets. Fresh laundry every fourteen days, no torn-up clothes, no wooden clogs but leather shoes and — the most important thing — the meal thick and usually a whole liter. Fools' paradise Dachau! No, it was too beautiful to be true" (1957, 147).

[4] Reprinted in Seydel, 295; Schneider 1973 and 1976, 162; Moll 1983, 116; Lau and Pampuch, 63; Kirsten and Kirsten, 143 and back cover.

[5] Reprinted in Schneider 1973 and 1976, 166–67; Moll 1983, 99–101.

[6] Reprinted in Kupfer-Koberwitz 1997, 525–28.

[7] Personal communication.

[8] Agamben reminds us: "The idea that the corpse deserves particular respect, that there is something like a dignity of death, does not truly belong to the field of ethics. Its roots lie instead in the most archaic stratum of law, which is at every point indistinguishable from magic. The honor and care of the deceased's body was originally intended to keep the soul of the dead person (or, rather, his image or phantasm) from remaining a threatening presence in the world of the living . . ." (79).

[9] Also printed in Seydel, 359, and Moll and Weiler, 77.

[10] Another very popular version reads: "Ri ra rutsch, / wir fahren mit der Kutsch, / wir fahren mit der Schneckenpost, / wo es keinen Pfennig kost, / ri ra rutsch, / wir fahren mit der Kutsch" (Ri ra rutsch, we ride on the coach, / we ride on the snail-coach, / it doesn't cost a penny / ri ra rutsch; Enzensberger, 71).

[11] Also printed in Seydel, 244; Moll and Weiler, 123; Lau and Pampuch, 55

Chapter 4

[1] Also printed in Kupfer-Koberwitz 1997, 536–37. According to the diary, this poem was written in July of 1944 (Kupfer-Koberwitz 1997, 329).

[2] Reprinted in Moll and Weiler, 71. There, this poem is printed with the mistaken annotation that it was "likely written in prison between 1940 and 1944."

[3] Reprinted in Schneider 1973 and 1976, 171; Moll 1983, 225; Moll and Weiler, 63.

[4] Reprinted in Schneider 1973 and 1976, 157; Moll 1983, 111. In Schneider (1973 and 1976) the poem appears under the title "Ein Häftling" (An Inmate), even though Schnog's original publication — most likely Schneider's source for the poem — entitles it "Der Häftling." It is probable that the change of title served to distinguish Schnog's poem from another poem entitled "Der Häftling" by Fritz Löhner-Beda, also in Schneider's collection (for a discussion of that poem, see chapter 2 above).

[5] Reprinted in Moll and Weiler, 146; Lau and Pampuch, 62 and back cover.

Chapter 5

[1] For example, Wolfgang Emmerich insightfully analyzes Werner Bergengruen's *Der Großtyran und das Gericht* (The Great Tyrant and the Court of Law), a work often held as exemplary of the oppositional nature of "inner emigration," in the following terms: "The result of the catharsis in the form of the high happy end is: we are all sinners . . . The murder committed and hidden by the great tyrant . . . appears as a sin among other sins, on a level with the faults of the small people . . . Accordingly, the great tyrant can well appear to the reader as a noble, spiritual, magnanimous, intelligent ruler, worthy of respect and admiration, for whom even the attributes of 'innocence,' 'pity,' and 'humaneness' are appropriate" (1976, 449).

[2] For a complete translation and discussion of this song, see for example Ritchie, 79–80.

[3] For more information on the Kulturbund, see Akademie der Künste; Steinweis 1993a and 1993b; and Rovit and Goldfarb, esp. 11–90.

[4] Gudrun Jäger's 1998 book on the history of the publication and of the critical reception of Kolmar's work shows how Kolmar's poems have been made to serve various needs, a number of them of questionable character and not always justified by the text or by the author's biography. The book further corrects a number of myths that have arisen in the context of Kolmar's work and life.

[5] Jäger cites Peter Gay in her description of Kolmar's background.

[6] For an overview of the literature on Kolmar, see Shafi 2003.

[7] Also printed in Kolmar 1980, 215; Kolmar 1987, 741. For a previously published translation into English, see Smith, 34.

[8] Chantal Müller has analyzed Kolmar's preoccupation with the possibilities of articulation, as exemplified in the title of the cycle, The Word of the Silenced Ones.

[9] Reprinted in Moll and Weiler, 41; Pampuch and Lau, 51.

[10] Printed in a slightly variant version in Gold, 2:78.

Appendix

[1] Translation reprinted with permission from Sander Gilman (see Gilman 1991, 229–31). Translation modified.

[2] Reprinted with permission from David Keir Wright in a letter to the author, 25 September 2003.

Works Cited

Aaron, Frieda W. 1990. *Bearing the Unbearable: Yiddish and Polish Poetry in the Ghettos and Concentration Camps.* SUNY Series in Modern Jewish Literature and Culture. Albany: State U of New York P.

Adler, Hermann. 1994. *Gesänge aus der Stadt des Todes: Todeslagergedichte aus dem Wilnaer Ghetto, 1941/42.* Berlin: Edition Hentrich. Originally published in 1945.

Adorno, Theodor W. 1986. "What Does Coming to Terms with the Past Mean?" First published in 1959. Translated by Timothy Bahti. In *Bitburg in Moral and Political Perspective,* edited by Geoffrey Hartman, 114–29. Bloomington: Indiana UP.

———. 1992. "Commitment." In *Notes to Literature,* vol. 2, edited by Rolf Tiedemann and translated by Shierry Weber Nicholsen, 76–94. New York: Columbia UP. Translation of "Kulturkritik und Gesellschaft," originally published in *Soziologische Forschungen in unserer Zeit,* edited by Karl-Gustav Specht. 1951.

———. 1995. "Cultural Criticism and Society." In *Prisms,* translated by Samuel and Shierry Weber, 17–34. Cambridge: MIT UP.

———. 1998. "Those Twenties." In *Critical Models: Interventions and Catchwords,* translated by Henry W. Pickford, 41–48. New York: Columbia UP.

Agamben, Giorgio. 1999. *Remnants of Auschwitz: The Witness and the Archive.* Translated by Daniel Heller-Rozen. New York: Zone Books. Original Italian: *Quel che resta di Auschwitz: L'archivio e il testimone.* Turin: Bollati Bollinghieri, 1998.

Akademie der Künste. 1992. *Geschlossene Vorstellung: Der Jüdische Kulturbund in Deutschland, 1933–1941.* Berlin: Edition Hentrich.

Améry, Jean. 1990. *At the Mind's Limits: Contemplations by a Survivor on Auschwitz and Its Realities.* Translated by Sidney and Stella Rosenfeld. Witnesses to War. New York: Schocken Books.

Anderson, Benedict. 1991. *Imagined Communities: Reflections on the Origin and Spread of Nationalism.* Revised edition. London: Verso.

Arendt, Hannah. 1948. "The Concentration Camps." *Partisan Review* 15, 7:743–63.

———. 1950. "Social Science Techniques and the Study of Concentration Camps." *Jewish Social Studies* 12, 1:49–64.

————. 1958. *The Origins of Totalitarianism.* 2nd enlarged edition. New York: Meridian Books.

Baer, Elizabeth, and Myrna Goldenberg, eds. 2003. *Experience and Expression: Women, the Nazis, and the Holocaust.* Detroit: Wayne State UP.

Baetens, Jan. 1997. "Free Writing, Constrained Writing: The Ideology of Form." *Poetics Today* 18, 1:1–14.

Bakhtin, Mikhail. 1986. *Speech Genres and Other Late Essays.* Translated by Vern. W. McGee. Edited by Caryl Emerson and Michael Holquist. Austin: U of Texas P.

Basoglu, Metin, ed. 1992. *Torture and Its Consequences: Current Treatment Approaches.* Cambridge: Cambridge UP.

Benz, Wolfgang, and Walter H. Pehle, eds. 1994. *Lexikon des deutschen Widerstandes.* Frankfurt am Main: Fischer Verlag.

Bernard, Catherine A. 2003. "Anne Frank: The Cultivation of the Inspirational Victim." In Baer and Goldenberg, *Experience and Expression: Women, the Nazis, and the Holocaust,* 201–25.

Bettelheim, Bruno. 1960. *The Informed Heart: Autonomy in a Mass Age.* New York: Free Press.

Biermann, Wolf, transl. 1994. *Großer Gesang vom ausgerotteten jüdischen Volk: Dos lied vunem ojsgerhargetn jidischn volk,* by Jizchak Katzenelson.1st edition. Cologne: Kiepenhauer & Witsch.

Bley, Wulf. 1934. *Das Jahr I: Rhythmus und Tatbestände des ersten Jahres nationalsozialistischer Staatsführung.* Berlin: Freiheitsverlag.

————. 1935. *Das Jahr II: Rhythmus und Tatbestände des zweiten Jahres nationalsozialistischer Staatsführung mit einem Vorwort des Minister-präsidenten Hermann Göring.* Berlin: Freiheitsverlag.

Bloch, Ernst. 1970. *Gesamtausgabe der Werke.* Vol 11: *Politische Messungen, Testzeit, Vormärz.* Frankfurt am Main: Suhrkamp.

Bollmus, Reinhard. 1970. *Das Amt Rosenberg und seine Gegner: Studien zum Machtkampf im nationalsozialistischen Herrschaftssystem.* Stuttgart: Deutsche Verlagsanstalt.

Bonheim, Günther. 2002. *Versuch zu zeigen, daß Adorno mit seiner Behauptung, nach Auschwitz lasse sich kein Gedicht mehr schreiben, recht hatte.* Würzburg: Königshausen & Neumann.

Boris, Georg, Edler von. *Die Lieder des Grauens.* ts./ms. 23486. Archive, KZ-Gedenkstätte Dachau, Dachau.

Bos, Pascale Rachel. 2003. "Women and the Holocaust: Analyzing Gender Difference." In Baer and Goldenberg, *Experience and Expression: Women, the Nazis, and the Holocaust,* 23–50.

Bower, Kathrin. 2000. "Claiming the Victim: Tokenism, Mourning, and the Future of German Holocaust Poetry." In *German Studies in the Post-Holocaust Age: The Politics of Memory, Identity, and Ethnicity,* edited by Adrian del Caro and Janet Ward. Boulder: U of Colorado P.

Breur, Dunya. 1997. *Ich lebe, weil du dich erinnerst: Frauen und Kinder in Ravensbrück.* Translated from the original Dutch (1983) by Rudie Leikes and Diete Oudesluijs. Berlin: Nicolai.

Buck, Theo. 1993. *Muttersprache, Mördersprache.* Aachen: Rimbauld.

Caruth, Cathy. 1995. *Trauma: Explorations in Memory.* Baltimore: Johns Hopkins UP.

———. 1996. *Unclaimed Experience: Trauma, Narrative, and History.* Baltimore: Johns Hopkins UP.

Cayrol, Jean. 1997. *Alerte aux ombres: 1944–1945.* Paris: Éditions du Seuil.

Celan, Paul. 2000. *Gesammelte Werke in sieben Bänden.* Edited by Beda Allemann and Stefan Reichert with the collaboration of Rolf Bücher. Frankfurt am Main: Suhrkamp.

Cixous, Hélène. 1979. "Poésie, e(s)t Politique?" *Des Femmes en Mouvements Hebdo* 4 (Nov. 30–Dec. 7): 29–32.

———. 1980. "Poetry is / and (the) Political." Translated by Ann Liddle. *Bread & Roses* 2, 1:16–18.

Coleman Nelson, Mary. 1977. "In Memoriam: Joost A. M. Meerloo, M.D., 1903–1976." *The Psychoanalytic Review* 64, 1:3–4.

Culler, Jonathan. 2001. *The Pursuit of Signs: Semiotics, Literature, Deconstruction.* London, Routledge. Originally published in 1981.

Pons Globalwörterbuch (German-English Dictionary), s.v. "rächen."

Dawidowicz, Lucy, ed. 1976. *A Holocaust Reader.* With introduction and notes by L. Dawidowicz. West Orange, NJ: Behrman House.

Daxelmüller, Christoph. 1994. "Kultur gegen Gewalt: Das Beispiel Konzentrationslager." In *Gewalt in der Kultur: Vorträge des 29. Deutschen Volkskundekongresses, Passau 1993,* edited by Rolf Brednich and Walter Hartinger, 223–69. Passau: Lehrstuhl für Volkskunde der Universität Passau.

Delbo, Charlotte. 1985. *La mémoire et les jours.* Paris: Berg International.

Denscher, Barbara, and Helmut Peschina. 2002. *Kein Land des Lächelns: Fritz Löhner-Beda, 1883–1942.* Salzburg: Residenz Verlag.

Des Pres, Terrence. 1976. *The Survivor: An Anatomy of Life in the Death Camps.* Oxford: Oxford UP.

Deutscher Militärverlag. 1965. *Strafdivision 999: Erlebnisse und Berichte aus dem antifaschistischen Widerstandskampf.* Berlin (GDR): Philipp Reclam jun. Leipzig.

Distel, Barbara. 1997. Foreword to *Dachauer Tagebücher: Die Aufzeichnungen des Häftlings 24814*, by Edgar Kupfer-Koberwitz. Munich: Kindler.

Eisen, George. 1990. *Children and Play in the Holocaust: Games among the Shadows*. 1st paperback edition. Amherst: U of Massachusetts P.

Elling, Hanna. 1978. *Frauen im deutschen Widerstand: 1933–45*. 1st edition. Frankfurt am Main: Röderberg-Verlag.

———, ed. and comp. 1990. *Mitten in tiefer Nacht: Gedichte aus Konzentrationslagern und Zuchthäusern des deutschen Faschismus, 1933–1945*. Frankfurt am Main: Verlag für Akademische Schriften.

Emmerich, Wolfgang. 1976. "Die Literatur des antifaschistischen Widerstandes in Deutschland." In *Die deutsche Literatur im Dritten Reich: Themen, Traditionen, Wirkungen*, edited by Horst Denkler and Karl Prümm, 427–58. Stuttgart: Reclam.

———. 1977. "'Massenfaschismus' und die Rolle des Ästhetischen: Faschismustheorie bei Ernst Bloch, Walter Benjamin, Bertolt Brecht." In *Antifaschistische Literatur: Programme, Autoren, Werke*, vol. 1, edited by Lutz Winkler, 223–90. Kronberg: Skriptor Verlag.

———. 1999. *Paul Celan*. Reinbeck bei Hamburg: Rowohlt.

Enzensberger, Hans Magnus, comp. 1979. *Allerleirauh: Viele schöne Kinderreime*. Frankfurt am Main: Insel Taschenbuchverlag.

Ertel, Rachel. 1993. *Dans la langue de personne: Poésie yiddish de l'anéantissement*. Paris: Éditions du Seuil.

Euler, Walter. 1956. *Ariel 3*. Darmstadt: Darmstädter Echo.

Fackler, Guido. 2000. *"Des Lagers Stimme" — Musik im KZ: Alltag und Häftlingskultur in den Konzentrationslagern, 1933 bis 1936*. Mit einer Darstellung der weiteren Entwicklung bis 1945 und einer Biblio-/Mediographie. Bremen: Edition Temmen.

Felmayer, Rudolf, ed. 1955. *Dein Herz ist deine Heimat*. Vienna: Amandus.

Felstiner, John. 1995. *Paul Celan: Poet, Survivor, Jew*. New Haven: Yale UP.

Forché, Carolyn, ed. 1993. *Against Forgetting: Twentieth-Century Poetry of Witness*. New York: W. W. Norton.

Freund, Florian, Franz Ruttner, and Hans Safrian, eds. 1992. *"ess firt kejn weg zurik . . .": Geschichte und Lieder des Ghettos von Wilna, 1941–1943*. Vienna: Picus.

Fricke, Gerhard, and Matthias Schreiber. 1988. *Geschichte der deutschen Literatur*. 20th edition. Paderborn: Schöningh.

Friedländer, Saul. 1993. *Reflections of Nazism: An Essay on Kitsch and Death*. Translated by Thomas Weyr. Bloomington: Indiana UP. Original French: *Reflétions du Nazisme*, 1982.

———. 1994. Trauma, Memory, and Transference. In Hartman, *Holocaust Remembrance: The Shapes of Memory*, 252–63.

———. 1997. *Nazi Germany and the Jews*. Vol. 1: *The Years of Persecution, 1933–1939*. New York: HarperCollins.

Frye, Northrop. 1990. *Anatomy of Criticism: Four Essays*. With a foreword by Harold Bloom. Princeton: Princeton UP. Originally published in 1957.

Garland, Caroline, ed. 1998. *Understanding Trauma: A Psychoanalytical Approach*. London: Karnac.

Gay, Peter. 1978. *Freud, Jews and Other Germans: Masters and Victims in Modernist Culture*. Oxford: Oxford UP.

Gilman, Sander, ed. 1971. *NS-Literaturtheorie: Eine Dokumentation*. Frankfurt am Main: Athenäum.

———. 1991. *Inscribing the Other*. Lincoln: U of Nebraska P.

Goes, Albrecht. 1991. Foreword to *In deinen Mauern wohnt das Leid: Gedichte aus dem KZ Theresienstadt*, by Ilse Weber. Gerlingen, Germany: Bleicher Verlag.

Gold. Hugo, ed. 1962. *Geschichte der Juden in der Bukowina*. 2 vols. Tel Aviv: Olamenu.

Goldenberg, Myrna. 2003. "Food Talk: Gendered Responses to Hunger in the Concentration Camps." In Baer and Goldenberg, *Experience and Expression: Women, the Nazis, and the Holocaust*, 161–79.

Grabner, Hasso. 1959. *Fünfzehn Schritte Gradaus: Gedichte*. Berlin: Aufbau Verlag.

Granof, Corinne, and David Mickenberg. 2003. "Complexity and Contradiction: An Introduction to *The Last Expression*." In *The Last Expression: Art and Auschwitz*, edited by David Mickenberg, Corinne Granof, and Peter Hayes, xi–xv. Evanston, IL: Northwestern UP.

Groll, Gunter, ed. 1946. *De Profundis: Deutsche Lyrik in dieser Zeit*. Munich: Verlag Kurt Desch.

Gubar, Susan. 2003. *Poetry After Auschwitz: Remembering What One Never Knew*. Bloomington: Indiana UP.

Habel, F. 2002. *Das große Lexikon der DDR-Stars: Schauspieler aus Film und Fernsehen*. Revised and expanded edition. Berlin: Schwarzkopf & Schwarzkopf.

Hartman, Geoffrey, ed. 1994. *Holocaust Remembrance: The Shapes of Memory*. Oxford: Blackwell.

———. 1996. *The Longest Shadow: In the Aftermath of the Holocaust*. Bloomington: Indiana UP.

Heidelberger-Leonard, Irène. 1996. *Ruth Klüger, weiter leben; Eine Jugend: Interpretation.* Oldenbourg Interpretationen 81. Munich: Oldenbourg.

Heilig, Bruno. 2002. "Das Buchenwaldlied." In Holm Kirsten and Wulf Kirsten, *Stimmen aus Buchenwald: Ein Lesebuch.* Excerpted from Bruno Heilig, *Menschen am Kreuz.* Berlin: Verlag Neues Leben, 1948.

Heiser, Dorothea, ed. and comp. 1993. *Mein Schatten in Dachau: Gedichte und Biographien der Überlebenden und Toten des Konzentrationslagers.* Munich: J. Pfeiffer.

Herf, Jeffrey. 1997. *Divided Memory: The Nazi Past in the Two Germanys.* Cambridge, MA: Harvard UP.

Herlinger (Weber), Ilse. 1929. *Die Geschichten um Mendel Rosenbusch: Erzählungen für jüdische Kinder.* Märisch-Ostrau [now Ostrava, Czech Republic]: Verlag Dr. R. Färber.

Hilberg, Raul. 1985. *The Destruction of the European Jews.* Revised and definitive edition. 3 vols. New York: Holmes & Mayer.

Hilzinger, Sonja. 1998. "'Das Wort der Stummen': Deutsch-jüdische Lyrik in Nazi Deutschland." *Menora: Jahrbuch für deutsch-jüdische Geschichte* 9 (1998): 70–99.

Hirsch, Marianne. 2000. "Surviving Images: Holocaust Photographs and the Work of Postmemory." In *Visual Culture and the Holocaust,* edited by Barbie Zelizer, 215–46. New Brunswick, NJ: Rutgers UP.

Hortzitz, Nicoline. 1995. "Die Sprache der Judenfeindschaft." In *Anti-semitismus: Vorurteile und Mythen,* edited by Julius H. Schoeps and Joachim Schlör, 19–40. Munich: Piper Verlag.

Humperdinck, Engelbert, ed. n.d. *Sang und Klang fürs Kinderherz: Eine Sammlung der schönsten Kinderlieder.* Berlin: Schönfeld's Verlagsbuch-handlung.

Ihanus, Juhani. 1998. "Dancing with Words: Transference and Countertransference in Biblio/Poetry Therapy." *Journal of Poetry Therapy* 12 (2):85–93.

Jäger, Grudrun. 1998. *Getrud Kolmar: Publikations- und Rezeptionsgeschichte.* Frankfurt am Main: Campus.

Johnson, Barbara. 1989. *A World of Difference.* Baltimore: Johns Hopkins UP.

Jones, Robert. 1969. "Treatment of a Psychotic Patient by Poetry Therapy." In *Poetry Therapy,* edited by Jack Leedy. Philadelphia: J. B. Lippincott Company.

Kahan, Bente. 1996. *Stemmer fra Theresienstadt.* Kristiansand, Norway: Lynor.

———. 1997. *Stimmen aus Theresienstadt: Lieder nach Gedichten von Ilse Weber und Songs aus den Kabaretts.* Dortmund: Verlag "Pläne."

———. 2000. *Voices from Theresienstadt: Ilse Weber and Cabaret Songs.* Ilse Weber translated by David Keir Wright. USA: Studio Magnetics.

Kahane, Claire. 2001. "Dark Mirrors: A Feminist Reflection on Holocaust Narrative and the Maternal Metaphor." In *Feminist Consequences: Theory for the New Century,* edited by Elisabeth Bronfen and Misha Kavka, 161–88. New York: Columbia UP.

Katzenelson, Jizchak. [Yitzhak].1980. *The Song of the Murdered Jewish People.* Translated by Noah H. Rosenblum. Ghetto Fighters' House, Israel: Hakibbutz Hameuchad Publishing House.

———. 1992 (©1951). *Dos Lid funm ojsgehargetn jidischn folk: Das Lied vom letzten Juden in der Nachdichtung von Hermann Adler.* Edited and translated by Hermann Adler. Berlin: Edition Hentrich.

———.1994. *Großer Gesang vom ausgerotteten jüdischen Volk: Dos lied vunem ojsgerhargetn jidischn volk.* Translated by Wolf Biermann. 1st edition. Cologne: Kiepenhauer & Witsch.

Kelly-Holmes, Helen. 2002. "German Language: Whose Language, Whose Culture?" In *Contemporary German Cultural Studies,* edited by Alison Phipps, 44–62. London: Arnold.

Ketelsen, Uwe-K. 1983. "Die dreißiger und vierziger Jahre." In *Geschichte der deutschen Lyrik vom Mittelalter bis zur Gegenwart,* edited by Walter Hinderer, 477–501. Stuttgart: Reclam.

———. 1985. "Die Literatur des 3. Reichs als Gegenstand germanistischer Forschung." In *Wege der Literaturwissenschaft,* edited by Jutta Kolkenbrock-Netz, Gerhard Plumpe, and Hans Joachim Schrimpf, 282–300. Bonn: Bouvier.

———. 1992. *Literatur und Drittes Reich.* Schernfeld, Germany: SH-Verlag.

Kiedaisch, Petra, ed. 1995. *Lyrik nach Auschwitz? Adorno und die Dichter.* Stuttgart: Reclam.

Kirsten, Holm, and Wulf Kirsten, eds. 2002. *Stimmen aus Buchenwald: Ein Lesebuch.* Commissioned by the Memorial Foundation Buchenwald and Mittelbau-Dora. Göttingen: Wallstein.

Kittner, Alfred. 1988. *Schattenschrift: Gedichte.* 1st edition. Aachen: Rimbaud.

———. 1996. *Erinnerungen, 1906–1991.* Edited by Edith Silbermann. Texte aus der Bukowina. Afterword by Theo Buck. Aachen: Rimbaud.

Klein, Katja. 1995. *Kazett-Lyrik: Untersuchungen zu Gedichten und Liedern aus dem Konzentrationslager Sachsenhausen.* Würzburg: Königshausen & Neumann.

Klüger, Ruth. 1994. *weiter leben: Eine Jugend.* Munich: Deutscher Taschenbuchverlag.

———. 2001. *Still Alive: A Holocaust Girlhood Remembered.* The Helen Rose Scheuer Jewish Women's Series, no. 7. New York: Feminist P. First English-language edition of *weiter leben,* 1992.

Kolmar, Gertrud. 1970. *Briefe an die Schwester Hilde (1938–1943)*. Edited by Johanna Zeitler. Munich: Kösel Verlag.

———. 1978. *Das Wort der Stummen: Nachgelassene Gedichte*. Berlin [East]: Buchverlag der Morgen.

———. 1980. *Frühe Gedichte (1917–1922) / Wort der Stummen (1933)*. Edited by Johanna Woltmann-Zeitler. Munich: Kösel Verlag.

———. 1987. *Weibliches Bildnis: Sämtliche Gedichte*. Munich: Deutscher Taschenbuch Verlag.

Kogon, Eugen. 1946. *Der SS-Staat: Das System der deutschen Konzentrationslager*. Frankfurt am Main: Europäische Verlagsanstalt.

Kozinn, Allan. 2003. "Hearing Music Silenced by the Nazis." *New York Times*. Critic's Notebook, The Arts section, March 26.

Kramer, Aaron, ed. 1998. *The Last Lullaby: Poetry from the Holocaust*. Syracuse, NY: Syracuse UP.

Kühn, Volker, ed. 1989. "Deutschlands Erwachen: Kabarett unterm Hakenkreuz, 1933–1945." Vol. 2 of Kleinkunststücke. Berlin: Quadriga Verlag.

Kupfer-Koberwitz, Edgar. n.d. *Die Sonne hinter Stacheldraht: Ein Erinnerungsbuch an das Lager Dachau in Versen*. ts./ms. 28738. Archive KZ-Gedenkstätte Dachau, Dachau.

———. [1946]. *Kette der Tage*. Stuttgart and Calw: Verlag Gerd Hatje.

———. 1957. *Die Mächtigen und die Hilflosen: Als Häftling in Dachau*. 2 vols. Vol. 1: *Wie es begann*. Stuttgart: Friedrich Vorwerk Verlag, 1957. Vol. 2: *Wie es endete*. Stuttgart: Friedrich Vorwerk Verlag, 1960.

———. 1997. *Dachauer Tagebücher: Die Aufzeichnungen des Häftlings 24814*. With a foreword by Barbara Distel. Munich: Kindler.

LaCapra, Dominick. 1994. *Representing the Holocaust: History, Theory, Trauma*. Ithaca, NY: Cornell UP.

———. 1998. *History and Memory after Auschwitz*. Ithaca, NY: Cornell UP.

———. 2001. *Writing History, Writing Trauma*. Baltimore, MD: John Hopkins UP.

———. 2004. *History in Transit: Experience, Identity, Critical Theory*. Ithaca, NY: Cornell UP.

Langer, Lawrence, L. 1982. *Versions of Survival: The Holocaust and the Human Spirit*. SUNY Series in Modern Jewish Literature and Culture. Albany: State of New York UP.

———. 1991. *Holocaust Testimonies: The Ruins of Memory*. New Haven, CT: Yale UP.

———. 1995. *Admitting the Holocaust: Collected Essays*. New York: Oxford UP.

Laplanche, Jean, and J.-B. Pontalis. 1973. *The Language of Psycho-Analysis.* New York: Norton.

Laqueur, Renata. 1992. *Schreiben im KZ: Tagebücher, 1940–1945.* Translated by Martina Dreisbach. Bremen: Donat. Originally 1971. PhD. diss., New York University.

Lau, Ellinor, and Susanne Pampuch, eds. 1994. *Draußen steht eine bange Nacht: Lieder und Gedichte aus deutschen Konzentrationslagern.* Frankfurt am Main: Fischer Taschenbuch Verlag.

Laub, Dori, and Nanette Auerhahn. 1984. "Annihilation and Restoration: Post-Traumatic Memory as Pathway and Obstacle to Recovery." *International Review of Psycho-Analysis* 11:327–44.

———. 1989. "Failed Empathy — A Central Theme in the Survivor's Holocaust Experience." *Psychoanalytic Psychology* 6, 4:377–400.

———. 1993. "Knowing and Not Knowing Massive Psychic Trauma: Forms of Traumatic Memory." *International Journal of Psycho-Analysis* 74:287–302.

Laub, Dori, and Daniel Podell. 1995. "Art and Trauma." *The International Journal of Psycho-Analysis* 76, 5:991–1005.

Levi, Primo. 1961. *Survival in Auschwitz: The Nazi Assault on Humanity.* Translated by Stuart Woolf. New York: Collier Books. Translation of *Se questo è un uomo,* 1958.

———. 1986. *I sommersi e i salvati.* Turin: Einaudi, 1986.

———. 1989. *The Drowned and the Saved.* Translated by Raymond Rosenthal. New York: Vintage Books. Translation of *I sommersi e i salvati.*

Leys, Ruth. 2000. *Trauma: A Genealogy.* Chicago: U of Chicago P.

Lewinska, Pelagia. 1993. "Water." In *Different Voices: Women and the Holocaust,* edited by Carol Rittner and Scott Roth, 88–91. New York: Paragon. Lewinska's text excerpted from her *Twenty Months at Auschwitz.* Translated from the Polish by Albert Teichner. New York: Lyle Stuart, 1968.

Lezzi, Eva. 2001. *Zerstörte Kindheit: Literarische Autobiographien zur Shoah.* Cologne: Böhlau.

Liebrand, Claudia. 2003. "'Das Trauma der Auschwitzer Wochen in ein Versmaß stülpen' oder: Gedichte als Exorzismus; Ruth Klügers *weiter leben.*" In *Jüdische Intellektuelle im 20. Jahrhundert: Literatur- und kultur-geschichtliche Studien,* edited by Ariane Huml and Monika Rappenecker, 237–48. Würzburg: Königshausen & Neumann.

Löhner-Beda, Fritz [Beda]. 1908. *Getaufte und Baldgetaufte.* Vienna: Huber & Lahme Nachfg.

———. 1909. *Israeliten und andere Antisemiten.* Vienna: Huber & Lahme Nachfg.

Luxemburg, Rosa. 1975. "Die Ordnung herrscht in Berlin." In *Politische Schriften,* vol. 2. Frankfurt am Main: Europäische Verlagsanstalt.

Mann, Thomas. 1945. "Warum ich nicht zurückkehre!" *Augsburger Anzeiger,* 12 October, letter. Reprinted in *Die große Kontroverse: Ein Briefwechsel um Deutschland,* edited by J. F. G. Grosser, 27–36. Hamburg: Nagel, 1963.

McGovern, William M. 1941. *From Luther to Hitler: The History of Fascist-Nazi Political Philosophy.* Cambridge, MA: Riverside P.

Meerbaum-Eisinger, Selma. 1995. *Ich bin in Sehnsucht eingehüllt: Gedichte.* Frankfurt am Main: Fischer.

Meerloo, Joost A. M. 1969. "The Universal Language of Rhythm." In *Poetry Therapy,* edited by Jack Leedy. Philadelphia: J. B. Lippincott.

Ménager, Yves, comp. 2001. *Paroles de déportés.* Paris: Les Éditions de l'Atelier/Éditions Ouvrières.

Mickenberg, David, Corinne Granof, and Peter Hayes, eds. 2003. *The Last Expression: Art and Auschwitz.* Evanston, IL: Northwestern UP.

Middlebrook, Diane W. 1991. *Anne Sexton: A Biography.* Boston: Houghton Mifflin.

Miller, Nancy K. 2004. "Ruth Klüger's *Still Alive: A Holocaust Girlhood Remembered;* An Unsentimental Education." In *Teaching the Representation of the Holocaust,* edited by Marianne Hirsch and Irene Kacandes, 386–95. New York: MLA.

Moll, Michael. 1983. "Gedichte aus nationalsozialistischen Gefängnissen, Ghettos, und KZs. Eine kommentierte Anthologie." Master's thesis, Westfälische Wilhelms-Universität zu Münster.

———. 1988. *Lyrik in einer entmenschlichten Welt: Interpretationsversuche zu deutschsprachigen Gedichten aus nationalsozialistischen Gefängnissen, Ghettos und KZ's.* Frankfurt am Main: R. G. Fischer Verlag.

Moll, Michael, and Barbar Weiler, eds. 1991. *Lyrik gegen das Vergessen: Gedichte aus den Konzentrationslagern.* Marburg, Germany: Schüren.

Morsch, Günter, ed. 1995. *Sachsenhausen-Liederbuch: Originalwiedergabe eines illegalen Häftlingsliederbuches aus dem Konzentrationslager Sachsenhausen.* Berlin: Hentrich.

Müller, Chantal. 1996. "Die Sprachproblematik in 'Die Dichterin' und 'An die Gefangenen.'" In *Klangkristalle; Rubinene Lieder: Studien zur Lyrik von Gertrud Kolmar,* edited by Heidy Margrit Müller. Bern: Peter Lang.

Nelson, Cary. 1989. *Repression and Recovery: Modern American Poetry and the Politics of Cultural Memory, 1910–1945.* Madison: U of Wisconsin P.

Nolan, Mary. 1988. The *Historikerstreit* and Social History. *New German Critique* 44:51–84.

Pareigis, Christina. 2003. *"trogt zich a gezang . . ." Jiddische Liedlyrik aus den Jahren 1939–1945: Kadye Molodovsky, Yitzhak Katzenelson, Mordechaj Gebirtig*. Munich: Dölling & Galitz.

Perk, Willi. 1970. *Die Hölle im Moor*. Frankfurt amMain: Röderberg Verlag.

———. 1979. *Die Hölle im Moor*. 2nd, improved edition. Frankfurt amMain: Röderberg Verlag.

Phillips, Adam. 1994. *On Kissing, Tickling, and Being Bored: Psychoanalytic Essays on the Unexamined Life*. Cambridge, MA: Harvard UP.

Pouzol, Henri, ed. 1975. *La Poésie concentrationnaire: Visage de l'homme dans les camps hitlériens, 1940–1945*. Paris: Éditions Seghers.

———, ed. 1995. *Ces voix toujours présentes: Anthologie de la poésie européenne concentrationnaire*. Paris: Presses Universitaires de Reims.

Rabinbach, Anson. 1991. "The Reader, the Popular Novel, and the Imperative to Participate: Reflections on Public and Private Experience in the Third Reich." *History and Memory* 3, 2:5–44.

Rahe, Thomas. 1999. *"Höre Israel": Jüdische Religiosität in nationalsozialistischen Konzentrationslagern*. Göttingen: Vandehoeck & Ruprecht.

Razdolina, Zlata. 1998. *"The Song of the Murdered Jewish People": After the Poem by Itzhak Katzenelson*. The Moravian Philharmonic. Victor Feldbrill. Israel: Acum.

Reichel, Peter. 1991. *Der schöne Schein des Dritten Reiches: Faszination und Gewalt des Faschismus*. Munich: Hanser Verlag.

Reiter, Andrea. 1989. "'Brot war eine Insel in dem Wassersuppenmeer . . .': Literary Imagination as a Means of Survival, as Reflected in Concentration-Camp Reports." *Forum for Modern Language Studies* 15, 2:123–38.

———. 2000. *Narrating the Holocaust*. Translated by Patrick Camiller. New York: Continuum.

Rich, Adrienne. 1993. *What Is Found There: Notebooks on Poetry and Politics*. New York: Norton.

Ringelheim, Joan. 1993. "Women and the Holocaust: A Reconsideration of Research." In *Different Voices: Women and the Holocaust*, edited by Carol Rittner and John K. Roth, 373–418. New York: Paragon.

Ritchie, J. M. 1983. *German Literature under National Socialism*. Towota, NJ: Barnes & Noble.

Rosenfeld, Alvin. 1980. *A Double Dying: Reflections on Holocaust Literature*. Bloomington: Indiana UP.

Roskies, David. 1984. *Against the Apocalypse: Responses to Catastrophe in Modern Jewish Culture*. Cambridge, MA: Harvard UP.

————. 1986. "Yiddish Writing in the Nazi Ghettos and the Art of the Incommensurate." *Modern Language Studies* 16, 1 (winter): 29–36.

————. 1994. "The Library of Jewish Catastrophe." In Hartman, *Holocaust Remembrance: The Shapes of Memory*, 33–41.

Roth, John K. 2003. "Equality. Neutrality. Patriarchy: Perspectives on Women and the Holocaust." In Baer and Goldenberg, *Experience and Expression: Women, the Nazis, and the Holocaust*, 5–22.

Rothberg, Michael. 2000. *Traumatic Realism: The Demands of Holocaust Representation*. Minneapolis: U of Minnesota P.

Rovit, Rebecca, and Alvin Goldfarb, eds. 1999. *Theatrical Performance during the Holocaust: Texts, Documents, Memoirs*. Baltimore: John Hopkins UP.

Saporta, José, and Bessel A. van der Kolk. 1992. "Psychobiological Consequences of Severe Trauma." In *Torture and its Consequences: Current Treatment Approaches*, edited by Metin Basoglu. Cambridge: Cambridge UP.

Scarry, Elaine. 1985. *The Body in Pain: The Making and Unmaking of the World*. Oxford: Oxford UP.

Schaeffer, Jean-Marie. 2001. "Genre." In *Dictionnaire des Genres et notions littéraires*. Paris: Encyclopædia Universalis et Albin Michel.

Schäfer, Hans Dieter. 1976. "Die nichtnationalsozialistische Literatur der jungen Generation im Dritten Reich." In *Die deutsche Literatur im Dritten Reich: Themen, Traditionen, Wirkungen*, edited by Horst Denkler and Karl Prümm, 459–503. Stuttgart: Reclam.

————.1983. *Das gespaltene Bewusstsein: Deutsche Kultur und Lebenswirklichkeit, 1933–1945*. Munich: Hanser Verlag.

Schärtel, Birgitt. 2000. "Begrüßungsrede für Max Mannheimer am 28. Januar 2000." Available online at: http://www.altmuehlnet.de/~an02216/juden/schartel.html.

Schiff, Hilda, ed. 1995. *Holocaust Poetry*. New York: St. Martin's Griffin.

Schlaffer, Heinz. 2002. *Die kurze Geschichte der deutschen Literatur*. Munich: Carl Hanser.

Schlenstedt, Silvia. 1989. "Suche nach Halt in haltloser Lage: die Kulturarbeit deutscher Juden nach 1933 in Deutschland und die Dichterin Gertrud Kolmar." *Sinn und Form: Beiträge zur Literatur* 41, 4:727–42.

Schlösser, Manfred, ed. 1960. *An den Wind geschrieben: Lyrik der Freiheit, 1933–1945*. Darmstadt: Agorà.

————, ed. 1961a. *An den Wind geschrie*ben: Lyrik der Freiheit, 1933–1945. 2nd, revised edition. Darmstadt: Agorà.

————, ed. 1961b. *An den Wind geschrieben: Lyrik der Freiheit, 1933–1945*. 2nd, improved edition. Darmstadt: Agorà.

————, ed. 1962. *An den Wind geschrieben: Lyrik der Freiheit, 1933–1945.* 1st paperback edition. Munich: Deutscher Taschenbuch Verlag.

Schneider, Wolfgang. 1973. *Kunst hinter Stacheldraht: Ein Beitrag zur Geschichte des antifaschistischen Widerstandkampfes.* 1st edition. Weimar: Nationale Mahn- und Gedenkstätte Buchenwald.

————. 1976. *Kunst hinter Stacheldraht: Ein Beitrag zur Geschichte des antifaschistischen Widerstandkampfes.* 2nd, revised edition. Leipzig: VEB E.A. Seemann Verlag.

Schnell, Ralf. 1976. *Literarische Innere Emigration, 1933–1945.* Stuttgart: Metzler.

Schnog, Karl. 1934. *Kinnhaken: Kampfgedichte, 1933/34.* Luxemburg: Malpaartes Verlag.

————. 1945. *Unbekanntes KZ: Erlebtes von Karl Schnog.* Stimmen aus dem KZ. Luxemburg: Bourg-Bourger.

————. 1947. *Jedem das Seine: Satirische Gedichte.* Berlin: Ulenspiegel Verlag.

Schoor, Kerstin. 1998. "'Jüdische Lyrik der Zeit': Kurt Pinthus' Lyrik-Anthologie in der Berliner *C.V.*-Zeitung vom April 1936." In *Deutschsprachige Exillyrik von 1933 bis zur Nachkriegszeit,* edited by Jörg Thunecke. Amsterdamer Beiträge zur neueren Germanisik 44. Amsterdam: Rodopi.

Schulte-Sasse, Linda. 2004. "'Living On' in the American Press: Ruth Kluger's *Still Alive* and Its Challenge to a Cherished Holocaust Paradigm." *German Studies Review* 27, 3:469–75.

Schumann, Gerhard, ed. 1944. *Lyrik der Lebenden.* Munich: Deutscher Volksverlag.

Schwarberg, Günther. 2000. *Dein ist mein ganzes Herz: Die Geschichte von Fritz Löhner-Beda, der die schönsten Lieder der Welt schrieb, und warum Hitler ihn ermorden ließ.* Göttingen: Steidl Verlag.

Segal, Lore. 2001. "Going on Living." Foreword to *Still Alive,* by Ruth Klüger. New York: Feminist P.

Seydel, Heinz, ed. and comp. 1968. *Welch Wort in die Kälte gerufen: Die Judenverfolgung des Dritten Reiches im deutschen Gedicht.* Berlin: Verlag der Nation.

Shachar, Isaiah. 1974. *The Judensau: A Medieval Anti-Jewish Motif and its History.* Warburg Institute Surveys. London: The Warburg Institute.

Shafi, Monika. 1995. *Gertrud Kolmar: Eine Einführung in das Werk.* Munich: Iudicium Verlag.

————. 2003. "Gertrud Kolmar (1894–1943)." In *Holocaust Literature: An Encyclopedia of Writers and Their Work,* edited by S. Lillian Kremer, 688–93. New York: Routledge.

Silva, Cara De, ed. 1996. *In Memory's Kitchen: A Legacy from the Women of Terezín*. Northvale, NJ: Jason Aronson.

Smith, Henry A. 1975. "Gertrud Kolmar's Life and Works." In *Dark Soliloquy: The Selected Poems of Gertrud Kolmar*, edited and with an introduction by Henry A. Smith, 3–52. Foreword by Cynthia Ozick. New York: Seabury P.

Sofsky, Wolfgang. 1997. *The Order of Terror: The Concentration Camp*. Translated by William Templer. Princeton: Princeton UP. Original German: *Die Ordnung des Terrors: Das Konzentrationslager*, Frankfurt am Main: S. Fischer, 1993.

Speer, Albert. 1976. *Spandau: The Secret Diaries*. Translated by Richard and Clara Winston. New York: Macmillan.

Stapel, Wilhelm. 1937. *Die literarische Vorherrschaft der Juden in Deutschland, 1918 bis 1933*. Schriften des Reichsinstituts für Geschichte des neuen Deutschlands. Hamburg: Hanseatische Verlagsanstalt.

Steiner, George. 1967. *Language and Silence: Essays on Language, Literature, and the Inhuman*. New York: Atheneum.

Steinweis, Alan E. 1993a. "Hans Hinkel and German Jewry, 1933–1941." *Leo Baeck Yearbook* 38: 209–19.

———. 1993b. *Art, Ideology, and Economics in Nazi Germany: The Reich Chambers of Music, Theater, and the Visual Arts*. Chapel Hill, NC: U of North Carolina P.

Sternberg, Hermann. 1962. "Der Steinbruch (Cariera de piatra): 1942–1943." In *Geschichte der Juden in der Bukowina*, edited by Hugo Gold, 75. Tel Aviv: Olamenu.

Stern-Wolfe, Mimi. 2000. *Composers of the Holocaust: Ghetto Songs from Warsaw, Vilna, and Terezín*. New York: Leonarda Productions.

Striar, Marguerite, ed. 1998. *Beyond Lament: Poets of the World Bearing Witness to the Holocaust*. Evanston, IL: Northwestern UP.

Strothmann, Dietrich. 1963. *Nationalsozialistische Literaturpolitik: Ein Beitrag zu Publizistik im Dritten Reich*. Bonn: Bouvier.

Szondi, Peter. 2003. *Celan Studies*. Translated by Susan Bernofsky with Harvey Mendelsohn. Stanford: Stanford UP. Original German edition, *Celan-Studien*. Frankfurt am Main: Suhrkamp, 1972.

Taterka, Thomas. 1999. *Dante Deutsch: Studien zur Lagerliteratur*. Philologische Studien und Quellen, no. 153. Berlin: Erich Schmidt Verlag.

Todorov, Tzvetan. 1984. *Mikhail Bakhtin: The Dialogical Principle*. Translated by Wlad Godzich. Minneapolis: U of Minnesota P. Original French: *Mikhaïl Bakhtine, le principe dialogique, suivi de: Écrits du Cercle de Bakhtine*, 1981.

———. 1996. *Facing the Extreme: Moral Life in the Concentration Camps.* Translated by Arthur Denner and Abigail Pollak. Metropolitan Books. New York: Henry Holt. Original French: *Face à l'extrême,* 1991.

Ullmann, Viktor. 1994. *Der Kaiser von Atlantis: Hölderlin Lieder.* Entartete Musik. Gewandhaus Orchestra. Conducted by Lothar Zagrosek. London: Decca Record Company.

———. 1996. *The Emperor from Atlantis.* Music from Terezín. Vermont Symphony Orchestra. Conducted by Robert DeCormier. New York: Arabesque Recordings.

Verdet, André, ed. 1995. *Anthologie des poèmes de Buchenwald.* Paris: Éditions Tirésias.

Vesper, Will, ed. 1940. *Die Ernte der Gegenwart: Deutsche Lyrik von heute.* Ebenhausen, Germany: W. Langewische-Brandt.

Weber, Ilse. 1978. *Ilse Weber — Theresienstadt.* Edited by Hanus Weber. Stockholm: Författares Bokmaskin.

———. 1991. *In deinen Mauern wohnt das Leid: Gedichte aus dem KZ Theresienstadt.* 1st edition. Gerlingen, Germany: Bleicher.

———. 2001. *Mendel Rosenbusch: Tales for Jewish Children.* Translated by Ruth and Hans Fisher. New York: Herodias. Original German: *Die Geschichten um Mendel Rosenbusch: Erzählungen für jüdische Kinder,* by Ilse Herlinger. Mährisch-Ostrau [now Czech Republic]: Färber, 1929.

Weil, Jirí. 1964. Epilogue to *. . . I never saw another butterfly . . . Children's Drawings and Poems from Theresienstadt Concentration Camp, 1942–1944.* New York: McGraw-Hill.

Wieviorka, Annette. 1994. "On Testimony." In Hartman, *Holocaust Remembrance: The Shapes of Memory,* 23–32.

Wisse, Ruth R. 1981. Introduction to *Burnt Pearls: Ghetto Poems of Abraham Sutzkever,* by Abraham Sutzkever. Translated by Seymour Mayne. Oakville, ON, Canada: Mosaic P / Valley Editions.

Wulf, Joseph. 1966. *Literatur und Dichtung im Dritten Reich: Eine Dokumentation.* Hamburg: Hanseatische Druckanstalt.

Young, James. 1988. *Writing and Rewriting the Holocaust: Narrative and the Consequences of Interpretation.* Bloomington: Indiana UP.

Zeiger, Melissa. 1997. *Beyond Consolation: Death, Sexuality, and the Changing Shapes of Elegy.* Ithaca: Cornell UP.

Index

Aaron, Frieda, 27, 47–48
Adorno, Theodor: on "poetry after Auschwitz," 1, 36–37, 68–69, 181
Adorno, Theodor, works by: "Commitment," 68, 93; "Cultural Criticism and Society," 36; "Those Twenties," 37, 68–69; "What Does Coming to Terms with the Past Mean?" 55
Agamben, Giorgio: on death, 117–18, 236 n. 8; on *Muselmänner*, 97–98
Améry, Jean: on being Jewish, 48–50; on the German language, 3; on religious belief in the camps, 45; on torture, 131, 133–34; on the uses of culture in the camps, 40–42
anti-Semitism: in the German Democratic Republic, 30; in language, 130
apostrophe, 90–93, 125, 178
Arendt, Hannah: on the attack on individuality in the camps, 4; on legal limbo in dictatorships, 80
Arendt, Hannah, works by: *The Origins of Totalitarianism*, 156
Auerhahn, Nanette. *See* Laub, Dori, works by: with Nanette Auerhahn

Baetens, Jan, 183
Bakhtinian criticism, 13, 231 n. 17
Bernard, Catherine, 55, 68
Bettelheim, Bruno, 137–38
Bloch, Ernst, 6

Boris, Georg von, 112
Boris, Georg von, works by: *Hunger*, 112–17; *Die Lieder des Grauens* (Songs of Horror), 134–38
Bos, Pascale, 11, 66, 68, 71
Bower, Kathrin, 69
Buck, Theo, 181

camp songs, 51, 61, 78, 108
cannibalism: responses to, 112–17
Caruth, Cathy: on trauma, 12
Cayrol, Jean, 24–28
Celan, Paul: as exemplary post-Holocaust poet, 69, 181–83; on the German language, 7–8
children's play, 121–22
Cold War, 22, 29–30, 155
Culler, Jonathan: on apostrophe, 91–93

Daxelmüller, Christoph, 24
death: relation to, in the Holocaust, 4, 14–15, 42, 112–26, 131, 175–80, 236 n. 8
Delbo, Charlotte, 40
dialogic criticism, 13–14, 19–20
Distel, Barbara, 94–95, 104

Eisen, George, 121–22
Elling, Hanna, 31
Emmerich, Wolfgang: on poetry from the camps, 23
empathy, 12–13, 84, 132, 138; empathic identification/empathic unsettlement, 12–13, 130, 137; empathic response

(and lack thereof), 84–85, 91, 101, 103, 132–33, 151

Forché, Carolyn, 27, 115, 181
Friedländer, Saul: on individual memory in the writing of history, 17, 26, 94; on the *Kulturbund,* 166

Garland, Caroline: on the individual response to trauma, 14, 231 n. 20
Gay, Peter, 167
German language, 1–8, 41; as a "Jewish language," 3–4. *See also* Klüger, Ruth: on the German language
German-Jewish cultural activity in the Third Reich, 22, 26, 153, 165–68
Germany: East and West, 22–23, 25–27, 29–31, 148, 151, 155–57
Gilman, Sander, 56–59, 69
Goes, Albrecht, 121, 162, 164
Grabner, Hasso: short biography, 76
Grabner, Hasso, works by: *Die Häftlingsnummer* (The Prisoner's Number), 72–77, 82
Granof, Corinne, works by: with David Mickenberg, *Complexity and Contradiction: An Introduction to The Last Expression,* 18
Gubar, Susan: on empathic unsettlement, 13, 231 n. 16; on the German language, 8; on "minute incidents," 18, 181; on photographs, 131; on poetry, 19, 182

Hartman, Geoffrey, 17, 70
Heidelberger-Leonard, Irène, 59, 62, 64

Hentschke, Heinz: *Gelungene Flucht* (Successful Escape), 173–75
Hilzinger, Sonja, 166
Hirsch, Marianne, 17
Hortzitz, Nicoline, 130
hunger, 108–17

imaginative acts, 14–16, 80–81, 83–85, 93, 99, 103, 125–26, 138, 150–51

Jäger, Gudrun, 5, 26, 165, 168
Jews: German-speaking, in the camps, 3–5; Nazi conception of, as authors, 5–6, 166–68; religious, 46–48, 71, 235 n. 3
Johnson, Barbara: on apostrophe, 91–92
Judensau motif, 130

Kahane, Claire, 12, 24, 37
Kelly-Holmes, Helen, 6
Ketelsen, Uwe, 153, 157, 160–61, 164
Kiedaisch, Petra, 36
Kittner, Alfred: short biography, 122
Kittner, Alfred, works by: *Friedhof Obodowka* (Cemetery Obodowka), 176–80; *Fünfundzwanzig* (Twenty-Five), 148–51; *Unterwegs* (On the Road), 122–26
Klein, Katja, 44
Klüger, Ruth: on Adorno, 33–34, 36; on the German language, 3–4, 20–21, 43
Klüger, Ruth, works by: *Auschwitz,* 60–69; *Der Kamin* (The Chimney), 56–69; *Still Alive,* 35–36, 51; *weiter leben,* 35–36, 51
Kolmar, Gertrud, 167–68; self-understanding as poet, 5

Kolmar, Gertrud, works by: *Im Lager* (In the Camp), 169–72
Kozin, Allan, 28
Kulturbund (Jüdischer), 153, 165–67
Kupfer-Koberwitz, Edgar: short biography, 94–95
Kupfer-Koberwitz, Edgar, works by: *Erinnerung* (Remembrance), 128–31, 138–39; *Gestreiftes Kleid* (Striped Cloak), 85–93; *Kette der Tage* (Chain of Days), 95–108

LaCapra, Dominick: on empathy, 12–13, 230 n. 15; on the Holocaust as traumatic event, 12–13, 40; on transference, 13, 231 n. 18
Langer, Lawrence, 17, 93; on the dangers of a positive meaning in the Holocaust, 32, 38–39, 42; on humiliated memory, 117; on Kolmar, 172; on literary form, 39
Laub, Dori, 13, 17
Laub, Dori, works by: with Daniel Podell, *Art and Trauma*, 14–16, 99, 101, 134; with Nanette Auerhahn, *Failed Empathy*, 11, 82, 84, 91, 132
Levi, Primo: on the *Musulmänner*, 98, 100; on religious belief in the camps, 45–46; on the uses of culture in the camps, 18, 37–39, 42, 45
Lezzi, Eva, 67
Liebrand, Claudia, 34
Löhner-Beda, Fritz: short biography, 77–78, 81
Löhner-Beda, Fritz, works by: *Der Häftling* (The Inmate), 78–83, 85; untitled, 83–85, 102
Luxemburg, Rosa, 75

Mann, Thomas, 3, 155
meaning: creation of, 11, 14–16, 38, 45, 47, 50, 68–67, 72, 75, 90; loss of, 96–97, 100–101, 133, 174
Meerloo, Joost, 9–11, 22, 26, 230 n. 12
Mickenberg, David. *See* Granof, Corinne
Moll, Michael, works by: with Barbara Weiler, *Lyrik gegen das Vergessen*, 31–32; *Lyric in einer entmenschlichten Welt*, 1, 33, 47, 53, 87, 124
Muselmänner (Muselmann), 95–101, 116, 134, 146; Agamben on, 97–98; Levi on, 98–100; responses in poetry to, 51, 53, 58, 66; Sofsky on, 99–100

Nelson, Cary, 19, 25–26
Nolan, Mary, 158–59
number. *See* prisoner's number

perpetrators: language of, 2–3, 8; naming (and not naming), 59–60, 66–67, 73, 82, 87–88, 91–93, 102, 106–8, 125, 137–43, 150–51, 168–69; perspective of, 17, 130–31, 139
phantasmatic connection, 11, 47, 84
Phillips, Adam, 78
Podell, Daniel. *See* Laub, Dori, works by: with Daniel Podell
poetry after Auschwitz, 1, 8, 36, 181. *See also* Adorno, Theodor: on "poetry after Auschwitz"
poetry therapy, 9–11, 19
Pouzol, Henri, 27
prisoner's number, 71–83, 235 n. 3

Rabinbach, Anson, 158

Rahe, Thomas, 46, 71
Reichel, Peter, 158–59, 161
revenge: fantasies of, 60, 69, 107–
8, 141, 143, 146, 148–51
Rich, Adrienne, 18
Ringelheim, Joan: on comparing
categories of victims, 49
Rosenfeld, Alvin, 7
Roskies, David: on Jewish
testimonial tradition, 48, 50;
on the perspective of the critics,
19–20, 60
Rothberg, Michael: on Langer,
234 n. 4, 234 n. 5; on
periodization of the Holocaust,
230 n. 8; on "traumatic
realism," 34–35

Scarry, Elaine, 133
Schäfer, Hans Dieter, 158–59,
161, 163–64
Schlenstedt, Silvia, 165–68
Schlösser, Manfred, 26, 28–29
Schneider, Wolfgang, 29–31, 83,
148
Schnog, Karl: short biography,
139–49; on Löhner-Beda,
Fritz, 77–78
Schnog, Karl, works by: *Deutsche
Freie Presse* (German Free
Press), 141–43; *Gelöbnis* (Vow),
140–41; *Der Häftling* (The
Inmate), 144–48; *Jedem das
Seine* (To Each His Own), 143–
48; *Nackte Aussage* (Naked
Testimony), 147–48; *Der
Steinbruch* (The Stone Quarry),
104–8
Schoor, Kerstin, 167
Schwarberg, Günther, 83
sentimentality, 34, 54–55; in
criticism, 12, 234 n. 3
Shachar, Isaiah, 130
Shafi, Monika, 168–69

Sofsky, Wolfgang, 78, 82–83, 99–
100, 128–33
Speer, Albert, 159
Steiner, George: on the German
language, 7
Steinweis, Alan, 165–66
sun (as symbol of life), 58–66
Sutzkever, Abraham, 50, 66
Szondi, Peter, 181

Taterka, Thomas: on criticism, 20;
on the dangers of
"authenticity," 17, 20; on
references to Dante in the
literature of survivors, 38
Todorov, Tzvetan, 35, 44;
on Améry, 41–42; on
transcendence, 38
traditional poetic form, 19, 158,
166–67, 172, 182–83
transcendence: discussions of,
15, 33–35, 38, 40, 42–43, 45,
80; poetic, 5, 10–11, 168,
234 n. 7; poetry as, 26
trauma, 2, 11–16, 19, 24, 37, 39–
40, 52–53, 71, 84, 91, 93, 100,
126, 128, 132–34, 138, 147,
181, 231 n. 20, 232 n. 26

Weber, Ilse: short biography, 119
Weber, Ilse, works by:
Theresienstädter Kinderreim
(Theresienstadt Children's
Rhyme), 118–22, 126
Weil, Jiří, 121
Weiler, Barbara. *See* Moll, Michael
Wieviorka, Annette, 46
Wisse, Ruth, 66
Wulf, Joseph, 155–56

Young, James, 14

Zeiger, Melissa, 183